MINORITY AND MAINSTREAM CHILDREN'S DEVELOPMENT AND ACADEMIC ACHIEVEMENT

An Alternative Research and Educational View

Edited by

Virginia Gonzalez

University Press of America,® Inc.
Lanham · Boulder · New York · Toronto · Plymouth, UK

Copyright © 2007 by
University Press of America,® Inc.
4501 Forbes Boulevard
Suite 200
Lanham, Maryland 20706
UPA Acquisitions Department (301) 459-3366

Estover Road
Plymouth PL6 7PY
United Kingdom

Library of Congress Control Number: 2007922679
ISBN-13: 978-0-7618-3766-4 (paperback : alk. paper)
ISBN-10: 0-7618-3766-3 (paperback : alk. paper)

Because Santiago–my new baby nephew–will become
a bilingual Spanish/English child,
this book is dedicated to him–in celebration
of his Christening as my baby godchild–and
to his proud mother, my sister Sofia.
Congratulations Santiago,
and welcome to this wonderful world!

CONTENTS

Part I

Socio-Cultural and Socioeconomic Status (SES) Factors Affecting
Minority and Mainstream Children's Development and
Academic Achievement

CHAPTER 1
A Multidimensional Perspective of Minority and Mainstream
Children's Development and Academic Achievement

CHAPTER 2
Socio-cultural Factors in the Family and School Systems
Mediating Minority Children's Development and Academic
Achievement

PART II
An Alternative Research View to the Study of
Development and Academic Achievement in Minority
and Mainstream Children

LIST OF TABLES

FOREWORD

This textbook edited by Dr. Virginia Gonzalez introduces and details alternative and comparative perspectives of culturally and linguistically diverse (CLD) students growth and development and their academic achievement levels. In this sense, it is innovative because it goes beyond the typical psychological and developmental texts that present and then document the uses and outcomes of behavioral perspectives on academic achievement of CLD (and for that matter mainstream) students.

The perspectives taken in this innovative text is that of the Ethnic Researcher. In this perspective the foci are more on internal factors such as biological influence and on external factors for example schools (in the sense of social transmission) and their nurturing and shaping individual growth and human variability in academic achievement. Dr. Virginia Gonzalez establishes theoretical and practical concepts to help best educate culturally and linguistically diverse and mainstream students in American schools.

The perspective of the Ethnic Researcher paradigm is used to appropriately describe what and how adjustments need to be made in order to best serve today students. This perspective is juxtaposed of course to the more behavioral views that support the shaping and controlling of development and human growth variability through environmental reinforcement contingencies. With the changing student population and the trends swiftly shifting to culturally and linguistically diverse students, perspectives of researching and understanding those communities are essential. In addition, the Ethnic Researcher perspective includes the effects of socio-economic status (SES) and socio-milieux on academic achievement of CLD students. Thus, this book spotlights new ways to understand CLD cultures in special light of those families and communities dealing with high rates of poverty.

To explore these two factors and those of SES, for example, on CLD students academic achievement, this text is organized into two sections or parts. Part 1, of the text provides a setting to view social, cultural, and SES factors impacting CLD and mainstream students development and academic achievement. Critical to SES, included are factors such as parent educational levels, occupations, degrees of literacy, number of years in the U. S. and further setting factors including the neighborhood in which families reside and resources the community has available for use. For example, the family environment in which the child is born and raised provides salient mediators for CLD and mainstream students as they learn and model achievement, and as they develop resiliency, success and failure potentials. Families give learned potential to their children academic successes or failures not only in schools but as well in society.

In this text Part 2, the Ethnic Researcher perspective is explored in depth and its utility is examined with gifted CLD students, various contemporary family structures including family perceptions and home conditions. Assessment practices pull together these various aspects detailed in Part 2. They stress alternative multiple measures which can be used with ease and at the same time provide additional data much needed to make decisions on placement in grades and groups.

One of the oys of reading and using this text is experiencing multiple lenses. Here we mean using multiple lenses to look at cultural and linguistic minority and mainstream development and academic achievement permits the reader to grasp concepts that both divide and bond CLD and mainstream students. For example, validating the home language and culture of CLD and mainstream students becomes critical for individual development and familial and community inclusion in teaching and assessment stands out as one of the most important elements of education. Insights into external factors on texts and cultures combined with internal factors such as biological and psychological problems introduced in the text help create more multiethnic and multicultural views of teaching and understanding language minority students who have particular language acquisition needs and who come from low SES environments. Also, through multiple lenses of the Ethnic Researcher approach with comparisons to the current traditional Behavioral approach, the reader sees the richness and depth to view CLD achievement and internal and external impacts on this achievement. The potential for learning about CLD and mainstream students from an Ethnic Researcher point of view has vast benefits towards our ever changing picture of education especially in light of the shift of demographics of CLD students entering schools in America today.

Educators, administrators and policy makers definitely have a powerful new resource to use to look at how to best serve CLD populations of predominantly low socio-economic families. The challenges of changing faces of students in our classrooms, communities and agencies has already occurred and are with us today. We must able to meet these challenges in classrooms, families and communities with our CLD and mainstream students and families.

This text, *Minority and Mainstream Children Development and Academic Achievement: An Alternative Research an Educational View* enlightens the audiences of professionals and practitioners. It is critical because it contains new, contemporary views of educating and mainstream students and working with families from culturally and linguistically diverse populations and the processes of learning about different learners from various backgrounds. In working with CLD populations, this book is a ust have edition and certainly a eeper for future reference, re-reading and research.

Thomas D. Yawkey, Ph.D.,
Professor of Curriculum and Instruction
Department of Curriculum and Instruction
The Pennsylvania State University
University Park, Pennsylvania

Christopher J. Meidl, Ph.D., Candidate
Department of Curriculum and Instruction
The Pennsylvania State University
University Park, Pennsylvania

December, 2006

PREFACE

The Tale Behind The Book

P resently the school population characteristics are shifting to represent culturally and linguistically diverse needs of students. Consequently faculty and graduate and undergraduate students in education and related areas in higher educational institutions, and teachers and administrators in the schools need to be knowledgeable about the comparative and alternative research and educationally applied framework presented in this book. This book responds to this contemporary challenge by:

1. Opening a new interdisciplinary niche that communicates the mainstream with the minority modules of literature. Mainstream literature reviewed in this book represents the traditional developmental psychology perspective. Minority literature discussed represents an Ethnic Research perspective (see Gonzalez, Brusca-Vega, & Yawkey, 1997 for further discussion of this view). This interdisciplinary view is presented as a viable solution to the challenge of working with the wide range of individual and culturally/linguistically diverse learning and developmental characteristics of minority and mainstream students. Then, this book discusses an alternative research and educational view to the study of development and academic achievement in children, encompassing all human diversity represented in minority and mainstream children

2. Proposing a state-of-the-art research methodology for studying diversity in development and academic achievement among *all* (i.e., mainstream and minority) students in the public school system

This book presents a unique, state-of-the-art, ecological, and multidimensional view of the differential effect of socio-cultural and socioeconomic factors on the development and achievement of minority and mainstream children. Alternative methodological paradigms for solving theoretical and educationally applied problems in assessment and instruction are proposed, discussed in light of literature, and demonstrated through actual research studies conducted with both minority and mainstream populations.

This project developed because of the author's experience in teaching graduate courses in minority and mainstream development, assessment, and instructional topics for education majors in US institutions across 15 years, as well as by mentoring graduate students completing collaborative research projects and their masters theses and dissertation studies. Throughout the years, a major theme emerged across course content generated and numerous research studies that I have supervised: the interaction effect between internal and external factors on the development and academic achievement of minority and mainstream young children. Since graduate students were influenced by this theme through exposure to course content delivered by their research mentor, it was not by coincidence that the research topics that students selected resulted in the emergence of a multidimensional and interaction ethnic research perspective.

In addition, the author has extensive experience in delivering papers at major national, international, and regional conferences in the areas of bilingual education, second language learning, academic achievement and assessment in ESL students, and early childhood development. These experiences have contributed to realizing the high demand among educators and researchers for seeking information and acquiring knowledge regarding the assessment and instructional applications of research on development and academic achievement in minority and majority young children.

Furthermore, no books could be located that present a comparative and alternative view between minority and majority children's development and academic achievement. There exist many psychological and developmental books that present a traditional conceptual paradigm, and few books that present an educational perspective only for minority students. However, a psychological and developmental research view with its educational applications for both populations does not exist in the literature. As mentioned above, presently the school population characteristics are shifting to represent non-traditional educational needs of culturally and linguistically diverse students. Then, more students and faculty in higher educational institutions as well as practitioners in the field need to be knowledgeable about the comparative and alternative framework presented in this book. A traditional mainstream perspective presented in most books of development and academic achievement with a focus on mainstream students is not sufficient anymore to respond to the changing demographic characteristics of the school population.

Thus, the target audience for this book is comprised of university professors, researchers, upper level undergraduate students, graduate students; and teachers, professionals and administrators in the schools, including: educators in general, bilingual and special educators, cognitive psychologists, developmental psychologists, educational psychologists, school psychologists, educational diagnosticians, counselors, speech pathologists, and other support professionals collaborating or serving diverse students in the US public schools.

Therefore, there is need for books that present innovative conceptual theoretical frameworks, and propose a state-of-the-art research view for studying the development and academic performance, and its assessment and instructional applications, for *all* students in the public school system (i.e., minority and mainstream young children).

The data-based studies illustrate methodological advances in the field of ethnic research providing solutions for traditional methodological problems (e.g., alternative assessments and innovative research designs and strategies) with three main objectives, to demonstrate:

1. The interaction effect of internal (i.e., developmental and psychological) and external (schooling, socio-cultural, and socio-economic) factors on the academic achievement of minority and majority children

2. The powerful effect of the political and historical factors pre-existing in the social and economic environment in which young children develop, which can put them at-risk for underachievement and developmental delays

3. The importance of affective/emotional and socialization or acculturation processes, and of family and school environmental factors on the development of young children

In sum, the main idea that will be discussed in this book is that students are put at-risk of failure in the school environment due to overlooking: (1) developmental psychological factors, and (2) external socio-historical factors, including socio-cultural and socioeconomic realities.

Book Themes

The major theme of the book centers on the study of developmental, socio-cultural, and socioeconomic status(SES) factors affecting minority and mainstream children's assessment and academic achievement.

Four derived sub-themes are represented across chapters including:

1. An Ethnic Research perspective of psychological and developmental factors affecting learning processes and academic achievement in minority and mainstream children, with a comparison of similarities and differences

2. External socio-cultural and SES factors affecting differently development and academic achievement in minority and mainstream children

3. Home and school environmental similarities and differences affecting minority and majority children's development, learning processes, and academic achievement

4. An alternative Ethnic Research view to the assessment and academic achievement in minority and mainstream young children

Related to these four sub-themes is a central point discussed throughout the book, that is, the central role of cultural identity and personality and emotional/affective factors (i.e., the child as a whole persona) on the developmental and academic achievement outcome of minority and mainstream young children. Thus, throughout the book it will be emphasized how critical is for educators to value the home language and culture of the young minority child, to validate their cultural identity, and to respect and nurture both individual and socio-cultural differences. That is, throughout the book a main idea will be supported: the importance for us educators to stimulate in young children the development of language as thinking, learning, communicative, and emotional tools for expressing their uniqueness within a meaningful, real-life, socio-cultural setting. Thus, language as a symbolic tool needs to be present at both the family and school contexts in order for both minority and mainstream young children to be successful learners and to grow as mentally healthy, and socially productive individuals.

Overview of the Book

This book is divided into two parts. Part I of the book is entitled A Socio-Cultural and Socioeconomic Status (SES) Factors Affecting Minority and Mainstream Children's Development and Academic Achievement. The first part encompasses the first two chapters and provides a conceptual theoretical framework for understanding the influence of internal (i.e., developmental and psychological) and external factors (i.e., schooling, socio-cultural including minority home language, and socioeconomic conditions—poverty) affecting minority and mainstream children's development and academic performance. The critical review of the literature presented in these two conceptual chapters emphasizes the assessment and instructional implications derived from contemporary research traditional and Ethnic Research perspectives.

In order to establish a context for the actual research studies presented in the second part of the book, this conceptual framework provides a critical discussion of a comparison of:

1. Internal psychological and developmental similarities and differences present in minority and mainstream children's learning processes and academic performance

2. External school and home environmental similarities and differences affecting minority and mainstream children's psychological development, learning processes, and academic performance

The first part of the book also contributes to the state-of-the-art of minority research by bringing together literature typically treated as two separate modules, stemming from researchers within:

1. A developmental psychology perspective, endorsing traditional methodological paradigms that do not typically represent the cultural and linguistic backgrounds of minority children studied

2. An Ethnic Research perspective, with alternative qualitative assessments and methodological procedures that tap the cultural and linguistic diversity of minority students (see Gonzalez & Yawkey, 1993; Gonzalez et al., 1997; and Gonzalez, Yawkey, & Minaya-Rowe, 20006, for further discussion of the Ethnic Research perspective)

Chapter 1 has the objective of bringing together these two separate modules of contemporary research literature by presenting a multidimensional model for understanding the importance of an ecological perspective to the study of the development and academic achievement in minority and mainstream children. Chapter 1 examines critically, under the light of research evidence, two most important overarching factors demonstrated to significantly influence minority children's development and academic achievement

The effect of low SES of the minority children's family on their development and academic achievement, separating cultural/linguistic diversity from poverty. The examination of the SES factor will encompass much more than the traditional parental income, which has been expanded in modern literature to the inclusion of the parental educational level, degree of literacy, and occupation; and the quality of the neighborhood and community resources. Emphasis will be given to critically review the literature on the effect of low SES on minority children's developmental and achievement levels, their vulnerability and resiliency related to external school and family mediational factors, and the discussion of low SES factors for underachievement and future adult economic productivity

The home and family socio-cultural reality in which minority children develop (e.g., number of siblings, birth order, care-giving practices, value and belief systems held by parents, immigration status of family members, family mobility, and parents' number of years of US residency). Emphasis is given to the critical review of the literature on the effect of the language used at home by parents and siblings for minority children's developmental and achievement levels

Chapter 1 provides a context for Chapter 2 on schooling, socio-cultural, and SES factors; all socio-historical external factors influencing differently development and academic achievement in minority and mainstream children. The second Chapter relates to the major theme of the book because it expands the discussion of socio-cultural factors affecting minority children's assessment and academic achievement. Chapter 2 discussed the specific case of school settings as catalysts for developing minority family and home and community partnerships through English-as-a-second-language (ESL) and *all* teachers assuming a mentoring role. As Chapter 1, this second Chapter also emphasizes how critical is for educators to value the home language and culture of the minority child, and to respect and nurture both individual and socio-cultural differences present in their home and family setting. That is, in this second Chapter, as throughout the book, a main idea is supported: the importance for us educators to stimulate in young children the development of first and second languages as learning, thinking, communicative, and emotional tools for expressing individual and developmental uniqueness within a meaningful, real-life socio-cultural setting. Thus, language as a symbolic tool needs to be present at both the family and school context in order for minority young children to be successful learners and to grow as mentally healthy, and socially productive individuals.

Part II of the book includes Chapter 3 through Chapter 7 and provides an alternative Ethnic Research view to the study of development, assessment, and academic achievement in minority and mainstream young learners. The second part of the book is entitled An Alternative Research View to the Study of Development and Academic Achievement in Minority and Mainstream Children. These five chapters illustrate the book central theme and four sub-themes, all discussed also in the first part of the book.

In the second part of the book, a collection of five data-based research studies illustrate alternative methodologies for accurately instructing and assessing development and academic achievement in minority and mainstream young learners are included. These studies provide alternative solutions for major methodological problems still present in contemporary studies conducted with young minority and mainstream children. Many of these research studies highlight the importance of affective/emotional factors, and socialization or acculturation processes, and family and school environmental factors on the wholistic psychological development of minority and mainstream children.

These five actual data-based studies illustrate methodological advances in the field of Ethnic Research providing solutions for traditional methodological problems (e.g., alternative assessments and innovative research designs and strategies) with three main objectives:

1. To illustrate the complexity of the interaction effect of internal (i.e., developmental), and external (i.e., socio-cultural and SES) factors on the academic achievement of minority and mainstream children

2. To highlight the powerful effect of socio-historical and political factors pre-existing in the socio-cultural and socio-economic environment in which young minority children are born, which in turn may become the most important at-risk environmental settings for developmental delays and subsequently academic failure (when positive mediational factors are absent, such as mentors in family and school settings). Some of these external positive and negative factors are present in the school and

home environments such as teachers' and parents' attitudes, their values and belief systems, their prejudices, their discriminatory biases, their cultural adaptation, their attributions for academic success and failure, their perceptual interpretations of children's behaviors, their educational constructs internalized within a socio-cultural setting (e.g., giftedness, intelligence, academic language, instructional methodologies, child raising styles, etc.)

3. To analyze what major similarities as well as cultural and linguistic differences exist when comparing research findings when studying minority and mainstream children's development and academic achievement. Emphasis will be given to contrast the different effect of internal psychological (i.e., developmental) and external (i.e., socio-cultural and socioeconomic) factors when comparing minority to mainstream young learners

Chapter 8 provides closure for the book in the form of conclusions referring to educational applications of contemporary Ethnic Research findings in the study of psychological and SES factors affecting the home and school cultural experiences of minority and mainstream children. The conclusions Chapter brings closure to the discussion presented throughout the book about the many controversial issues and dilemmas in the study and education of minority and mainstream young learners. The main idea discussed in this conclusions Chapter is that minority students are put at-risk of failure in the school environment due to overlooking developmental psychological factors, and external socio-historical and socio-economic factors. Concluding remarks in relation to the state-of-the-art of research conducted on minority children's development an academic achievement support the need for conducting more data-based studies endorsing an ecological, multidimensional, and interaction framework. Finally, some recommendations for much needed research for broadening our current understanding of the interacting effects of external factors (i.e., SES and socio-cultural) with internal factors (i.e., developmental and psychological) are highlighted for the case of minority children's development.

Acknowledgments

I want to express my deepest thanks to the contributors for this book. First, my appreciation goes to Dr. Thomas Yawkey, Professor of Education at the Pennsylvania State University, who contributed Chapter 2 to this book. His expertise and talent as a researcher in the area of development and achievement of minority learners is transparent in the important issues discussed in Chapter 2. In adsdition, Dr. Yawkey has collaborated with me for the past 15 years, and as a mentor, colleague, and friend has inspired and contributed to the development of the Ethnic Researcher approached in so many joint publications (e.g., Gonzalez, & Yawkey, 1993; Gonzalez, et al., 1997, 2006). In Chapter 2 of this book, Dr. Yawkey co-authors with Dr. Chih-Sheng Chen, a discussion of the important role of teachers as mentors when serving minority students. Chapter 2 centers on the main theme of the book: socio-cultural factor in the family and school mediating minority children's development and academic achievement. Dr. Chen was a former graduate student of Dr. Yawkey, and he is now an Associate Professor at Southern Taiwan University of Technology, Taiwan.

My deepest thanks go to my collaborators for Chapter 3, Patricia Bauerle and Dr. Ellen Riojas Clark. Patricia is a school psychologists, a long-time research collaborator, whom I supervised when she was a graduate student at the University of Arizona. Dr. Riojas Clark, a longtime colleague and friend, is a Professor at the Division of Bicultural-Bilingual Studies, College of Education and Human Development at The University of Texas at San Antonio. They both collaborated with me on data collection and analysis and contributed their expertise for the completion of the study.

I also want to acknowledge the contributions of three of my former graduate students at The University of Arizona, College of Education, Educational Psychology Department. They are: (1) Dr. Nina Williams who collaborated with me on Chapter 5 entitled Parents' Perceptions and Home Environmental Factors Influencing Potential Giftedness in Monolingual Low and High SES Preschoolers, (2) Susan Leadem, who collaborated with me on Chapter 6 entitled Developmentally Adequate Assessment Practices when Screening Classroom Performance in Kindergartners, and (3) Ellen Demas, who collaborated with me on Chapter 7 entitled Academic Resilience in Young Children: Understanding the Relationship Between Temperament and Quality of the Parent-Child Relationship. Nina completed her doctoral degree in Educational Psychology, and Susan and Ellen completed their master degrees in Educational Psychology; all under my supervision. It was a pleasure to work with them as a mentor and research collaborator, they were very motivated and talented researchers who took an Ethnic Researcher approach to study mainstream low SES young children.

I also want to acknowledge the help with professional typesetting from Ms. Susan Peabody. Here diligent work helped to improve the quality of this book.

Finally, I want to acknowledge the help of editors and anonymous external reviewers, associated with University Press of America (UPA) who made possible the publication of this book. Their suggestions to improve the book proposal are appreciated, and did indeed help to make the content of the book of higher quality.

Best wishes and successes,

Virginia Gonzalez, Ph.D.

PART I

SOCIO-CULTURAL AND SOCIOECONOMIC STATUS (SES) FACTORS AFFECTING MINORITY AND MAINSTREAM CHILDREN'S DEVELOPMENT AND ACADEMIC ACHIEVEMENT

1

A MULTIDIMENSIONAL PERSPECTIVE OF MINORITY AND MAINSTREAM CHILDREN'S DEVELOPMENT AND ACADEMIC ACHIEVEMENT

ಙಞಬ

Virginia Gonzalez

The objective of this introductory Chapter is to discuss a multidimensional model for understanding the importance of an Ethnic Researcher perspective to the study of the development and academic achievement in minority and mainstream children. This first Chapter provides a context for the second Chapter on socio-cultural factors, present at home and school, which influence differently development and academic achievement in minority children.

This first Chapter relates to the major theme of the book that centers on the study of developmental, socio-cultural, and socioeconomic status (SES) factors affecting minority and mainstream children's assessment and academic achievement. More specifically, this first Chapter presents an Ethnic Researcher perspective when discussing psychological and developmental factors, interacting with external cultural/linguistic, SES, and home and family factors; all influencing minority and mainstream children's development, learning processes, and academic achievement. This first Chapter analyses closely the confounding effects of SES with parenting and cultural and linguistic minority factors.

A central idea discussed in Chapter 1 is the important role of identity or personality and emotional factors (i.e., the child as a whole persona) on the developmental and academic achievement outcome of minority and mainstream young children. Thus, Chapter 1 emphasizes how critical is for educators to value the home language and culture of the young minority child and to respect and nurture both individual and socio-cultural differences. That is, in this Chapter and throughout the book a main idea will be supported: the importance for us educators to stimulate in young children the development of language as a thinking and emotional process, and its use in real-life as a social communicative and learning tool. Thus, language as a symbolic tool needs to be present in both family and school contexts in order for both minority and mainstream young children to be successful learners and to become school achievers, and socially productive individuals.

Moreover, this first Chapter brings together two separate modules of contemporary research literature by presenting a multidimensional perspective of the interaction of internal (i.e., psychological—affective/emotional processes such as socialization, cultural identity, and cultural adaptation) and external factors (i.e., political and socio-historical factors such as poverty and family structure) that may place minority and mainstream children at-risk of developmental delays and underachievement. These two modules of literature typically treated separately, have been generated by researchers within:

1. A developmental psychology perspective, endorsing traditional methodological paradigms that do not represent the cultural and linguistic background of minority children studied

2. An Ethnic Researcher minority perspective, with alternative qualitative assessments and methodological procedures that tap the cultural and linguistic diversity of minority students (see Gonzalez, Brusca-Vega, & Yawkey, 1997; Gonzalez & Yawkey, 1993; and Gonzalez, Yawkey, & Minaya-Rowe, 2006, for further discussion of the Ethnic Researcher perspective)

Furthermore, this first Chapter discusses critically an important issue: What does it mean to be at-risk of developmental and academic achievement problems? Special attention is given to the effect of poverty in minority and mainstream children's developmental and academic achievement levels. Findings of contemporary research studies are examined for comparing similarities and differences between poor minority and mainstream children' development. The critical discussion centers on the confounding effect of poverty with cultural and linguistic differences present in minority children. In addition, the examination of SES factors includes much more than the traditional parental income, which has been expanded in modern literature to the inclusion of parental educational levels, parents' literacy levels and occupations; and to some related family structure factors such as the quality of the family structure and the parent-child relationship, as well as to the quality of the neighborhood and community resources. Moreover, this first Chapter gives special attention to the interaction of SES factors with formal and informal contexts for learning and language development that minority children are exposed to. Five central factors within the home cultural context are analyzed in light of contemporary literature, such as the role of:

1. The language used at home by parents and siblings for minority children's developmental and achievement levels

2. Parental cultural child-rearing styles

3. Parental value and belief systems

4. Siblings as cultural mediators (including birth order and number of siblings)

5. Immigration status of family members (including family mobility, and parents' number of years of US residency)

Moreover, in Chapter 1, emphasis is given to a critical review of the literature on the effect of low SES on minority children's developmental and academic achievement levels, and future adult economic productivity. The concepts of vulnerability and resilience are used for analyzing central issues:

1. The mediational and buffering effects of mentors and advocates for minority and mainstream children living below poverty levels

2. The moral responsibility of educators to nurture poor minority and mainstream children's development and consequently to reduce their risk of underachievement

The mediational effect of mentors and advocates in the home, school, and community settings links this first Chapter to the socio-cultural factors present in the school system that are analyzed more in depth in the second Chapter. Chapter 2 extends the scope of Chapter 1 to a lively critical discussion of the role of teaching as mentoring for developing community partnerships between home and school contexts leading to increasing developmental and academic performance in at-risk minority children.

Thus, two main sections are included in Chapter 1: the first one refers to a multidimensional Ethnic Researcher perspective for increasing our understanding of the interaction between internal (i.e., psychological) and external factors (i.e., SES and cultural/linguistic and family structure related factors) on minority children's development and academic achievement. This first section also discusses methodological variations in data collection and data analysis procedures across theoretical perspectives: traditional developmental psychology and the Ethnic Researcher approach.

The second section centers on a discussion of the confounding effect of poverty (or low SES) and cultural and linguistic differences in minority children's development and academic achievement. Demographic data of the growing numbers of minority low SES children in the US public school serves as a springboard for understanding the relation of poverty with mediational factors within the individual (i.e., in relation to concepts of vulnerability and resiliency) and external mediational factors present in the home and family and school settings (i.e., mentors and advocates). In this second section we also discuss the socio-cultural, physical, and psychological context of family affecting the quality of the parent-child relationship, the parents' child rearing styles, the parents' mental health, and ultimately (and most importantly) the use of the minority language at home by parents and siblings. Finally, a third section presents conclusions in relation to similarities and differences between minority and mainstream children's development and academic achievement, and suggests some research questions that still remain open for future studies.

A Multidimensional Ethnic Researcher Perspective for Increasing Our Understanding of Minority Children's Development and Academic Achievement

Contemporary researchers endorse developmental and ecological models that take into consideration multidimensional variables stemming from the interaction of internal and external factors. The use of this multidimensional approach results in more complex research methods and strategies that allows to study: (1) higher-level thinking and problem-solving processes; and (2) developmental trends with more elaborated control for contextual factors and individual differences (through the combination of longitudinal and cross-sectional strategies resulting in sequential studies). For instance, Garcia Coll (1990) proposed that the transaction between the organisms or psychological variables present within the child and the contextual system is very dynamic. More specifically she highlighted the interaction of at-risk biological factors (e.g., prematurity), social at-risk factors (i.e., low SES), and cultural factors (e.g., minority values and beliefs, child-rearing techniques, caretakers' behaviors, and parents' perceptions and developmental goals).

In addition, this transaction between biological, social, and cultural factors (representing interactions between internal and external factors) may create effective or ineffective home environments for minority children to become resilient or at-risk of developing learning problems. Trying to shed light on the particular interactions resulting in resilient or at-risk situations for minority students, Masten and Coatsworth (1998) conducted a data-based study, and concluded that:

> Children who have good internal and external resources tend to get off to a good start in school [whereas] children who enter school with few resources, cognitive difficulties, and self-regulatory problems often have academic problems, and get into trouble with teachers, and are at-risk for disengaging from normative school and peer contexts. (p. 216)

The contemporary view of the interaction between internal (i.e., representing biological and psychological domains) and external factors (representing SES and socio-cultural domains) affecting minority children's development is related to the developmental principles of range of reaction and canalization. As discussed previously by Gonzalez and Yawkey (1993), these two principles are very useful for explaining the dynamic interaction among SES, socio-cultural, psychological, and biological factors influencing minority children's development. More specifically, the principle of range of reaction proposes that there is flexibility and plasticity within biological factors, so that the child is born with a *potential* to develop and learn (*genotype* or genetic endowment), rather than with already acquired or fixed values for his/her skills and abilities across developmental areas. The complementary principle of canalization states that the particular external environment in which the child lives (e.g., home and family setting, and school culture) will provide a positive or negative degree of stimulation for the child's genetic *potential*. The resulting degree of actualization of this *potential* is influenced by the *interacting* effect of inseparable internal *and* external factors canalizing the child's genetic endowment. Then, ecological or external factors are important mediating processes canalizing or actualizing the genetic predisposition of children into skills, abilities, and adaptive strategies, which result in resilience. This achievement is called developmental competence.

In relation to the interacting effect of external factors on internal *potential*, Hill and Sandfort (1995) concluded, after reviewing social science research across disciplines, that a low family income compromises children's physical growth, cognitive development and socio-emotional functioning. Low family income decreases the achievement of children when they are in school and puts them at heightened risk of dropping out of school early (p. 91). The researchers developed a conceptual model of how poverty affects children's development across the life span, finding a causal pathway linking conditions of parental family or external events with childhood poverty to adult capabilities and performance (i.e., earnings, wage rate, work hours, and family income). That is, as shown by Hill and Sandfort (1995), "poverty exerts its effects through a process involving a chain of causal linkages" (p. 93).

In addition, this causal model also identifies confounding factors (often measured by social science research studies) that have an effect on developmental outcomes, education, and adulthood abilities and accomplishments. These confounding factors are defined by Hill and Sandfort (1995) as "circumstances that can confound estimates of the effects of childhood poverty" (p. 101). These confounding factors encompass: (1) parents' characteristics such as low parental education, single-parent family, parental marital disruption, race, and parental unemployment; and (2) duration of poverty (i.e., persistent versus transitory poverty). Hill and Sandford (1995) also noted the existence of many other confounding factors often not measured by social sciences studies, such as: (1) parental characteristics in relation to academic and social skills, and (2) parenting skills in relation to health behaviors in child caring (e.g., whether they fix nutritious meals, and whether they seek medical advice during early signs of health problems in their child, etc.).

Thus, contemporary research studies are presenting cumulative evidence for the importance of studying the interaction between: (1) internal child's characteristics across developmental domains (i.e., biological, physical, psychological-cognitive, social, emotional), and (2) external factors present in the school and family environments (i.e., SES and socio-cultural such as the parents' characteristics—educational level, occupation, and the family structure such as the language used at home).

Methodological Variations Across Disciplines

Aside from the need to conduct multidimensional studies, taking into consideration the powerful effect of external factors on minority children's internal potential; there is also a critical need for using valid and reliable methodological procedures for representing the social, cultural, and linguistic characteristics of this population. The most common problem in this area is that studies stem from different disciplines, and rarely present an interdisciplinary approach. Therefore, available studies represent a very diverse set of theoretical paradigms and philosophies endorsed, and consequently also select a wide variety of research methodologies. This methodological variation across disciplines and existing problems has been noted by several researchers before (e.g., see Gonzalez, 2002; Messick, 1995; Moss, 1992). For instance, Hill and Sandfort (1995) noted the methodological problems present when comparing research findings conducted with minority children across disciplines:

> Compiling evidence across a number of disciplines presents challenges [since they] tend to differ not only in their theoretical paradigms and acceptable measures but also in their analytical approaches. These differences included variation not only in statistical estimation techniques but also in their general approach to drawing samples and employing control variables. (p. 98)

Studies representing the Ethnic Researcher paradigm tend to include more valid and reliable methodologies such as alternative assessments that represent the culture and language of minority children and their families. Within this paradigm, more powerful and robust results are obtained when combining standardized and qualitative assessments for data collection, and when using complementary statistical and qualitative models for data analysis. For instance, I have used qualitative measures for the methodological control of cultural and linguistic factors (see e.g., Gonzalez, 1994, 1995, 2005, 2006; Gonzalez, Bauerle, & Felix-Holt, 1996). However, there is still a scarcity of these alternative models when studying minority children.

Most social sciences studies try to control for some important confounding factors, as listed above (e.g., parental characteristics and duration of poverty). However, they do not take into control biases introduced by traditional standardized measures (e.g., intelligence quotient IQ tests) that do not account for the effect of culture and language on minority children's development. Even if studies use regression analysis for controlling confounding factors (by including them as additional predictors), methodological problems with standardized tests introduce biases and make results invalid for minority populations, when compared with norms standardized with mainstream groups.

Moreover as noted by McLoyd (1998), studies using regression models for controlling some parental demographic characteristics, overstate the true effect of income because of the mutual association that parental income and child outcomes share with unmeasured parental characteristics (p.190). This problem is especially acute for minority children, since parental characteristics and SES family levels are also associated with cultural and linguistic factors, which are left unmeasured in most studies.

As demonstrated by the research studies included in Part II of this book (and in previously published research studies, see e.g., Gonzalez, 2005, 2006), when developmental, cultural, and linguistic factors are controlled for by valid alternative measures, Hispanic, bilingual, low SES children perform at higher cognitive developmental levels than mainstream, middle-high SES, monolingual counterparts. Moreover, when using one-way ANOVA and multiple linear regression models (as demonstrated by the research studies included in Part II of this book, and in previously published research studies, see e.g., Gonzalez, 2005, 2006), I have found SES to be a more significant predictor of cognitive development than cultural or linguistic factors for Hispanic, bilingual, low SES children. It is important to note that cognitive development was measured with alternative instruments (particularly verbal and non-verbal concept formation, the Qualitative Use of English and Spanish Tasks QUEST, see Gonzalez, 1991, 1994, 1995 for a description of QUEST).

Furthermore, developmental outcomes, such as cognitive development, are difficult to measure validly using standardized tests (for an extended discussion of this topic see Clark & Gonzalez, 1998; Gonzalez, 1996; Gonzalez & Clark, 1999; Gonzalez, et al., 1997; Gonzalez & Yawkey, 1993). Biases and lack of construct and content validity are especially problematic when assessing minority and mainstream, young, low SES children. That is, developmental factors compound the effect of cultural, linguistic, and SES factors on minority children's performance in traditional standardized tests (see e.g., Gonzalez, 2005, 2006). As stated by Hill and Sandfort (1995), "different age-specific aspects of cognitive ability appear to develop at different rates during childhood [and] many of the standard indicators of cognitive ability are age-specific" (p. 103). That is, when conducting longitudinal studies, researchers face the challenge of measuring development over a period of time. That is why alternative assessments are useful tools because they can be adapted to become flexible and sensitive to measure developmental changes over time in minority children.

Another problem is that most studies use only one measure of cognitive abilities and development—typically an intelligence quotient or IQ traditional, standardized test, such as the Wechsler Scales or the Stanford Binet test. Instead a battery of assessments would be needed that also includes other developmental areas besides cognition (e.g., emotional and affective processes) as well as different informants (e.g., parents, teachers, peers). In addition, besides measures of IQ, studies of ecological factors influencing cognitive development should focus on the assessment of potential for learning processes, rather than on learning outcomes measured by IQ tests (see Gonzalez, 1996 for an extended discussion of this topic). Furthermore the effects of poverty on cognitive development can also be measured by academic performance outcomes, such as using qualitative assessments of mathematics and reading abilities during the early elementary grades.

By using measures of cognitive development that represent validly cultural and linguistic factors; the specific qualitative differences of how culture, language, age, and low SES affect cognitive processes can be uncovered (see e.g., Gonzalez, et al., 2006). However, most studies still use more simplistic and surface level methodologies, showing that poor minority children scored lower on IQ standardized tests when compared with minority and/or mainstream children from middle and upper-middle income families. Instead of actual differences in the cognitive developmental outcomes of minority, low SES children, these studies do show methodological problems with their measures. The presence of uncontrolled and confounding factors in these measures, stemming from cultural and linguistic domains, make results invalid for the population of minority, low SES children (for an extended discussion of this topic see Gonzalez, 2002). The situation is even worse when studying socio-emotional development in minority children from low SES backgrounds due to even a more acute scarcity of developmental studies conducted within a wide range of social science disciplines. The effect of poverty on children's impaired socio-emotional development is mediated by parental behaviors impacted by economic stress in the family. For instance, Elder, Conger, Foster, and Ardelt (1992), found that "economic stress increases parental stress, which in turn causes depression in children" (cited in Hill & Sandfort, 1995, p. 105). McLoyd (1998) showed that "economic hardship increases maternal psychological distress, which in turn interferes with their abilities to nurture their children" (cited in Hill & Sandfort, 1995, p. 105). Moreover, as noted by Hill and Sandfort (1995), these studies "evidence that poverty contributes to behavior problems, dependency and feelings of unhappiness and anxiety" (p. 106).

Another factor affecting the accuracy of insight into the cognitive developmental performance of young children is the instrument's sensitivity to tap individual differences, and to allow the evaluator to measure and value cultural and linguistic diversity. Alternative assessments can be adapted to represent and measure validly and reliably the cultural and linguistic factors affecting minority children's development. For instance, QUEST allows the evaluator to use the first-and-second languages of the minority child as a simultaneous methodology for administration and response. This procedure results in the use of *code switching* (i.e., use of both Spanish and English within the same sentence) and *code mixing* (i.e., use of Spanish and English in consecutive independent sentences) by both the evaluator providing instructions as well as the minority child providing verbal responses. This alternative language of administration and language of response methodology has demonstrated to be a significant predictor of Hispanic, low SES children; making possible the methodological control of cultural and linguistic confounding factors (Gonzalez et al., 1996; Gonzalez, 2005, 2006). Moreover, the use of alternative instruments sensitive to individual differences can also assist in accurately assessing individual changes when using longitudinal or sequential designs. The accurate measure of individual differences is particularly important in minority children because they are associated with cultural and linguistic diversity and developmental factors.

Thus, as discussed in this section, a multidimensional perspective needs to be taken into consideration when studying minority students. The wide variation of disciplines, with their researchers attempting to study the development of minority students, introduces a similarly wide variety of methodologies. Different disciplines endorse a variety of theoretical paradigms and philosophies while using a diverse set of measures and data analysis procedures. Another problem when conducting research with minority students is the presence of confounding factors in relation to the control and/or measure of ecological variables (e.g., SES, language, and culture). Presently, problems still exist with the validity and reliability of standardized tests of cognitive, linguistic, social, and emotional development, which do not represent cultural and linguistic variables and SES factors, and do not tap individual differences and developmental changes present in this population. In the section below, we will review more closely the definition of theories and discuss how they can vary in their perspectives when used to study development and academic achievement in minority children.

Definition of Theories

Theories provide the structure or framework of general laws and principles that are internally consistent and include: (1) axioms (i.e., formal statement of the assumptions, postulates, self-evident beliefs), (2) generalizations from proven hypotheses based on valid data and logical derivations, and (3) definitions of concepts. Then, theories provide explanations and predictions logically derived from axioms, generalizations, and definitions of concepts that represent connections between facts or data measuring behaviors and the cause-effect relations or associations between variables or factors studied. It is important to note that different theoretical frameworks may use the same labels of concepts or constructs but they may have different connotations or meanings. That is why is so important for theories to define operationally terms used, behaviorally based and measurable definitions that also need to be operationally defined by researchers when conducting a study.

Scientific theories offer explicit and logically organized categories, and formally organized schemes or taxonomies that researchers can use to conduct systematic analysis and comparisons among data (Thomas, 1996). Categories or taxonomies used for data coding can be produced in two manners: (1) inductively (i.e., pre-conceived at the time of planning a study) for the case of experimental or quasi-experimental and descriptive or correlation studies; or (2) deductively (i.e., discovered once data is produced and coding categories are derived from content represented in data) for the case of qualitative studies such as case studies, ethnographies, historiographies, content analysis, etc.

Theoretical frameworks are research-based and data-driven and offer factual support based on a large body of evidence for its conceptual definitions and cause-effect relations and associations between variables or factors. It is important to analyze the strength of evidence in terms of confidence of sources (in relation to validity and reliability of methodological design for research studies and its data collection and analysis characteristics), and also types and amount of evidence offered as proof for a theory. That is, series of studies using a variety of research designs, and data collection and analysis methodologies, and conducted by multiple researchers should be provided as proof for a theory. According to Leedy and Omrod (2005), scientific research in the social sciences such as education has many characteristics, it: (1) seeks to find answers and conclusive evidence for research questions or hypotheses stated; (2) is based on systematic and disciplined inquiry that follows scientific research methodology for its design and data collection and analysis procedures; and (3) is organized, structured, and testable based on data and previous theoretical knowledge.

Researchers generate ideas for research questions based on prior knowledge of scientific literature, and reflections and observations about social and cultural contextual reality of professional and personal experiences related to the phenomenon under study. When researchers are trained, they are initiated into an academic discipline that trains their minds to think systematically and reflect about daily life experiences and their naturalistic observations of the phenomenon under study in relation to their prior knowledge about literature on the topic and research methodology. That is, based on natural observations of behaviors under study and related experiences in the real social and cultural world, researchers generate explanations or rationales for behaviors based on prior knowledge of the literature and theories on this topic, and prior personal and professional experiences. Then, there is subjectivity involved when researchers select a theoretical perspective which endorses particular research methodologies for designing a study, starting from the statement of research questions. This subjectivity involved in research activities is related to the issue that the most important tool for research is the researcher's brain, and her/his understanding of theories and models, prior knowledge and experiences, and his/her cultural values and beliefs about the constructs they are studying.

These explanations in turn generate well-defined hypotheses or research questions that can be testable using the scientific research method that systematically and in an organized and structured manner follows data collection and analysis procedures to answer the research questions posed. These research questions identify variables or factors (constructs or concepts) that represent measurable behaviors that can be operationally defined or described, identify relations (cause-effect or associations) with other factors or constructs, and can be systematically tested through data.

Moreover, as discussed below, different theoretical approaches accept or reject different types of research designs, and data collection and analysis methodologies as proof for a theory. So, there is always a certain degree of subjectivity in what methodologies become acceptable for offering proof or evidence for specific theories. Finally, theories that create new methodologies in the process of generating proof for its validity, in turn become stronger theories that can create methodological tools for contributing with new knowledge and opening new research areas and questions. Then, a theory becomes more fertile if it goes beyond replication studies and continues to have historical significance over an extended period of time.

More importantly, best theories do not only explain past events, but also can predict future events through the generation of hypotheses or research questions. These explanations of past behaviors and the prediction of future behaviors needs to occur not only at the level of generalizations, but also at the specific level of individual behaviors or cases. Then, a theory can have theoretical or general principles that contribute to the creation of new knowledge, as well as specific educational applications and recommendations for guiding educational practitioners (i.e., teachers, counselors, social workers, psychologists) in solving daily classroom problems, for guiding parents with developmental advice, and for supporting other professionals serving children such as pediatricians, nurses, social workers, etc. Theories can also contribute with derived products that have practical implications such as tests, instructional materials for children, training materials for professionals, etc.

Parsimony is another important characteristic of theories. That is, theories should be economical and provide explanations and predictions of behaviors and the cause-effect relations and associations between variables using the simplest possible processes. The more abstract and complicated the theory is, the more difficult it becomes to test hypotheses or research questions through data collection and analysis. However, at the same time, theories should be complex enough to be falsifiable or offer the possibility to uncover new and intuitive results that may be unexpected, serendipitous, and even contradictory; which may result in creative and novel approaches. This later characteristic is also connected with the adaptability of a theory, that is its capacity to include new data, and to re-interpret and revise guiding principles in light of new data.

The Start of a Theory: A Model

In contrast to a theory that is data-based and offer proven relations between variables, a model is just a tentative set of hypotheses or research questions that have not been yet proven by data but derive logically from an abstraction or representation of reality, or from possible explanations of behaviors and its causes and association to variables. In contrast, as explained in the section above, research questions that have been empirically tested and validated in light of data and a series of studies. A theory provides a body of evidence that demonstrates the existence of extensive empirical studies that have been conducted to test, refine, and revise the model hypothesized.

Observations and descriptions of behaviors in its natural environment can be viewed as the springboard for theory building. Natural observations reported as qualitative and descriptive studies can serve as a fertile ground for generating hypotheses or research questions, and for identifying variables involved in a cause-effect relation or association between variables.

Comparison of Theories

In the same manner that researchers introduce subjectivity to data collection and analysis, which fit their values and beliefs about the topic under study and its theoretical explanation, they also introduce biases to theory comparison. When we compare theories we need to define a philosophical framework and its dimensions and criteria and standards against which we will analyze similarities and differences (Thomas, 1996). Researchers choose standards in relation to their values and beliefs and theoretical predilections. And in turn, standards selected guide the judgments, criticisms, and comparisons that researchers make between theories. New theoretical perspectives can emerge as responses to unsatisfactory features in traditional theories, such as the lack of inclusion of socio-cultural differences in child development and learning (e.g., first language other than English, bilingual home environments, low income family households, minority cultural value systems for child rearing, etc.).

Furthermore, new technology has opened possibilities for collection and analysis of large amounts of data representing multiple cause-effect relations and association among a vast number of variables (Leedy & Omrod, 2005). New computer capabilities for automatic statistical software packages have resulted in large numbers of researchers undertaking complex multivariate statistical studies. New statistical tests have also open possibilities for combining qualitative and quantitative research designs into mixed methodologies that can analyze in-depth cases within a large number of subjects. Mixed methodologies also provide for researchers an opportunity to examine behaviors from multiple methodological windows, such as a variety of data collection instruments and research and data analysis designs. These multiple methodologies result in more valid interpretations of data patterns in a meaningfully manner, and consequently in more valid and reliable studies.

Nature Versus Nurture

One of the central criteria used to compare similarities and differences between theories is the nature versus nurture domain. The two most important causal explanations or meaning generated for explaining data and behaviors include hereditary or biological (internal) factors and environmental or socio-cultural (external) factors. These external and internal factors represent a nature versus nurture relation, and traditional theoretical positions include: (1) Environmentalists (i.e., emphasizing the individual's experiences and learning processes in determining development), (2) Preformationists (i.e., part of the hereditarian tradition, environment has no influence, and emphasis is on innate traits), and (3) Predeterminists (i.e., part of the hereditarian tradition, environment has little influence, and emphasis is on heredity for development).

A more contemporary approach is an Interactionist position, which emphasizes the active role of the individual in how the boundaries set by heredity and maturation interacts with the environmental influences. Within this Interactionist view, there are two important developmental principles (as explained earlier in this Chapter): (1) range of reaction, referring to the limits imposed by the genotype on the kinds of phenotypes (i.e., aspects of the genetic endowment that are visible through physical characteristics, such as color of eyes and hair, potential for a range of minimum and maximum height and weight in relation to nutrition and other environmental influences) that are influenced by the different environments; and (2) canalization, referring to the extreme environmental conditions that can modify genotypes (i.e., genetic codes). In addition, in relation to the principle of canalization, there are three types of complex correlations between the genotype and the environment: (1) passive, in which the family environment matches the individual's genotype; (2) reactive, in which genetic differences in an individual are supported by the environment (e.g., deaf child born to deaf parents); and (3) active, in which the individual modifies the environment to fit his/her genotype.

Within a contemporary Interactionist view, there are many open areas for research, such as to understand how wide are the boundaries set by heredity for various aspects of development, what environmental factors are more significantly affecting heredity and how these potentials manifest as behaviors and developmental abilities and skills learned, how the interaction of heredity and environment reflects into different developmental stages within the life span, and understand the processes by which the interaction of nature and nurture takes place, to name a few areas.

A form of Interactionist view is represented by Humanistic theories which provide a view of development and growth that is flexible and dynamic, and sees development as an unlimited potential to grow. Inner motivations and feelings drive individuals to achieve self-realization and to seek environmental conditions that satisfy their basic physical and emotional needs. Humanist theories believe that the child's original nature is one of positive striving to actualize an inner essence that is good and constructive, with interest, talents, and emotions. Humanistic approaches view individuals as free wills that can choose and display creative power, development is a positive striving to actualize an inner essence that is good and constructive. A traditional Piagetian perspective imposes limits to development based on maturation.

A Socio-Constructivistic theory, following a Vygotskyan perspective, provides also an Interactionist view of development with emphasis on socio-historical factors in which an individual develops exposed to experiences in the social institutions of the culture (e.g., school, family, church, etc.), and the child's own developmental history within the unique opportunities and demands presented by his/her culture (i.e., the child's own ontogenic development). For instance, Vygotsky (1986) postulated that children needed to use action to create internalizations that form thought. Besides criteria necessary for comparing theories such as the nature versus nurture domain, and the resulting Interactionist view, theories also provide a structure for research methodology as discussed below.

Theories Provide Taxonomies for Research Methodology

The two most important theoretical causal explanations discussed above, external and internal factors, include meaningful interpretations, and the development of attributions, inferences, and causal explanations for patterns or clusters of findings based on trends in the data and behaviors measured. In addition, theories provide structure to data analysis or behaviors studied and measured by the development of taxonomies or categories for data analysis.

Theories can also have different ways of representing concepts, definitions, and principles. Some representational tools can be verbal or non-verbal, and may include words, diagrams, figures, metaphors, and analogies. Some examples of metaphors for understanding the concept of "theory" follow. A theory is like "a lens" to filter out meanings in patterns of behaviors observed and measured in data. A theory is also like a "map" that guides the researcher's representations of behaviors in the research methodologies and guiding principles used for choosing and developing standardized and/or alternative measurement tools and categories for data collection and analysis. And so, when a researcher chooses a particular theoretical framework or perspective to collect and analyze data, there is a particular "tint" or angle that the data interpretations will produce. This is so because a theory can only represent selected aspects of the multidimensional complexity of reality, an approximation of "the truth" about a topic. This is the rationale behind multiple contradictory explanations for the same phenomenon or topic studied under different theoretical approaches, because the researcher chooses a particular school of thought to represent reality and select research methodologies to measure behaviors and to analyze data collected. Even more interesting is the issue that different researchers endorsing different theoretical frameworks would accept different research methodologies to collect and analyze data (e.g., standardized versus qualitative measures) as "evidence" or proof of validation of research questions or hypotheses. The most important tool for conducting research is actually, not the actual methodologies used, but the brain of the researcher, who is subjectively making decisions about what is "proof" and what "interpretations" to make about patterns of statistical or qualitative data.

Thus, in this first section of Chapter 1, an overview of the Ethnic Researcher perspective has been discussed in relation to multidimensional theories that take into account the interaction between nature and nurture. This contemporary perspective uses alternative research methodologies to study development and academic achievement in minority children in a more valid and reliable manner.

The Confounding Effect of Poverty and Cultural and Linguistic Differences in Minority Children's Development and Academic Achievement

The second section of Chapter 1 applies the Ethnic Researcher perspective, with its multidimensional and Interactionist view, to analyze the confounding effect of poverty and cultural/linguistic differences in minority children's development and academic achievement. Even though some minority children and their families can cope with the stress of poverty and become resilient, the vast majority of them become at-risk of academic underachievement. Childhood poverty negatively impacts academic achievement, school performance, placement, and years of completed education. Low family income tends to be positively related to children's poor academic achievement (e.g., Alwin & Thornton, 1984; Patterson, Kupersmidt, & Vaden, 1990; all cited in Hill Sandfort, 1995), especially during early childhood and with cumulative effects spreading throughout adolescence and adulthood (especially when poverty spans a long period of time). As reported by Corcoran, Gordon, Laren, and Solon (1992; cited in Hill Sandfort, 1995), "Increasing the proportion of childhood years a male spends in poverty reduces his adulthood earnings, family income, and family income/needs by 50% and decreases his adulthood wages ad work hours by 25-30%" (p. 118).

Moreover, younger children are at a higher risk for stronger negative effects of poverty on their academic achievement, with poverty negatively affecting mediating factors present in their family environment (e.g., parental characteristics). Some studies even show some higher likelihood of poor children to be at-risk for special education placement (e.g., Chaikind & Corman, 1991; cited in Hill & Sandfort, 1995), especially when other biological at-risk conditions were also present (e.g., low birth weight). In addition, evidence exists of a positive relationship between family income and years of school completion in young children (e.g., Duncan, 1993; Hill & Duncan, 1987; Kennedy, Jung, & Orlando, 1986; all cited in Hill & Sandfort, 1995). This positive relationship remains even when studies control for other mediating or potentially confounding factors (e.g., race and parental educational levels, neighborhood conditions).

In addition, school characteristics and teachers' behaviors also influence low SES children's achievement. More specifically, teachers' attitudes, school values, school and classroom climate are significant factors influencing low SES children's achievement, especially when they are from minority backgrounds (e.g., see McLoyd, 1998 for a review of contemporary research on this topic). Moreover, according to Alexander, Entwisle, and Thompson (1987, cited in McLoyd, 1998), Kindergarten and first grade teachers were found to have lower achievement expectations for low SES students. Teachers' expectations were based on their non-cognitive negative perceptions of the low SES children's speech and dress patterns (using these misleading clues as behavioral signs of lack of cognitive maturity). Then, as reported by Alexander and collaborators (1987), these negative attitudes in teachers translate into less positive attention, fewer learning opportunities, and less reinforcement of instances of good performance. These negative perceptions, expectations, and attitudes are more likely to be present in middle-class teachers, who are more prone to hold racial and social class biases, stemming from their unfamiliarity with poor and minority students' language and culture.

Furthermore quality of education is also another mediating factor present in the extra-familial environment that can significantly affect achievement levels in poor children. As reported by McLoyd (1998), the Head Start program has shown the power of early childhood high quality stimulation, resulting in superior academic readiness skills during preschool and primary grades. However, these cognitive and academic skills may be lost by the third or fourth grade if high quality school programs are discontinued. Thus, as concluded by McLoyd (1998), "although preschool intervention offers some protection from the negative effects of poverty, over the long run, it does not bestow levels of cognitive and academic competence comparable to those seen among non-poor children in the general population" (p. 195).

In conclusion, there is yet scarcity of studies that control for confounding cultural and linguistic factors interacting with poverty, and which use valid measures for minority groups. As stated by Hill and Sandfort (1995), the few studies using mostly traditional and single measures show that "childhood poverty is an important impediment to the physical growth, cognitive development, and socio-emotional development of children" (p. 106). It is also important to understand what aspects of poverty processes, and their accompanying mediating factors affecting the family and neighborhood-community structure, may have similar or different effects on the developmental opportunities that mainstream and minority children may have. Finally, as remarked by Hill and Sandfort (1995), "low parental income substantially increases the risk of dropping out of high school, delaying completion of high school, delaying college entry and completion, and overall receiving fewer total years of completed education" (p. 112).

In sum, there is need to conduct studies that broaden our understanding of the interacting effects of poverty and other mediating factors (i.e., biological, psychological, and family and community structure) on the achievement and cognitive and socio-emotional development of minority children. Developmental *processes* influenced by cultural and linguistic factors need to be studied further within a multidimensional and ecological paradigm by ethnic researchers (e.g., bilingualism, knowledge acquisition, problem-solving ability, cultural thinking style, social style of interpersonal relations, cultural value and belief systems, bicultural identity, self-esteem and self-concept).

Demographic Data on Minorities

As reported by Hodgkinson (1992), the Census data of 1990 show that states with a higher growth rate tend to have a high minority population, especially minority youth. I will just focus on the two immigrant groups highly represented in the 1980s and 1990s decades, Hispanic and Asian. Population estimates of the native residents done by the US Census Bureau (2000) based on the 1990 US census, report that by July 1, 1999, Hispanics comprise 8.2% of the population, with a median age of 18.6 years; and Asian/Pacific Islanders-non Hispanic, 1.6%, with a median age of 13.7 years. The much higher rate of growth of non-traditional (i.e., Hispanic, and Asian/Pacific Islanders) groups is due to both high legal and illegal immigration trends, and a higher fertility rate. With white-non Hispanic still accounting for 76.8% of the US population, but with an older median age of 37.7 years; with Asian/Pacific Islanders and Hispanics representing the younger populations.

According to Hodgkinson, by the year 2010, "minorities will encompass more than half of the population of twelve states and the District of Columbia." Projections done by the US Census Bureau (2000), foresee that 45.5% of the US resident population would be composed of minorities (Hispanic 23.1%; Black-non Hispanic, 13.2%; American Indian-non Hispanic, .8%; and Asian/Pacific Islander-non Hispanic, 8.4%).

Thus, the American population has been changing dramatically during the 1980s and 1990s, especially among four states that have the highest proportion of minorities New York, California, Texas, and Florida. Over half of the population in California, Texas, and Florida will be minority well before the year 2010. Moreover, projections of the US population for the 1990-2010 period forecasts that the white, non-Hispanic youth will decrease by 3.8 million, while the Hispanic youth will increase by 2.6 million (Hodgkinson, 1992). Hispanics are projected to increase to 14.8% of the US population by 2015. The US Census Bureau (1997) reported that the Hispanic population will increase in approximately 74% between 1995 and 2015.

Demographic Data on Immigrants

Population estimates of the foreign-born done by the US Census Bureau (2000), consistent with the 1990 population estimates report that Hispanics of any race would account for the larger percentage (43%), followed by white-non Hispanic (25.3%), and by Asian/Pacific Islander-non Hispanic (24.5%). According to the US Bureau of the census (1992), the decades of the 90s (7.3 million) and 80s (4.4 and a half million) show the largest number of immigrants legally admitted since the 1920s (4.1 million), 1910s (5.7 million), and 1900s (8.7 million).

According to an Immigration and Naturalization Service Report (2000), immigration trends during the period of 1981-1996 show a total of 13.4 million of legal immigrants admitted, with the largest proportion repre-sented by Mexico (3.3 million), Asian/Pacific Islanders (i.e., Philippines, Vietnam, China, Korea; with less than 1 million each), and Latin Americans (i.e., Mexico, Dominican Republic, El Salvador, and Cuba; with less than a million each). This new reality of immigration trends has also increased dramatically the number of minority or English-as-a-second-language (ESL) students in the US public schools.

Presently, adult immigrants who are illiterate do not have a real chance to enter the US labor market. Their children, both foreign and US-born, may have an opportunity to earn a living in the US technological society if they do not drop out of school. Dropouts are more likely to be unemployed than high school graduates and to earn less money if eventually they can find a job (US Department of Education—DOE, National Center for Education Statistics—NCES, 1999). High school dropouts are also more likely to receive welfare moneys (US DOE, NCES, 1998) and to be female, single-parents at younger ages (US, DOE, NCES, 1996). There are also other social implications of young adults dropping out of high school, because a disproportionate proportion of dropouts are represented in the nation's prison and death row inmates (US Department of Justice, Office of Justice Program, Bureau of Justice Statistics, 1994).

Parental Characteristics: Home Cultural Context

Following on the analysis of the confounding effect of poverty on cultural and linguistic differences in minority children, it is central to discuss the home cultural context and parental characteristics affecting development and academic achievement. As discussed in the section above, the need for assuming an ecological view when studying minority students is especially highlighted by the fact that most of them come from a low socioeconomic status (SES) background. As defined by McLoyd (1998), "Unlike poverty, SES signifies an individual's, a family's or a group's ranking on a hierarchy according to its access to or control over some combination of valued commodities such as wealth, power, and social status" (p. 188). Many parental characteristics such as occupation, educational level, prestige, power, and lifestyle denote numerous mediating factors associated with SES, which significantly affect children's development and academic achievement. It is important to note that these environmental factors interact with other mediating individual factors such as age, gender, race, and ethnicity. And for this reason, research findings obtained when studying majority populations cannot be generalized to minority groups.

Recent demographic data also supports the urgent need to study the effect of low SES on minority children's development. Then, studies showing poor quality and good quality cultural family factors related to SES will be discussed, in relation to the family structure and the parent-child relationship. Special emphasis will be given to the interaction of the characteristics of the parents' and children's personalities, and to the impact of low SES background on the children's academic and economic productivity. Closure will be given to this section by discussing the need for conducting research on the interaction of low SES and developmental variables, for the specific case of minority young children.

The Socio-Cultural, Physical, and Psychological Context of Family

The parents' SES is also related to the number of years of residency in the US, and therefore to whether they are immigrants or first, second, third (or more) generation in the US. Then, the level of acculturation can interact with the presence of poverty, which in turn influence parental stress levels. Levels of cultural adaptation will determine whether or not minority parents are able to access mainstream resources and to become fully-fledged participants within the mainstream society. For instance, Wang (1993) studied Hispanic (first-and-second generation Caribbean families—i.e., Cuban, Puerto Rican, or Costa Rican), African-American, and Anglo second-grade children from low and middle-class SES backgrounds, living in Orlando, Florida. Wang found that cultural familial factors related to SES were better predictors of the child's metacognitive developmental skills rather than the child's ethnicity. The cultural family factors identified by Wang (1993) were: (1) family structure such as family size, child's birth order, parents' marital status, parental divorce and separation, and language spoken at home; and (2) parent-child interactions such as whether parents assisted in their child's homework

More specifically, Wang found that "SES supersedes ethnicity as a predictor for a child's metacognitive development" (p. 87). Wang defined and measured metacognitive development as a social construction that stimulates the development of learning strategies and executive processes to monitor and guide performance in cognitive tasks during early childhood. He concluded that "the same pattern of SES effects was apparent for all three ethnic groups. That is, children from higher SES families" (regardless of ethnicity) had higher overall metacognitive scores than children from lower SES families (p. 87). Similar findings were also reported by Walker, Greenwood, Hart, and Carta (1994), who showed that differences found between Hispanic and African-American children from low SES backgrounds were attributable to their SES-related factors (socio-cultural contexts such as the home, community, and school environments), rather than to their minority or cultural background.

Even household characteristics related to small family size can enable parents to develop higher quality home environments and influence more positively their children's development (Blake, 1989, Zuravin, 1988, cited in Garret, Ng'andu, & Ferron, 1994). This leads to the idea that household characteristic such as the family composition in terms of number of siblings and the presence of mother/father companion, and other adults (e.g., extended family members) can significantly impact the child's development outcome. For instance, Garrett and colleagues (1994) found a very high correlation between the adult-child ratio and the number of siblings. They also found all maternal characteristics (i.e., age, ethnicity—White or Hispanic, or African American—educational level, academic ability in terms of IQ, and self-esteem) to be significantly associated with the quality of the home environment.

Poverty can also have a negative effect on the quality of the family structure and the parent-child relationship. According to Takeuchi, Williams, and Adair (1991, cited in Garrett et al., 1994), poverty can indirectly affect parents' behaviors resulting in marital conflict, psychological distress, clinical depression, loss of self-esteem and feelings of mastery, and withdrawal from friends and family. The higher incidence of single mothers among minority children is also associated with a high-risk and stress for children's development, primarily because of multiple demands and limited time and energy resulting in overworked mothers (Garfinkel & McLanahan, 1986, cited in Garrett et al., 1994).

Moreover, the child's characteristics can also interact with the parents' ability to create a higher or lower quality family environment and parent-child relationship. For instance, the temperament fit between the parents and the child, or the challenges imposed by taking care of a premature or low birth weight child, can significantly impact the quality of the parent-child relationship. For instance, Garrett and colleagues (1994), found some of the child's characteristics (i.e., being male is negatively associated, and being older has a positive relationship) to have a significant effect on the quality of the home environments of poor Hispanic, African American, and White families.

Hence, the issue of the complexity of at-risk factors affecting poor children's developmental outcomes, and whether or not they are able to cope with environmental stress needs to be further studied. As discussed throughout this article, an urgent need presents itself to maintain a multidimensional approach to research. For instance, Masten and Coatworth (1998) emphasized the need to study the interacting effect of recurrent or changing child's characteristics and ecological factors on resilience. Examples of recurrent child's characteristics that need to be further studied are temperament and personality traits, unique individual needs, and self-regulation of attention, emotion, and behaviors. Examples of changing child's characteristics that need to be studied are developmental stages, interests, attitudes, perceptions, and values and belief systems. Examples of ecological factors open for research are the quality of parent-child relationship, and the effect of mentors and other educational opportunities for success.

Therefore, there is still a major task ahead for researcher studying minority children's development: to discover the interacting effect of SES factors and internal potential that may result in resilient or vulnerable conditions. More specifically, researchers still need to uncover the different transitional or recurrent risks affecting minority children, and which are the protective mechanisms at different ages and points in development. That is, well adapted parents, or any other committed and effective adult present, can function as scaffolds to provide opportunities, protective mechanisms, and emotional support for children exposed to at-risk ecological factors (such as poverty) to develop resilience. Masten and Coatworth (1998) highlighted the importance of providing at-risk children with a protective ecological environment, especially during infancy and early childhood because "there is no such a thing as an invulnerable child" (p. 216). They acknowledged that conducting experimental research for implementing change in the dynamic developmental and ecological factors influencing adaptive and resilient process is challenging, especially because of the complex role of culture on minority children's development.

In sum, poverty can be a high-risk factor for the development of minority children, and could have a negative impact when significant mediating processes (e.g., the quality of the attachment between parents and child), facilitating successful adaptation, are damaged. The availability of committed, involved, nurturing, and competent parents is crucial and provides powerful adaptive systems that can protect the minority child's development.

Family Structure and Quality of Parent-Child Relationship

Presently, researchers have put forth ecological and developmental models of the dynamic interplay of the child's experiences and the internal child's factors. For instance, Bradley, Whiteside, and Mundfrom (1994) studied premature, low birth weight, low SES children in a three-year longitudinal study. Their findings showed that stress present in the external environment increased the risk of these children to present developmental problems, increasing their susceptibility to risk for a wide variety of physical, mental, and social problems; and for reducing their resiliency and producing morbidity or susceptibility for problems due to a combination of biological and environmental risks. Resilience refers to individual variations in response to at-risk conditions such as psychological characteristics of children who can resist conditions of poverty, as well as protective home environmental characteristics in four areas: (1) aspects of caregiving and home contexts that provide sustenance for health and biological integrity; (2) stimulation for adaptive functioning, support for emotional integrity; (3) structure for responding to individual's needs, capabilities, and behavioral styles; and (4) surveillance for timing and structure. Resilient children present some temperamental characteristics that produce positive responses from caregivers, and tend to have fewer habits that produce stress in caregivers. Then, poverty interacts with associated negative home and parental characteristics to reduce resilience and increase the odds of adverse developmental outcomes in children with biological at-risk conditions (such as premature children).

The most important at-risk ecological variables were shown to be the parental characteristics such as low levels of education in mothers, occupation in parents (related to income), parental depression and chronic stress, and absence of emotional bonds in marriage and external family networks that may offer social support in time of need of parents (for financial assistance, for offering child care help, to provide emotional support, etc.). Some characteristics of the home environment also were associated with resilience or morbidity in young children such as presence of adult males in the household, density of household (number of rooms in relation to number of people living in the house), moving more than once a year (related to stability of residence), and availability of toys and other educational materials in the household. It is important to note that most participants of Bradley and collaborators (1994) study were minority (African-American and Hispanic) and only about 10% of premature, low birth weight children living in poverty were reported as resilient. Bradley and collaborators (1994) noted:

> There is evidence that the impact of poverty is not consistent across all socio-cultural groups. Other cultural, language, demographic, and psychological factors interact with SES to help determine the pattern of parenting [and more importantly] the quality of the home environment is not uniform across families living in poverty. (p. 347)

More specifically, Bradley and collaborators noted the presence of mediating and protective factors such as "the caregiving context that may serve as protective mechanisms" (p. 359), which may provide low SES children with adequate sustenance, stimulation, support, and structure. They concluded by stating the need "to determine particular relations among risk and protective mechanisms in different socio-cultural groups living in poverty" (p. 359).

It follows that the parents' SES strongly affects their behaviors and child rearing practices, through some mediating variables such as parental educational levels and occupational attainments, as well as home language use in relation to academic or literacy activities stimulated at home. For instance, Duncan, Brooks-Gunn, and Kato (1994) studied cognitive development by comparing the performance of infants and toddlers (0 to 3 years of age) from minority, Hispanic and African-American and majority backgrounds. They found that two major mediating factors (i.e., psychological effects of poverty on parents' characteristics and the provision of educational resources to children) had a negative impact on the children's cognitive development (measured by IQ tests such as Weschler Preschool and Primary Scale of Intelligence, WPPSI; Wechsler, 1967). These two mediating factors also were found to predict the presence of behavioral problems (measured by behavioral problem checklists).

More specifically, Duncan and colleagues (1994) showed that the detrimental psychological effects of poverty on maternal characteristics are related to female headship of households, and inability to develop coping strategies for adapting to the at-risk conditions of poverty. Duncan and colleagues' (1994) study also demonstrated that the presence of poverty can affect negatively the mental health of parents, leading to some problems such as clinical depression. Moreover, they found that the low SES background of parents negatively affected their ability to provide educational resources for their children (a second mediating factor). These educational resources were related to: (1) the learning and stimulation environment at home (i.e., the amount and quality of time parents spend with their children, the emotional health of parents, the level of stimulation, the physical environment at home, and the affective and warmth provide in the parent-child relationship); (2) the low-income neighborhoods in which low SES families lived (related to the quality of public schools, community resources such as parks and recreation facilities, police protection, peer influences such as role models and parental monitoring); and (3) the duration, degree, and timing of poverty (with cumulative effects of poverty).

That is, as reported by Duncan and colleagues (1994), "children in persistently poor families have 9.1-point lower IQs [and] there were highly significant detrimental effects of being poor both early [during either 12 or 24 months] and late [during either 36 or 48 months]" (p. 307). In addition, the neighborhood level of economic deprivation can be interactive with family poverty, and can have a detrimental effect on the child's cognitive development (Duncan et al, 1994). Thus, the Duncan and colleagues' (1994) study exemplifies the importance of understanding external, family structure factors that mediate the negative effect of low SES on young children's development. Moreover, the detrimental effects of poverty can endure over a length of time, and can even impair productivity during adulthood; through limiting the achievement of poor minority children's full potential and ultimately hindering their educational attainment (Hill & Sandfort, 1995). So, several mediating characteristics present within the family environment (e.g., the quality of the parental characteristics) interact with other factors present in the community environment (e.g., community, school, etc.) in which, poor, young, minority children live and develop.

The Role of Home Minority-Language on Development & Academic Achievement: A Socio-Constructivistic Perspective

In a natural socio-cultural environment setting such as home, children learn language and concepts simultaneously, with language providing a symbolic tool for expressing non-verbal and verbal thoughts. Language is added to non-verbal thinking and concepts during the second year of life providing children the ability to move from more concrete and perceptual ideas to more abstract and metacognitive ways of thinking during the preschool years. Language provides the capacity of abstraction and displacement from the immediate time and space allowing the individual to communicate ideas at a distance via media (*written*: e.g., books, messages, newspapers, magazines, computers, etc.; *oral*: e.g., phone, radio, etc.; *visual*: e.g., videos, photos, drawings, graphs, figures, symbolic play, art crafts, etc.).

With the onset of language, toddlers and preschoolers can start manipulating real-life experiences, by using language to shape, categorize, store, and recreate experiences. Young children can recall and transform past experiences from memory through their symbolic play and other forms of representation (e.g., drawings, dialogue, questions, dreams, and recollection of previous experiences through language, role playing, and acting out, etc.). Infants and toddlers develop awareness of the onset of language and become sensitive for how language provides for them conventional mapping for verbal expression of thoughts, so they can engage in the communication of their verbal and non-verbal ideas through an intentional and observable mean: words. Preschool children have the newly acquired ability to develop labels and verbal networks for better developing and communicating their thoughts. Thus, educators need to nurture the natural function of language by using concrete and developmentally appropriate materials to think and talk about subject areas and topic knowledge.

Several authors (see e.g., Delgado Gaitan, 1994; Ogbu, 1982; Suarez-Orozco, 1989) have presented continuity and discontinuity theories as an explanation for the degree of cultural adaptation of minority parents and children to the public US school system, which in turn impact the children's developmental level attained. In fact, the degree of acculturation of minority families and their children is reflected in their home language use, their daily cultural practices, and the particular values socially communicated verbally and non-verbally by parents to their children. That is, the particular language used at home helps parents to socialize their children, helping as a major tool to transmit implicitly cultural values to children. In fact, Shatz (1991) asserted that "language is a powerful tool of parenting...Not only do parents use language to tell their children directly what is acceptable social behavior, but their language also includes indirect information about social values" (p. 139). Shatz also considered that language reflects practices of social interactions among individuals as well as in relation to social institutions. Thus, the way in which language is used at home also reflects different cultural ways of socializing children, which are called by Shatz (1991) "communicative modes" or styles, related to cultural content transmitted such as social values. Moreover, Ochs and Schieffelin (1984) concluded that how language was used by adults carries implicit information about how to function within a particular social system.

The differences in degrees of acculturation between different generation Hispanic families are also present in the different patterns of home language use. In the case of Hispanic immigrant parents, the primary use of English by children for communicating with siblings at home has an impact on family structure and quality of communication with parents. Children of Hispanic immigrant parents tend to be raised speaking Spanish to their parents at home, but prefer to use English when communicating with peers. In contrast, first-generation Hispanic parents participating in Delgado

Gaitan's (1994) study spoke English as their primary language, and Spanish was spoken only with relatives who were monolingual Spanish (typically of a previous immigrant generation such as grandparents). As Delgado Gaitan (1994) observes "not only had English become the first language in one generation but Spanish language loss was significant in most cases..." (p. 79).

Interestingly, even though language loss occurs only after one generation, the traditional Hispanic values survive across intergenerational socialization practices even when using English, but only in relation to the context of interpersonal family relations. As a result, some similarities and differences between first-generation and immigrant parents occur; especially in relation to the dual cultural identity model presented by first-generation Hispanic parents, who also model cultural values for succeeding in the mainstream school culture. Thus, Hispanic children can be exposed to a monolingual English environment at home, but still develop a bicultural identity that allows them to adapt to social environments with diverse value systems.

As mentioned above, the language used at home by parents may also communicate cultural values and belief systems in relation to educational goals and developmental expectations for their children. For instance, Delgado Gaitan (1994) conducted some ethnographic interviews to Hispanic immigrant parents with low educational levels, and discovered some "cultural myths" held in relation to language development in infants. She stated, "parents agreed that although children received facile attention as infants, verbal communication with babies was 'silly' because they believed that children could not understand them until later—after they began to talk" (p. 75). Despite this finding, she also pinpointed that "The more educated ... immigrant parents...verbally engaged their children very early. They said that they had learned that talking with children in early years was important to develop language skills" (p. 75).

Delgado Gaitan (1994) also provided immigrant and first-generation Hispanic parents the opportunity to participate in a parent/community organization. Even before their participation in the parent program, the first-generation Hispanic parents engaged infants in conversations and gave preschoolers verbal instructions or explanations of activities. This first-generation, Hispanic parents also provided their children with some stimulation for critical thinking skills in relation to academic activities only, but not for social interpersonal relations in which conflict with traditional Hispanic values may occur. For example, a child's willingness to express his/her opinions and ideas would not be penalized, but would be encouraged by first-generation Hispanic parents within the context of an academic activity. That is, a parent helping his/her child with homework would extend the child's questions, and would probe his/her observations about academic related content. In contrast, a child's willingness to participate in an adult conversation with family members, would not be seen as an example of assertiveness, valued from a mainstream cultural perspective. This socially unacceptable behavior from the Hispanic cultural perspective of family interactions would result in a parent's request for the child to show "respect" towards his/her elders and not to "interrupt" the conversation.

So, cultural exposure to the mainstream American society has resulted in Spanish language loss, however the maintenance of cultural values is still present in first-generation Hispanic parents and their second-generation children. With two different criteria in relation to the mainstream academic context and the more traditional socio-cultural view of interactions still present within the minority family, it is interesting to note that there is however, a duality for the retention of values. Hence, even though language loss occurs more rapidly, cultural values tend to survive in the duality of the bicultural experiences that the mainstream school culture and minority family contexts offer to monolingual English Hispanic children. Thus, Hispanic children may have retained cultural values and beliefs of the minority culture; but yet be proficient monolingual, as well as bicultural, English speakers. As Delgado Gaitan (1994) explains, "possibly the parents' own acculturation experiences have made them incorporate a sense of reality and the need to accommodate both values in a way that allows them to fit both worlds: family and society" (p. 81).

Thus, in every culture and at every SES level, every parent tends to have the ultimate goal of socializing their children to adapt to the cultural values present in their social reality. Then, for a minority child to be successful in the school mainstream culture, he or she needs to internalize assertiveness, independence as a thinker, and develop inquiry and critical thinking skills. The dissonance of these mainstream values with the minority Hispanic culture would be accommodated by parents in their socialization efforts, because they had develop social knowledge about the cultural discontinuities between the mainstream school and minority family contexts. That is, parents would present to their children the need to adapt their behaviors and implicit value systems in order to meet the different social realities of the contrasting contexts in which they live. As a result, Hispanic children were socialized to become *bicultural,* in order to be successful in meeting the needs of culturally discontinuous social environments in which they were expected to be successful. As stated by Delgado Gaitan (1994), "the tacit expectation on the part of the parents is that both can and should coexist and do not necessarily detract from one another" (p. 82).

As reported by Delgado Gaitan (1994), in comparison, before participating in the parent program, immigrant Hispanic parents with low educational levels just allowed their children to observe daily activities with no verbal communication involved (e.g., eating, preparing meals, etc.). The lower level of education of these immigrant parents, especially of the mothers, was reported by Delgado Gaitan (1994) to have an impact on how language was modeled and taught at home to the children. Immigrant parents fear the change of family values, and felt a tension on the degree of acculturation experienced by their children as they get older, and the displacement of their Hispanic traditional values. This fear and tension, as mentioned above, was not present within the first-generation Hispanic parents, who had resolved this tension by developing in themselves and in their children a bicultural identity. As concluded by Delgado Gaitan (1994), the most important difference between first-generation and immigrant parents was the presence, or absence correspondingly, of social and cultural knowledge of the mainstream school system. Only the first-generation parents were able to guide their children into a successful mainstream school culture adaptation, as mentor or mediators to bridge their minority and mainstream experiences into a meaningful bicultural identity.

Even though some differences were found by Delgado Gaitan (1994) when comparing first-generation and immigrant Hispanic parents, she also found continuity in the set of traditional cultural values still used to socialize their children. Most importantly all the parents wanted for their children was to become successful in their academic activities in the mainstream school culture, and were willing to make accommodations in their degree of acculturation in order to socialize their children to adapt to their bicultural experience. What she found to be critical was to present to parents the opportunity to make their own personal decisions about the acculturation degree that they were willing to acquire. Only then were parents able to negotiate the discontinuities allowed to still maintain their ethnic minority identity and pride, which led them into feeling powerful and legitimized (instead of alienated and isolated from access to the mainstream society).

It is interesting to note that language per se is not used solely by parents to socialize their children (i.e., their bilingual or minority language ability), but rather that the *cultural* styles or modes of communication, and appropriate or valued non-verbal behaviors, are the tools that transcend into *biculturalism*. For instance, Schatz (1991) found that specific pragmatic patterns of social language used by Korean, German, and American parents were more important than general linguistic similarities between their languages for affecting the specific patterns of language acquisition in their children. More specifically, she found that parental language style reflected cultural values transmitted to toddlers, such as the specific selection of model verb system transmitting values. As an example, the selection of verbs such as *must* connotes a semantic and pragmatic meaning of *obligation*, versus *may* connotes *possibility*. German mothers used more verbs connoting obligation and necessity than did American mothers, and this pattern of frequency use was already reflected in the vocabularies of their toddlers, conveying implicitly to these German and American children different underlying social values. She concluded by stating that "even societies that share a common language can use it in ways that may result in different outcomes for child development" (p. 151).

Thus, as pointed out by Schatz (1991):

Differences in cultural values can be carried not only by differences in the specific forms of two languages, but also by parental lexical choices and by the relative frequency of the forms and meaning expressed...[within] societies [that] differ in cultural beliefs about socialization (p. 149).

In sum, the more traditional view of considering language the only tool for the transmission of cultural values to children (e.g., see Ochs & Schieffelin, 1984) is too simplistic. There is need to consider that even monolingual English first-generation parents can transmit the duality of traditional Hispanic values as well as mainstream cultural values, even though they are using only English as a communication and socialization tool. Then, we can think of minority or diverse ways of using English, such as tinting the mainstream language with minority communication styles and minority non-verbal modes of communication. For instance, the use of *code mixing* and *code switching* and culturally appropriate Hispanic non-verbal behaviors may tint with a "coat of cultural values" the English language used at home by parents. In reality, mainstream English and mainstream culture is not modeled by parents within the family environment. Instead a new minority bicultural identity is created in which children learn how to appropriately behave within a minority family with a specific degree of acculturation.

In conclusion, in contrast to the discontinuity and disadvantaged view, there is the advantage position that Hispanic families trying to integrate two cultural systems also stimulate in their children a greater cognitive and social flexibility. Their bicultural children can, as a result, adapt to the discontinuities of home and school cultures, since they can successfully accomplish situational problem-solving processes. Finally, as discussed in this section, to the extent that ethnicity and socio-cultural adaptive strategies are independent from SES variables, the effect of poverty on minority children's development and achievement should be studied within the context of the mediating factors present in the family and school environments.

Parental Educational Values & Beliefs as Social Constructs

The presence of poverty does not mean that the cultural background of parents and children is necessarily diminished. As discussed above, in many instances the low SES background does affect the quality of the family structure and parent-child relationship. However, a number of minority parents are able to develop successful coping strategies and mechanisms, which help them to become resilient and to offer a good quality and nurturing family environment for their children. These resilient parents instill in their children minority cultural values and goals (which are preserved within a bicultural identity) and maintain high educational aspirations for their children. Minority, low SES parents can stimulate successfully the development of their children by nurturing their social and emotional development within a well structure family environment.

Furthermore, according to Garrett and colleagues (1994) low SES parents have the capability to react constructively to financial constraints, and be able to function as positive mediators for their children to become resilient to ecological at-risk conditions. For instance, the mother's resourcefulness to get social services and to preserve her physical and mental health will have a tremendous impact on the child's biomedical, cognitive, emotional, and social development (McBarnette, 1988; Dorris, 1989, cited in Garrett et al., 1994). That is, the mother's ability to secure prenatal care and adequate nutrition and to avoid substance abuse or other external risks during pregnancy are key factors affecting her children's development. Similarly, the father's behavior will also have an important impact on the child's overall development, especially in terms of the father's ability to maintain mental health in the presence of stress factors (e.g., unemployment, economic hardship). That is, the father's avoidance of social isolation can also result in the avoidance of an abusive or neglectful parent-child relationship (Elder, Caspi, & Van Nguyen, 1986, cited in Garrett et al., 1994).

In sum, research findings show that even though parents may be poor and have low levels of formal education, they can provide for their children a stable and well structure environment. These resilient low SES parents model for their children strong moral values, and stimulate them to develop ethnic pride; helping to promote in their children normal, advanced or even gifted developmental levels (see e.g., Clark & Gonzalez, 1998; Gonzalez & Clark, 1999).

The Coping Strategies and Resourcefulness of Parents

Socio-cultural factors exert their influence within a family structure in which parents mediate their children's behaviors for their adaptation to the wider social system. Examples of socio-cultural factors are belief and value systems, attitudes, acculturation levels, socialization goals and practices for modeling behaviors, communication styles, language use at home, interpersonal relations and experiences, and problem-solving and stress coping strategies. In order to adapt successfully to the US public school system, minority parents and their children have to develop socio-cultural strategies for balancing the continuities and discontinuities present between the minority family structure and the mainstream school cultures.

As defined by DeVoss (1982), adaptive strategies are observable behaviors occurring within a particular socio-cultural setting that are appropriate within the patterns and perceptions of the social group. Harrison, Wilson, Pine, Chan, and Buriel (1990) proposed an interrelation between the family environments provided by ethnic minority parents, socialization goals, adaptive strategies, and child behavioral outcomes. Harrrison and colleagues (1990) argued that minority families would present different patterns of adaptive strategies, which would be related to their higher risk to come from a lower SES background. They presented some examples of adaptive strategies, such as the presence of an extended family, biculturalism, and ancestral worldview. Moreover, as suggested by Harrison and colleagues (1990), "these adaptive strategies foster the child-rearing goals of positive orientation to the ethnic group and socialization for interdependence, which in turn enhance the developmental outcomes of cognitive flexibility and sensitivity to discontinuities among ethnic minority children" (p. 347).

As mentioned in the section on the SES effects on minority children's development, the significant effect of socio-cultural factors found by some previous studies needs to be considered. For instance, Walker and colleagues (1994) found a cumulative effect of the socio-cultural contexts of home, community, and school (influenced by SES) to be linked to the presence of at-risk factors in academic achievement levels in minority children. Most significantly, they found that Hispanic and African-American, low SES children's performance in reading and spelling standardized tests, and verbal ability tests (in receptive and spoken language measured by home observations and standardized vocabulary tests) was lower in comparison to minority and majority middle SES children's performance. Their four-year longitudinal study's findings indicated that the quantity and quality of interactions between the child and his or her parents and teachers, related to the stimulation resources available, was very important in the early language learning experiences of minority, low SES children. As they noted, "children from lower SES families continued to demonstrate lower performance on language and reading-related achieve-ment across grades in the elementary school. This performance was surprisingly stable, suggesting lower trajectories across time" (p. 617).

Even though the language and achievement measures used by Walker and colleagues seem to have been sensitive to SES factors, especially the standardized measures may have been biased against the Hispanic and African-American minority groups. That is, showing differences among different SES groups in their performance in standardized measures does not reveal the underlying effect of socio-cultural processes on their cognitive and linguistic performance. Moreover, due to lack of construct and content validity of language and academic achievement standardized tests, these instruments may be tapping different abilities in different minority groups. For instance, these standardized tests may be measuring degree of acculturation instead of cognitive ability in minority children (see Gonzalez, 1996; Gonzalez et al., 1997; Gonzalez & Yawkey, 1993, for further discussion of this topic).

Furthermore, Garcia Coll (1990) proposed that one of the most important sources of influence on the developmental process in minority children is the particular set of cultural belief and value systems held by adult caregivers. For instance, she mentioned the presence of extended and dependent families within the Hispanic culture, who fosters children to develop interpersonal dependency in attachment and separation processes. She considered these ideologies to be related to the cultural hierarchy of the priorities held by minority parents' goal, which lead to alternative developmental pathways in their children. She found that among minority low SES parents, the top developmental priority became survival and physical health; followed by stimulating their children to develop behavioral capacities for economic self-maintenance and other minority cultural values (i.e., traditional ideologies such as strong familism and collectivism). Garcia Coll stated that "minority mothers might not only have different developmental goals for their infants but might "perceive, react, and behave very differently to their infants' cues, behaviors, and demands" (p. 272). Thus, as Garcia Coll (1990) highlighted, there is need to understand the underlying processes that cause at-risk minority infants to display developmental problems; as well as to understand the underlying or mediating factors creating buffering effects of poverty resulting in resilient children.

As noted by Ogbu (1982), parents have cultural knowledge of the socialization goals for their children, in relation to what verbal and non-verbal behaviors may work for interacting with societal institutions and systems. According to Ogbu (1982), the family ecology of ethnic minorities suffer from ethnic stratification of relative fixed membership, which is based on an underclass or a lower ethnic stratification status. He uses the term "castelike minorities" for these underclass ethnic groups, such as low SES Hispanics who suffer from oppression, discrimination, and racism as a standard for judging social position and rewards. Thus, the family ecology show beliefs about the meaning of being poor, as well as being a member of an ethnic minority group, and what behaviors and attitudes are appropriate for adapting to their challenges.

Ethnic minorities also suffer from negative stereotypes and attributions as well as from a controversial deficit explanation when compared with the "standards" of mainstream populations. In fact, the different family and social ecology surrounding ethnic minority children would result in different developmental patterns (in comparison to mainstream children) that would in actuality be adaptive strategies for their different (but not deviant or inferior) social reality. It is in fact the presence of mediating factors within the family ecology (e.g., quality of the parent-child relationships, role models and mentors, mental health of parents; as discussed in the previous section) that plays the role of protective factors against at-risk external environments. This mechanism of family protection may result in resilient outcomes in some low SES ethnic-minority families and their children. As noted by McLoyd (1998):

Parenting that is strict and highly directive (i.e., well-defined house rules, clear sanctions for breaking rules, close supervision), combined with higher levels of warmth, helps poor, inner-city children resist forces in their extra-familial environments than in ordinary circumstances contribute to low levels of achievement. (p. 194)

As stated by Harrison and colleagues (1990), similarities exist within the cultural adaptation mechanisms present among ethnic-minority families (including Hispanics, African Americans, American Indian/Alaskan Natives, and Asian/Pacific Americans). These similarities result from their need to develop adaptive strategies for gaining access to benefits provided by European American cultural and social institutions (e.g., education, medical care, political and legal services, employment, etc.). According to Harrison and colleagues (1990), among Hispanic families one of the most important socio-cultural adaptive strategies is the presence of extended family members as a problem-solving and stress-coping system in order to face daily normal and crisis situations. For instance, extended family members can help with tangible resources such as income, childcare, and household maintenance; and also with non-tangible resources such as emotional support through interpersonal relations of attachment and affiliation (Harrison et al., 1990).

In fact, strong familism within the Hispanic culture includes "strong feelings of identification, loyalty, and solidarity with the parents and the extended family" (p. 352). The Hispanic sense of family and community includes also non-relatives within the extended family, such as "compadres" (godparents) as well as close friends; with whom frequent contact and reciprocal interpersonal relations of strong familism are cultivated through-out the years. As reported by Sabogal, Marin, Otero-Sabogal, Marin, and Perez-Stable (1987), preferred language used at home was associated to the level of acculturation of Hispanic familism, in relation specifically with their familial obligations and family referents. However, they found that their perception of family support remained constant regardless of language used at home. And so it can be seen that cooperation, obligation, sharing, and a social/psychological dependence are some of the socialization goals and value systems modeled and transmitted to Hispanic children by their extended family members and parents. These common ethnic minority values are in sharp contrast to the mainstream cultural values of competition, autonomy, individualism, and self-reliance.

Moreover, the use of older siblings as "surrogate parents" is also quite common among the socio-cultural adaptive strategies of Hispanic families in order to allow low SES mothers to work outside the home at least part-time. Another adaptive socio-cultural strategy is the presence of alternative family arrangements so that adults can share the bread winner role. Thus, many times Hispanic families go through a "physical or material transition" (as coined by Harrison et al., 1990) in order to acquire the mainstream language and adapt to the educational and occupational demands of the mainstream society (resulting in loss of the minority language).

In sum, "cultural transition" (as coined by Harrison et al., 1990) is the most difficult socio-cultural process of adaptation faced by Hispanic families. Most commonly, the traditional values will still remain mostly intact within the private family interaction patterns, but a duality of bicultural adaptation will have to be developed for acculturating success-fully to the mainstream society. Thus, instead of complete assimilation, it seems that Hispanic families value the integration of bicultural experiences.

Conclusions: Similarities and Differences Between Low SES Minority and Mainstream Children' Development

Based on the critical literature review discussed throughout Chapter 1, and related to the theme of this book, there is need to understand the powerful influence of ecological factors (including SES and socio-cultural factors such as culture and language) on minority students' development and academic achievement. This literature supports the view that studies need to be conducted from an Ethnic Researcher perspective, endorsing a developmental, multidimensional, and Interactionist view (i.e., interaction of internal or biological and psychological and external or ecological factors on development, learning, and achievement). That is, we need to increase our understanding of ecological school, home/family, SES, and cul-tural/linguistic factors positively and negatively impacting learning and development in minority children. There is need to produce ecological research, from an Ethnic Researcher perspective, for documenting how schools can separate cultural and linguistic differences from underachievement, developmental delays, and learning problems; and how not to confound poverty with cultural and linguistic differences. There is need to realize that minority students are put at-risk of dropping out by schooling and/or family factors failing to nurture their developmental and achievement potential. The ecological systems can positively or negatively mediate the impact of poverty and socio-cultural factors (i.e., cultural and linguistic diversity and low SES levels) on minority students' development and academic achievement.

In order to reduce drop out rates among minority students and increase their potential for resiliency, research trends show the need to increase positive mediating factors present in the school and family environments; such as role models, mentors, and advocates and high-quality education. More research needs to be conducted on the effect of high-quality educational programs that appropriately respond to cultural and linguistic diversity and are integrated to alternative assessments. These high-quality educational programs will also integrate school, family, and community ecological systems by infusing respect and value for cultural and linguistic diversity among educators, and by providing parents and community leaders with appropriate communication channels. The creation of a reciprocal adaptation process in the most important environments (i.e., family, school, and community) in which minority students develop can provide them with opportunities to adapt and integrate the cultural and linguistic diversity lived at home and in their minority communities, with their psychological and educational needs at school.

Moreover, we need to further study the powerful effect of high-quality educational programs on minority students' achievement, which nurture their potential for developing critical thinking and problem-solving abilities across content areas. The opportunity created by high-quality instruction to achieve at high standards of learning and developing can positively mediate poverty and socio-cultural factors affecting minority students. The ultimate goal of studying the effect of high-quality instruction on minority students' learning and development is to: (1) reduce the risk of dropping out of school and enter middle class America, and (2) provide a genuine educational opportunity to achieve national high academic standards for *all* students.

Thus, we need to conduct further research on how minority students learn; and on how the integration of schooling, family, and community experiences can increase their resiliency and learning, developmental, and achievement levels. By increasing our theoretical and educationally applied understanding of this problem of national importance, we can generate valuable and cost-effective conceptual and applied recommendations. For instance, this research avenue can result in the creation of: (1) a profile of at-risk and resilient characteristics of minority students and schooling factors, (2) recommendations for screening and assessments that are valid and reliable, and (3) a set of recommendations for high-quality instruction.

Some suggestions for opening research questions for future studies are provided within a contemporary Interactionist view. For instance, there are many open areas for research, such as to understand how wide are the boundaries set by heredity for various aspects of development, what environmental factors are more significantly affecting heredity and how these potentials manifest as behaviors and developmental abilities and skills learned, how the interaction of heredity and environment reflects into different developmental stages within the life span, and how to increase our understanding of the processes by which the interaction of nature and nurture takes place, just to name a few areas.

Hence, the issue of the complexity of at-risk factors affecting poor children's developmental outcomes, and whether or not they are able to cope with environmental stress and become resilient needs to be further studied. As discussed throughout this book, an urgent need presents itself to maintain a multidimensional approach to research. Examples of more permanent child's characteristics that need to be further studied are temperament and personality traits, unique individual needs, and self-regulation of attention, emotion, and behaviors. Examples of changing child's characteristics that need to be studied are developmental stages, interests, attitudes, perceptions, and values and belief systems. Examples of ecological factors open for research are the quality of parent-child relationships, parental cultural values about education and child rearing practices, the effect of home language, and the effect of mentors and other educational opportunities for success.

Therefore, there is still a major task ahead for researcher studying minority children's development: to discover the interacting effect of SES factors and internal potential that may result in resilient or vulnerable conditions among minority young children. More specifically, researchers still need to uncover the different transitional or recurrent risks affecting minority children, and which are the protective mechanisms at different ages and points in development. That is, well adapted parents, or any other committed and effective adult present, can function as scaffolds to provide opportunities, protective mechanisms, and emotional support for children exposed to at-risk ecological factors (such as poverty) to develop resilience. It is in fact the presence of mediating factors within the family ecology (e.g., quality of the parent-child relationships, role models and mentors, mental health of parents; as discussed in the previous section) that plays the role of protective factors against at-risk external environments. This mechanism of family protection may result in resilient outcomes in some low SES ethnic-minority families and their children.

In sum, there is need to conduct studies that broaden our understanding of the interacting effects of poverty and other mediating factors (i.e., biological, psychological, and family and community structure) on the achievement and cognitive and socio-emotional development of minority children. Developmental *processes* influenced by cultural and linguistic factors need to be studied further within a multidimensional and ecological paradigm following an Ethnic Researchers perspective (e.g., bilingualism, knowledge acquisition, problem-solving ability, cultural thinking style, social style of interpersonal relations, cultural value and belief systems, bicultural identity, self-esteem, self-concept).

References

Bradley, R. H., Whiteside, L. Y., Mundfrom, D. J. (1994). Early indications of resilience and their relation to experiences in the home environments of low birthweight, premature children living in poverty. *Child Development*, 65, 346-360.

Clark, E. R., & Gonzalez, V., (1998). *Voces* and voices: Cultural and linguistic giftedness. *Educational Horizons*, 77(1), 41-47.

Delgado Gaitan, C. (1994). Socializing young children in Mexican-American families: An intergenerational perspective. In P.M. Greenfield & R. R. Cocking (Eds.), *Cross-cultural roots of minority child development* (pp. 55-86). Hillsdale, NJ: Lawrence Erlbaum Associates.

DeVoss, G. A. (1982). Adaptive strategies in US minorities. In E. E. Jones & S. J. Korchin (Eds.), *Minority mental health* (pp. 74-117). New York: Praeger.

Duncan, G. J., Brooks-Gunn, J., & Kato, P. K. (1994). Economic deprivation and early childhood development. *Child Development*, 65, 296-318.

Garcia Coll, C. T. (1990). Developmental outcomes of minority infants: A process-oriented look into our beginnings. *Child Development*, 61, 270-289.

Garrett, P., Ng'andu, N., & Ferron, J, (1994). Poverty experiences of young children and their quality of their home environment. *Child Development*, 65, 331-345.

Gonzalez, V. (1994). A model of cognitive, cultural, and linguistic variables affecting bilingual Hispanic children's development of concepts and language. *Hispanic Journal of Behavioral Sciences*, 16 (4), 396-421.

Gonzalez, V. (1995). *Cognition, culture, and language in bilingual children: Conceptual and semantic development.* Bethesda, MD: Austin & Winfield.

Gonzalez, V. (1996). Do you believe in intelligence?: Socio-cultural dimensions in intelligence assessment in majority and minority students. *Educational Horizons,* 75(1), 45-52.

Gonzalez, V. (2002). Advanced cognitive development and bilingualism: methodological flaws and suggestions for measuring first-and-second-language proficiency, language dominance, and intelligence in minority children. In J. A.

Castellano, and E. Diaz. (Eds.), *Reaching new horizons: Gifted and talented education for culturally and linguistically diverse student* (pp. 47-75). Needham Heights: Allyn & Bacon.

Gonzalez. V. (2005). Cultural, linguistic, and socioeconomic factors influencing monolingual and bilingual children's cognitive development. In Gonzalez, V., & Tinajero, J.V. (Co-Editors). *National Association for Bilingual Education (NABE) Review of Research & Practice*, Vol. 3 (pp. 67-104).Mahwah, NJ. Lawrence Erlbaum Associates.

Gonzalez, V. (2006). Profiles of cognitive developmental performance in gifted children: Effect of bilingualism, monolingualism, and SES factors. *Journal of Hispanic Higher Education*, Vol. 5 (2), 142-170. Thousand Oaks, CA: Sage.

Gonzalez, V., Bauerle, P, & Felix-Holt, M. (1996). Theoretical and practical implications of assessing cognitive and language development in bilingual children with qualitative methods. *Bilingual Research Journal,* 20 (1), 93-131.

Gonzalez, V., Brusca-Vega, R., & Yawkey, T. (1997). *Assessment and instruction of culturally and linguistically diverse students with or at-risk of learning problems: From research to practice.* Needham Heights, MA: Allyn & Bacon.

Gonzalez, V., & Clark, E. R. (1999). *Folkloric* and *historic* views of giftedness in minority children. In V. Gonzalez (Vol. Ed.), *Language and cognitive development in second language learning: Educational implications for children and adults* (pp. 1-18). Needham Heights, MA: Allyn & Bacon.

Gonzalez, V., & Yawkey, T. (1993). The assessment of culturally and linguistically diverse students: Celebrating change. *Educational Horizons*, 72(1), 41-49.

Gonzalez, V., Yawkey, T.D., & Minaya-Rowe, L. (2006). *English-as-a-Second-Language (ESL) teaching and learning: Classroom applications for Pre-K-12th Grade students' academic achievement & development.* Needham Heights, MA: Allyn & Bacon.

Harrison, A. O., Wilson, M. N., Pine, C. J., Chan, S. Q., & Buriel, R. (1990). Family ecologies of ethnic minority children. *Child Development*, 61, 347-362.

Hill, M. S., Sandfort, J. R. (1995). Effects of childhood poverty on productivity later in life: Implications for public policy. *Children & Youth Services Review*, 17(1/2), 91-126.

Hodgkinson, H. H. (1992). *A demographic look at tomorrow.* Washington D.C.: Institute for Education Research.

Immigration and Naturalization Service Report (2000). *Immigration statistics by country of origin.* Washington DC: US Government Printing Office.

Masten, A., S., & Coatsworth, J. D. (1998). The development of competence in favorable and unfavorable environments. *American Psychologist*, 53(2), 205-220.

McLoyd, V. C. (1998). Socioeconomic disadvantage and child development. *American Psychologist*, 53(2), 185-204.

Messick, S.(1995). Validity of psychological assessment: Validation of inferences from persons' responses and performances as scientific inquiry into score meaning. *American Psychologist, 50*(9), 741-749.

Moss, P. A. (1992). Shifting conceptions of validity in educational measurement: Implications for performance assessment. *Review of Educational Research, 62*(3), 229-258).

Ochs, E., & Schiefellin, B. B. (1984). Language acquisition and socialization: three developmental stories. In R. Shweder & R. LeVine (Eds.), *Culture theory: Essays on mind, self, and emotion* (pp. 276-320). Cambridge, MA: Cambridge University Press.

Ogbu, J. (1982). Cultural discontinuity and schooling. *Anthropology and Education Quarterly, 13*(4), 290-307.

authentic assessment (pp. 1-18). Albany, NY: State University of New York Press.

Sabogal, F., Marin, G., Otero-Sabogal, R., Marin, B., & Perez-Stable, E. J. (1987). Hispanic familism and acculturation: What changes and what doesn't. *Hispanic Journal of Behavioral Sciences, 9*, 397-412.

Shatz, M. (1991). Using cross-cultural research to inform us about the role f language in development: Comparisons of Japanese, Korean, and English, and of German, American English, and British English. In M. H. Bornstein (Ed.). *Cultural approaches to parenting* (pp. 139-153). Hillsdale, NJ: Lawrence Erlbaum Associates.

Suarez-Orozco, M. (1989). *Central American refugees and US high schools: A psychological study of motivation and achievement.* Stanford, CA: Stanford University Press.

Thomas, R. M. (1996). *Comparing theories of child development* (4th ed.). Pacific Grove, CA: Brooks Cole.

US Census Bureau (1997). *Statistical Abstract of the United States: 1996.* Washington DC: US Government Printing Office.

US Census Bureau (2000). *Projections of the resident population by race, Hispanic origin, and nativity.* Washington DC: US Government Printing Office.

US Department of Education, National Center for Education Statistics (1999). *The condition of education* (NCES 99-022). Washington D.C.: Government Printing Office, Indicators 11 and 12.

US Department of Education, National Center for Education Statistics (1998). *The condition of education* (NCES 98-013). Washington D.C.: Government Printing Office, Indicator 34.

US Department of Education, National Center for Education Statistics (1996). *Dropout rates in the United States: 1994* (NCES 96-863) by M. McMillen & P. Kaufman. Washington D.C.: Government Printing Office.

US Department of Justice, Office of Justice Programs, Bureau of Justice Statistics (1994). *Comparing federal and state prison inmates: 1991* (NCJ-145864) by C. W. Harlow. Washington D.C.: US Government Printing Office.

Vygotsky, L. S. (1986*). Thought and language.* Cambridge, MA: MIT Press.

Walker, D., Greenwood, C., Hart, B., & Carta, J. (1994). Prediction of school outcomes based on early language production and socioeconomic factors. *Child Development*, 65, 606-621.

Wang, A. Y. (1993). Cultural-Familial Predictors of Cildren's metacognitive and Academic Performance. *Journal of Research in Childhood Education*, 7(2), 83-90.

Wechsler, D. (1967). *Wechsler Preschool and Primary Scale of Intelligence (WPPSI)*. San Antonio, TX: Psychological Corporation.

2

SOCIO-CULTURAL FACTORS IN THE FAMILY AND SCHOOL SYSTEMS MEDIATING CHILDREN'S DEVELOPMENT AND ACADEMIC ACHIEVEMENT

෨෬

Chih-Sheng Chen and Thomas D. Yawkey

The second Chapter provides a theoretical conceptual framework for understanding socio-cultural factors in the school environment influencing minority children's developmental and achievement levels. Chapter 2 provides a rich discussion of contemporary perspectives on family-school involvement and mentoring for positive influencing minority children's development and academic achievement. This contemporary view highlights changes from traditional "deficit" to contemporary "difference" perspectives arising from socio-developmental theories of Bronfenbrenner (1979) and Vygotsky (1962, 1968).

Research results abound documenting the potential outcomes of English as a second language (ESL) teachers helping minority family involvement as mentors and mediators within community-based contexts called societies. Following an Ethnic Researcher perspective, this second Chapter advocates for ESL teachers to serve as mentors in their effective roles as mediators between minority families, students, and schools. For ESL teachers to serve as effective mentors and mediators, they need to recognize the many communication barriers that are culturally based and implicitly and explicitly arise between minority families and schools, and learn how to use strategies to negotiate and establish communication modes and processes (e.g., develop trust and cooperation, recognize family concerns and feelings).

Three major sections are presented in this second Chapter, including: (1) family involvement and ESL teachers as mediators; (2) communication barriers between home and school contexts and strategies for cultural mediators and mentors to overcome them; and (3) Epstein's family involvement model, with emphasis on practices and procedures for ESL teachers. In the conclusions section, closure is provided for this second Chapter by discussing the similarities and differences between the home minority culture and the mainstream school culture. Synthesis is reached by discussing the effects of socio-historical and psychological factors on the minority children's assessment and academic performance.

The second Chapter relates to the major theme of the book because it expands the discussion of socio-cultural factors affecting minority children's assessment and academic achievement. Chapter 2 discussed the specific case of school settings as catalysts for developing minority family and home and community partnerships through ESL and *all* teachers assuming a mentoring role. As Chapter 1, this second Chapter also emphasizes how critical is for educators to value the home language and culture of the minority child, and to respect and nurture both individual and socio-cultural differences present in their home and family setting. That is, in this second Chapter, as throughout the book, a main idea is supported: the importance for us educators to stimulate in young children the development of first and second languages as learning, thinking, communicative, and emotional tools for expressing individual and developmental uniqueness within a meaningful, real-life socio-cultural setting. Thus, language as a symbolic tool needs to be present at both the family and school context in order for minority young children to be successful learners and to grow as mentally healthy, and socially productive individuals.

Introduction

On January 6, 2005, Ms. Margaret Spellings, Secretary of U.S. Department of Education, gave an opening statement at Senate Confirmation Hearing. In her opening statement, Secretary Spellings referenced that parent, student and school need to cooperate with each other. She, as a mother of two children, stressed, arents must be active participants in a child's education. They deserve information about their child's school, they deserve to know who is teaching their child, and they deserve options when their schools are not serving their children (Department of Education, 2005, p. 8). Clearly, Secretary Spellings sounded the content of this article for the need: (a) to view English as a second language (ESL and *all*) teachers as mediators or negotiators between schools and their families, (b) to expand drastically parents' options and links with the schools and teachers, and (c) to use what works in improving the effectiveness of culturally and linguistically diverse minority parent involvement and collaboration with the schools based on scientific research.

This article provides information to stimulate teachers to become advocates for helping minority families in their cultural adaptation process, and through establishing a collaborative relationship with family members, together to help ESL students to achieve at higher developmental levels.

Some Potential of Minority Family Involvement and ESL Teachers as Mediators: Examining Selected Research

The potentials of family involvement and recognition of important links between families and schools has greatly increased over the past decade. This decade highlights a change from "deficit" to "difference" (Yawkey, in preparation). Briefly, prior to and during the 1990 , parent involvement perspectives focused on harnessing parents to programs where they were trained, their behaviors monitored and retrained as necessary to bring targeted behaviors to criterion. Underlying these curricular intentions was a "deficit" view of parent involvement (Edwards & Warin, 1999). On the other hand, from 1999 to the present, parent involvement was opened to a "difference" perspective, in which the family was viewed as working collaboratively with the school and together they can nurture the student to become a responsible citizen who can contribute to society (Edwards & Warin, 1999). Family involvement viewed from a "difference" perspective helps to reduce the distance between family and school, and to highlight their inter-relationship as proposed by more contemporary family systems theories such as Bronfenbrenner's (1979) and Vygotsky's (1962, 1978) approaches.

Fresh Views of Minority Families: Some Foundations and Research.

This contemporary "difference" perspective highlights the view of family involvement underlying the ESL standards proposed by the most important professional organizations such as the Teachers of English to Speakers Of Other Languages (TESOL, 1997), and the American Council for Teachers of Foreign Languages (ACTFL, Lewelling & Rennie, 1998); and also recommendations derived from many scientific research studies such as the ones conducted by Powell (1989) and Page (1999). This new view takes or recognizes "differences" among minority families as factors helping with English-as a-second-language (ESL) students development, academic achievement, and school involvement. For example, within the TESOL (1997) standards for pre-Kindergarten to Grade 12, teachers are professionally asked to bridge from the cultures of ESL students and their families to school. Essentially, teachers are being urged to play the role of cultural mediators and brokers between the minority families and the mainstream school culture. In similar fashion, the ACTFL standards entice all foreign language teachers to serve as cultural brokers and mediators for ESL students and their families. ACTFL new standards of communication, cultures, communities, connections, and comparisons clearly point to this newer "difference" perspective of families, and for that matter, highlights the importance of teachers recognizing and embracing a "difference" perspective when serving students from diverse cultures and languages.

From a scientific research perspective, there are several studies of interest that take a contemporary "difference" perspective to family school involvement. For example, Powell (1989) showed that the outcomes of family and school working together bring positive benefits for children. These outcomes are based on maintaining and increasing positive and consistent relations between *all* families and schools. This consistency and persistency of family and school relations are critical to increasing family school involvement and students' educational outcomes such as effective-ness in promoting higher levels in learning, development, and academic achievement. Moreover, Pape (1999) noted that building strong and positive relations between family and schools yield higher parental ratings, which in turn can increase the morale of teachers. Relatedly, the results of many studies (e.g., Gettinger & Guetschow, 1998; Karther & Lowden, 1997) showed that outcomes of *all* families working collaboratively with schools result in achievement gains in students. As Secretary Spellings pointed out, and as studies have shown (Cassity & Harris, 2000), genuine participation of minority families in schooling activities must be increased due to the benefits that this collaboration brings to students and society. The need is greater than ever for ESL and *all* teachers to act as mediators or brokers to create "bridges" between the minority families and the mainstream school culture, and to self reflect in order to develop healthy and welcoming atmospheres in schools (Woodlief, 2002).

In sum, Secretary Spellings comments and results of scientific research have been influenced by several significant insightful theories of contemporary family ecology (Bronfenbrenner, 1979) and families as critical participants in socio-cultural development (Vygotsky, 1962, 1978). These two major theories of family ecology are surveyed in the section below, and some educational implications are drawn for improving minority family involvement practices in schools.

Bronfenbrenner Family Ecology

A developmental psychologist, Bronfenbrenner (1979) viewed children social and cognitive development as:

1. An initial series of relations and connections between and among family members

2. A series of reciprocal impacts among external factors such as race, ethnic group/s, culture/s of family members and so forth

So, a child at birth and onward is embedded within these relations similar to Russian matrioshka dolls, where each one is enclosed in the other and another and another and so forth (Keyes, 2000). Bronfenbrenner illustrated this concept graphically using five environmental systems and their interrelations: microsystem, mesosystem, exosystem, macrosystem, and chronosystem.

Briefly, the microsystem contains immediate settings that impact the student. These settings include: home, religious institutions, neighborhood, school, community and so forth. So, the social development (including attitudes, opinions, and beliefs of ESL students and *all* students) impact and are impacted by these settings and what is said and done within them. The reciprocal nature of home impacting neighborhood and neighborhood impacting home show these interrelations.

As we examine further the microsystem, the immediate environmental settings have great and long lasting impacts on ESL students. For example, whether stated or implied, the teacher verbal and nonverbal communication influences the ESL students social and academic performance. And, the ESL students behaviors impact in similar respect the teacher attitudes,

The mesosystem, the second relationship, focuses on two or more connections as settings for participatory and reciprocal actions of ESL and *all* students. A significant example for ESL students is their connections with home and school or home, school, and neighborhood.

Another example is the relation between home, school, and peers. Consider that an ESL teacher has requested a conference with the minority family member and ESL student. Depending on how much work the ESL teacher has done prior to this conference request with this minority family, the outcomes of the conference definitely impact the minority family's feelings and attitudes of schooling and home parenting situations.

Further, a teacher, in the lunchroom spots a baby bottle with milk in the lunch box of a seven-year old ESL student. After questioning the Hispanic, the teacher found out that this was his bottle. And, the ESL teacher informed the school nurse and social worker of this observed behaviors and opinions toward the ESL student. This innermost structure, in a sense, becomes the center most matrioshka doll in the series of dolls or settings all impacting and all having reciprocal relationships.

These connections and interrelations are real and impact this Hispanic boy, the teacher in the lunchroom, the school nurse, the social worker, and the family member. With some natural bridging, this teacher might have known that it is quite a common practice for family members to put condensed milk into baby bottles for older children (Ariza, 2002). This example emphasizes the great need for ESL and *all* teachers to serve as mediators, negotiators, or advocators and bridge between schools and minority homes. Within the mesosystem, the transitioning is critical between the relationship dealing with ESL classroom social behaviors, which are culturally embedded, and minority families which may be misinterpret as "inappropriate" classroom behaviors and expectations of the ESL teachers (Geenen, Powers & Lopez-Vasquez, 2001).

With the exosystem, these relations or connections between the student and other external situations or events in his or her social and cultural environment are indirect. That is, these settings really do not directly affect the ESL student. They are subtle. However, the events occurring within the socio-cultural setting put pressure on and indirectly impact the ESL students or any student. For example, a minority family member becomes ill and is unable to work for a sustained period of time or the minority parent is arrested for a traffic violation and must go to court hearings. Another example is posed by the lost of a job by a family member due to a lengthy illness, which impacts the ESL student in a variety of ways. Even though these events do not involve the student directly, these situations do impact the student because they impact what happens in these external socio-cultural settings, such as the family home setting (Bronfenbrenner, 1979). These interrelations within the exosystem are connected and mutually share impacts because of these relations.

The macrosystem, the fourth system, has a number of systems that are lower in order, but yet demonstrate similar content and form. These lower-order systems appear at various levels such as culture, subculture, religion, history, other societal institutions such as marriage, birth of a child, and so forth. In a sense, these connected, lower-order systems contain belief systems or ideologies that have meanings or contextual consistencies (Bronfenbrenner, 1979). For example, the American mainstream culture is individualistic and lower-order systems demonstrate this consistency in social institutions and settings such as schools, restaurants and so forth. Whereas, more traditional cultures such as Greek, Chinese, Russian, Hispanic and so forth are more collectivistic and interlock lower-order consistencies with emphases on group thoughts, feelings and beliefs. An example can illustrate this difference in lower-order systems between the American mainstream culture and more traditional cultures. More specifi-cally, three new Russian students came for the first day in January to a high school social studies class. That day was test day, so each of these newcomers received a separate test. In turn, these three students huddled together and discussed the questions and arrived at final group, not individual, answers to the test questions. The high school teacher having understandings of the macrosystem and its consistencies was able to understand these interrelations and consistencies within cultural context. So, the teachers' familiarity with cultural differences between macrosystems gave a "happy ending" to the story.

The fifth and final system of family development is the chronosystem. The Greek word, "chrono" denotes time. Bronfenbrenner (1979) added to a socio-historical element or context to this concept. From a family systems perspective, chronosystem gives meaning and understanding of social or cognitive concepts of ESL students as a function, outcome or impact of time on their social or cognitive development. For example, all of us have had experiences with ESL students or know of teacher colleagues who work with ESL students from war torn countries who have witnessed horrors and experienced terrors in their former countries of origin. This horror or terror at an early age has a different impact on ESL students than these same experiences but at the adolescent years of development. These influences or impacts differ because of different times at which they occurred and in different socio-historical contexts.

In the next section, Vygotsky (1978) socio-cultural theory of language development of individuals wthin family and school settings are examined. Briefly, the highlights of Vygotsky orientation are examined with a focus on family, adult-peer, and peer-peer interactions and their contributions to language learning and development.

Vygotsky Socio-Cultural Theory: Family Context and Language/Cognitive Development

For ESL teachers, Vygotsky is a household name for "small group involvement" and "community building and learning" and so forth. For ESL teachers, Vygotsky ideas of grouping to benefit ESL students and non ESL students are very well known in numerous ESL programs (Yawkey, in preparation). In understanding the ideas of ESL teacher as mediators between individuals, family, school, and society we focus on his perspectives of socio-cultural theory and how selected concepts relate with our ESL work in developing our roles as ESL advocators and mediators for ESL students and their families.

Similar to Bronfenbrenner, Vygotsky was also developed deeply into and researched the fields of developmental psychology, sociology, and linguistics. As a developmental psychologist, Vytgotsky emphasized language acquisition, development, and literacy within cultures, schools and communities. His writings include a most famous text, *Language and Thought*, published in 1962 and another very famous and well-read text, *Mind in Society*, published in 1978. Both major contributions were published after his death in 1934.

Across these major texts and other writings, Vygotsky focused squarely on culture. Vygotsky's studies were mainly focused on culture that provides the foundations and all subsequent studies in language learning as a socio-cultural communication process, cognitive development in relation to language and cultural processes (i.e., semantics and pragmatics), and the understanding of beliefs and attitudes in relation to cultural factors. There are several major concepts critical to Vygotskyian socio-cultural perspectives: (1) culture as product, (2) culture as process, and (3) the zone of proximal development and its context.

First, culture became an imperative for it shapes our thinking, communication practices, linguistic structures, knowledge, beliefs, attitudes and practices. In culture as product, Vygotsky (1962, 1978) noted its powerful effects on thought, language and social practices and costumes. For example, cultures have their particular distinctive ethnic food including types of food products used, their preparation, and ways to serve these foods. Couchenhour and Chrisman (2000) noted the importance of these cultural foods as examples of cultural outcomes. For instance, Japanese with sushi, Middle Eastern cultures with pita bread, and so forth. Ways of serving differ depending on culture, for example Japanese, Korean, Chinese (and other Asian cultures) with chopsticks; Americans with forks, knives and spoons. So, from this perspective, culture develops and shapes our thinking and other processes because we are immersed in "a sea" of cultural content (Brown, 1992). And this cultural setting as product does the shaping and molding and impacting cognitive, language, and socio-emotional development from a Vygotskian perspective.

Second, in addition to templates as products, culture provides the processes for our thinking and understandings. For Vygotsky, cultural processes of thinking are acquired by language and in particular social interaction between adults and children and between and among peers. In Vygotsky (1978) terms, this social level was termed inter-psychological. Both of these principles of language as products and process are critical because language role is to enhance cognitive development. In addition, the framework for language is a cultural template. And, finally all higher forms of language begin as actual communicative interactions between individuals (Vygotsky, 1978). The latter idea is important to all school context and ESL programs. More explicitly, for ESL students, in home settings, families and siblings; and in school settings, teachers and peers; are most important for language acquisition, development, and cognitive growth (Grabe & Stoller, 1997). As we examine the implications of Vygotskyian thought for ESL teachers when working with minority families as advocates and mediators, this idea of culture as process becomes the building blocks for promoting family school involvement.

Third, the zone of proximal development (ZPD), as well, is a cultural construct. Vygotsky (1978, p.86) gave the following definition for the construct of ZPD and its relationship with culture. The ZPD is the "distance" between the actual developmental level as determined by independent problem solving and the level of potential development as determined through problem solving under adult guidance or in collaboration with more capable peers (ibid, p.86). Lets pull together this construct of the ZPD with fulfilling the educational needs of ESL students and the role of ESL teachers. Vygotsky is saying that the difference between the ESL students *current level* of second language (L2, and the first language—L1) and their more advanced *potential level* of L2 (and L1) is described by the ZPD. The movement to their *potential levels* is navigated or managed by ESL and *all* teachers, peers, families, siblings, and significant others (for descriptive details, see Couchenour & Chrisman, 2000; Grabe & Stoller, 1997). With this ESL realization, the potential for ESL students becomes unlimited especially with ESL teachers as advocates and mediators of culture. For these ESL teachers it is key to understand the bridges that can be built from *current to potential* developmental levels through the support and help or "scaffolding role" of advocates and mediators among cultures (Yawkey, in preparation).

In looking across Bronfenbrenner and Vygotsky social-based models, there are several operational fundamentals that can be identified, and implications used in order to develop ESL teacher ideas of their important roles as mediators and advocators of family involvement. For the benefit of ESL students and ESL and *all* teachers, these operational fundamentals are identified and explained in the next section.

Some Implications of Fresh Views: Bronfenbrenner and Vygotsky Operational Fundamentals at Work for ESL Students

The following implications are developed from the brief overviews of both Bronfenbrenner and Vygotsky family and cultural models. In the descriptions of the implications, links are made with ESL programs and their teachers and to their roles of advocates and cultural mediators. Within each implication, roles of the ESL teacher as cultural mediator and broker are explained.

Multifaceted L2 Development

ESL students development of L2 illustrates many multifaceted factors that influence L2 acquisition and development in many ways. From Bronfenbrenner perspectives, these ways of influence focus on their interrelations with and connections to the L2 (and L1) learner. Vygotsky argument would center of course on culture/s as the primary points affecting the development of L2 and L1. For purposes of discussion, lets focus on culture since it is the core of the Vygotskyian argument for language and cognitive development and one of many factors for Bronfenbrenner family ecology that contributes to ESL students growth.

From the point of view of Bronfenbrenner relations between and among systems, culture plays a role as well. Although more than a question of assimilation or adaptation, native culture impacts and affects the L2 learner; American culture likewise affects the L2 learner. As native and American cultures impact ESL students, they together influence cognitive development and language and of course, other systems impact ESL students as well from family to neighborhood to greater community.

The Vygotskyian imperative follows a similar note of Gibson (1984) that different cultures impact individuals differently. In other words, being immersed in a native culture in family and neighborhood settings complete with native language/s and religions/s, and then in American culture in school and elsewhere, provides multiple cultural standards. These multiple cultural standards provide diversity for cultural products and processes such as ways of doing things (i.e., ethnic food as a cultural product), perceiving and believing in ideas (i.e., values and beliefs as cultural processes), and evaluating these and other products and processes.

Even though products of relationships between cultural systems can be viewed as a positive and contributing phenomenon to individual development and learning, the result may have a negative impact on English as a L2 learning among ESL students. For example, if the minority family has continuing and frequent conflicts between native and American cultures, confusion and negativity may result which could impact negatively the L2 learner's development and academic achievement within mainstream school culture. Whether conflicts are big or small, the ESL teacher as advocate can negotiate these conflicts with minority family members based on developing trust and cultural knowledge for the academic benefit ESL students.

These roles of ESL teachers as advocates and mediators are critical for solving cultural conflicts that inevitably arise not only between minority and mainstream groups, but also within diverse ethnic groups (such as Puerto Ricans and Mexicans within Hispanics, and Japanese and Koreans within Asians) represented within a single cultural minority group (such as Hispanics or Asians). We, as ESL teachers, need to become aware of cultural and linguistic differences between and among different minority groups in order to avoid overgeneralizations leading to stereotypes (e.g.,

Puerto Rican versus Mexican dialectal variations with its similarities and differences, or Columbians versus Cubans versus Puerto Ricans' cultural traditions for celebrating holidays, such as their ethnic food). Stating that all Hispanics eat tortillas at home, for instance becomes a stereotypical attribution that is very far from the actual cultural traditions of multiple ethnic groups encompassed within the broader minority category of Hispanics. Not all Spanish speaking families coming from Central and South American, Mexico and Puerto Rico share the same ethnic food in terms of preferred produce, preparation procedures, and serving modalities. Some countries based their diets in potatoes, rice, or corn; depending on their geography and traditional crops. For instance all Andes countries (including Ecuador, Colombia, Peru, Bolivia) have a large production of dozens of kinds of potatoes and their diet is impacted by this geographical fact of nature.

Our position is that we as ESL teachers need to embrace pluralism, and therefore respect and celebrate, and learn from the diversity of cultures and languages that all ESL students bring to our classrooms. Moreover, we as ESL teachers need to become knowledgeable about the diversity within minority groups and try to consciously avoid overgeneralizations and stereotypes resulting from lack of knowledge and familiarity with diversity. As ESL educators, it is our responsibility to take charge, and make a personal commitment, to learn about cultural diversity, both directly or informally from the minority families, and more explicitly from exposing ourselves to formal learning opportunities (i.e., professional development sessions, academic and authentic readings—novels, newspapers, audio or audiovisual media such as tapes and movies, trips, visits to ethnic neighborhoods and communities in the U.S., and ultimately exposure to a L2 learning experience). In sum, the best of cultures produces L2 and L1 learners who are culturally pluralistic (i.e., an individual who understands cultures, cultural patterns and moves with ease between and among various cultures; Gonzalez, Brursca-Vega, & Yawkey, 1997; Yawkey, in preparation). It is our imperative as ESL educators to become pluralistic citizens in order to better serve ESL students and to increase the degree of school involvement of their minority families.

Social Interaction as L2 Development

ESL students linguistic, social, and cognitive growth occur through interactions between them and external factors in the environment such as schools and ESL teaches. Within Bronfenbrenner Family Systems approach, the ESL teacher as advocate could easily nurture native language (and English language) development within classroom settings. By simply learning and speaking key native languages occurring in an ESL classroom, a teacher can show legitimacy and respect for the native cultures and languages spoken by her or his ESL students. This is one of many ways in which the ESL teacher demonstrates her or his positive role as advocate, and cultural broker and mediator. For example, in a study conducted by Yawkey, Jackson, Wang, and Chuang (2003), one major difference between a group of ESL teachers that were exposed to training in their role of cultural brokers, and counterparts who did not receive training, was for the degree of using native cultures and languages in their classrooms.

For Vygotsky, Bronfenbrenner and other developmental psychologists and applied linguists such as Schinke-Llano (1993), languaging and thinking are entities that develop in an interrelated manner, and are impacted by and within interactive settings such as families, siblings, peers , teachers and so forth. In agreement, Brown's (2000) surveys studies show that L2 (and L1) acquisition/s and development evolve and are impacted by conversational discourse within a social interactive setting between teachers and ESL students, family members and siblings, and so forth.

Interactive ZPD Settings for L2 Development

Both Bronfenbrenner and Vygotsky models emphasize the outcomes and impacts of individuals within interactive, connected settings. For Bronfenbrenner socio-cultural settings influence L2 and thinking development through influences from individuals from the larger social environment, even when not in direct contact, but in the form of social institutions or cultural products and processes In this instance, the references are via media such as video or television where the ESL student has opportunities to see and through imagination interact with cultural heroes such as baseball players as Yao Ming, the Chinese athlete and Sammy Sosa, the Puerto Rican Hispanic athlete. In these instances, cultural heroes via media or textbooks and readings provide interactive settings for developing L2 learning and teaching. For Vygotsky socio-cultural settings influence L2 and thinking development through significant others acting as role models and mediators, by providing nurturance to the individual's potential for learning within social interactive settings, and then by providing scaffolding for continual development in the ZPD. For example, parents or siblings, or ESL teachers can act as role models and social learning mediators for ESL students to develop their skills and abilities to the highest degree of learning potential.

In addition, other ideal interactive ZPD settings include cooperative learning groups where L2 and L1 learners engage in tasks, negotiate them and take on roles within these settings. The ESL teacher as advocator can use any number of ways to group students based on a Vygotskyian approach. For example, and for ESL groupings with potential for ZPD application, Walqui (2000) described four possible grouping systems with ZPD potentials:

1. Modeling between L2 learner and more capable peers or ESL teachers having greater English language capacities

2. Interaction between L2 and L1 peers that have similar language developmental levels

3. Interaction between L2 and L1 students for stimulating social and emotional development, with one demonstrating strong commitment, psychological strength, and goal directedness

4. Interaction between L2 and L1 students, with one showing greater command of a particular subject area than his/her peer, such as mathematics. The former acts as a tutor in this subject area using L1 (i.e., "learning by teaching")

Within interactive and other ZPD settings for L2 development, Bronfenbrenner (1979) noted that, "if one member of a dyad undergoes developmental change, the other is also likely to do so." (p. 65). As pointed out by the four possible grouping systems with ZPD potentials, both the tutor and the tutee benefit greatly from this collaborative peer interactive situation, in which the social learning setting facilitates "learning by teaching" for the tutor and "learning from role modeling and scaffolding" for the tutee.

Cultures' Knowledge for L2 Development

Another mode or way to develop the ESL teacher role of cultural mediator relative to Bronfenbrenner and Vygotsky ideas is to use cultural content as instructional materials within classroom settings. Useem (1999) summed up the use of culturally relevant instructional materials and curriculums for the case of immigrant students within classroom settings with the term Third Culture Kids or simply, TCKS. Useem echoed the incredible potential of using immigrant L2 learners (and minority families) in our classes for developing sound understanding of cultures on first hand bases.

Using Bronfenbrenner and Vygotsky perspectives, ESL students have the natural exposure to cultures, facilitating the development of cross cultural skills, adaptability, knowledge, and understandings of two or more cultures (Rader & Sitting, 2003). These understandings become advantages that ESL teachers can use as "cultural resources" or TCKS to develop cultural and linguistic skills and attitudes across cultural groups. These advantages also provide opportunities to ESL students to tell and showcase their languages and cultural materials and at the same time develop self-confidence and pride while discussing their cultures with their peers. This assists ESL teachers to expand their roles as cultural brokers and mediators between and among cultures. Plus, we as ESL teachers learn much from ESL students' discussions of their cultures that help sharpen our role as cultural mediators.

Taking the role of ultural neutrality damages and detracts from the role of ESL teacher and mediator. To remain neutral to avoid perceived stereotypes or biases from bubbling forth into the classroom is not a viable alternative because remaining "neutral" communicates the message to ESL students that their cultural and linguistic diversity is been "ignored" (Yawkey, in preparation). With similar reasoning Marshall (2002) added another caution concerning "remaining neutral." Marshall said that "neutrality" says to ESL and *all* students that the ESL teacher is disconnect-ing himself or herself from cultural roots including his own culture heritage/s. The notion of "remaining neutral" in Marshall terms has negative influences on ESL students and on the role of ESL teachers as advocates for minority families and students.

In sum, following Bronfenbrenner and Vygotsky perspectives, we as ESL teacher need to assume the role of advocates of ESL students, and we must help minority families become knowledgeable about their rights and the rights of their children. As outlined by Aiza (2002) further understandings to help minority families and advance roles of ESL advocacy include:

1. Expecting sound education for *all* ESL students

2. Reading materials sent home by schools in native languages they can understand

3. Being a part of any and all actions involving their children in school settings, such as disciplinary actions and academic grouping decisions

4   Playing an active part in informational meetings at classroom and building levels

In the next section, we focus on selected communication barriers that arise between minority families and schools, and we provide suggestions to develop positive and strong roles as ESL teachers and to make the commitment to serve as cultural mediators and mentors to minority families and students.

Communication Barriers: Overcoming These Barriers as Cultural Mentors and Mediators

Some Perspectives on Communication

Being misunderstood happens daily to all of us when we talk, teach and discuss ideas. This miscommunication happens because speakers and listeners can interpret the same message differently (Berger, 2000). Within communication processes, we exchange common elements of communication that we know such as: symbols (e.g., using words), signs (e.g., showing body language such as folding arms in talking), and behaviors (e.g., increasing intensity of our voices; Gamble & Gamble, 1982; Merriam-Weber, 2000). Potentials for miscommunication and misinterpretation are doubled and tripled when cultural and linguistic considerations come into play because individuals use personal baselines from one culture to analyze another cultural setting and system of behaviors and actions (Ariza, 2002). Floyd (1998), Gettinger and Guetschow (1998), and Wheeler (1992) identified several major communication barriers that arise between schools and minority families. In turn, these perceived barriers provide rationales for explaining how schools attempt to explain barriers perceived when communicating with minority families. As we will read below, minority families are deeply interested in their children education, but instead avoid to do so because of cultural and language barriers (Ariza, 2000).

Each of the barriers is explained in the following sub-sections: minority L1 fluency, family protection, uncomfortable feelings, negative schooling, differential treatment, and life constraints (Floyd, 1998; Gettinger & Guetshow, 1998; Wheeler, 1992). In addition, each barrier is explained thorough the use of examples of how ESL teachers serving as cultural mediators can use activities to help reduce or ameliorate each of these communication barriers. For these examples, see the sub-heading *As Mentors*, beneath each communication barrier.

Minority L1 Fluency

When families speak languages other than English, they are often not as likely to participate in schools compared to English speaking families (Gettinger & Guetshow, 1998). Aronson (1996) referred to this barrier as issues of culture and language. Minority families often times feel that they do not speak good English and many say that they do not understand the American culture well enough to feel comfortable in discussions with school staff. They feel that their cultures and native languages may cause miscommunications with the teacher. If they come to school, they find it difficult and frustrating to communicate their desires, feelings and thoughts with teachers. And it is quite well known that when families permit their perceived non-English fluencies to interfere with their communication with school personnel or school participation, these behaviors are viewed by educators as being indifferent and not caring about their children or their achievement in schools (Chavkin & Gonzalez, 1995).

As ESL Mentors

ESL teachers can reduce the perceptions of English language inadequacies and advocate and become cultural brokers by having memos and other print materials translated into native languages. These materials include announcements of conferences, newsletters, school policies, parent letters from schools and so forth and serve as avenues for open communication with minority families and communities. The ESL mentor also analyzes the school climate to see if it plays roles in developing or influencing minority families inadequate feelings of communicating in English. For example, do school personnel avoid speaking to minority families and individuals in the school halls and offices? Are their signs in native languages explaining the locations of the office, cafeteria, layground and so forth? These methods open up thoughts of communication difficulties with school personnel or with minority families. And, we move from avoiding communication to using communication with minority families. Open communication is critical as we move to provide ESL mentoring with our minority families (Berger, 2000).

Family Protection

This is the strong desire of families to protect themselves and their children. For many families emigrating from other countries, America is very unfamiliar and an alien place to them. They have already experienced some unpleasant situations with discrimination. Therefore, when families perceive that their children many be criticized if they come to discuss their student progress they may not attend. In addition and in some cultures, families come to school only when their children have acted inappropriately and/or received poor grades (Epstein, 1996). Furthermore, most diverse families view their children as representing family pride. Therefore, perceived criticisms of their children by school personnel are denied in order to protect their families' interest. When school staff request a meeting with minority families to talk about children's learning difficulties, the majority of times minority family members refuse to communicate with the schools (Rosenthal & Sawyers, 1996). These actions of school personnel respond to mainstream cultural perceptions and reinforce the separation of minority families from schools and the misperception that they do not care about the education of their children; and vice versa minority families are reinforced by negative school communication to continue maintaining their distance and distrust with school settings.

As ESL Mentors

ESL teachers in their roles of cultural brokers can begin to reduce this communication barrier by holding cultural fairs and spotlighting different cultures using native languages, authentic materials and minority speakers representing these various cultures. Here, and by inviting the minority families and greater minority community to participate, ESL teachers acting as cultural mediators build bridges to demonstrate positive intercultural understandings and relations.

Uncomfortable Feelings

Most minority families do not feel comfortable with schools or with school personnel. Minority families see teachers, especially those from a mainstream cultural background, as having paramount power and do not wish to communicate with school personnel. In context, these minority families do not wish to interfere with this power or their authority. In addition, school personnel as power figures, may easily be linked with immigration personnel and decide not to communicate with teachers and other school personnel.

However, minority families respect teachers and think teachers educate their children well. For example, in traditional cultures such as Chinese families consider teaching as a sacred job. So, in a sense, teaching and education serve a higher spiritual purpose rather than an economic or tangible purpose. In their native countries, school personnel were often expected to decide all matters, from teaching to discipline. Therefore, minority families who communicate with school personnel often times nod their heads and refuse to express their opinions and thoughts. Ariza (2002) pinpointed that minority families may not actually know their rights for acting as collaborative decision makers and advocates for providing the best possible educational experiences for their children, because they misperceived that teaching is the sole responsibility of the schools.

As ESL Mentors

ESL teachers acting as cultural mediators can avoid this communication barrier with minority families and their children. Experienced ESL teachers who act as cultural brokers know that many minority families wish to communicate to school personnel through interpreters or through their children who are drafted to serve as interpreters for their parents. For these purposes, uncomfortable feelings are reduced when ESL teachers ask bilingual interpreters to serve in this capacity. Ariza (2002) pinpointed that using children of the minority family as interpreters may weaken culturally established authority and hierarchy levels within families. The bilingual interpreter knowing cultural hierarchies respects them in their roles as a liaison between school and minority family and community. Uncomfortable feelings are also reduced when ESL teachers make home visits and actually attempt to develop trust relations between school and minority family (Berger, 2000).

In addition, Berger (2000) recommended attempting to reduce the atmosphere and appearances of school staff as Corporate Executive Officer (CEOs). Reducing the appearances of authority is critical to begin developing the roles of mentor and cultural broker. Inviting minority families in to discuss school activities and affairs becomes important to reducing uncomfortable feelings about schools and the appearance of authority. Also, this invitation to minority families for visits to the school do much to reduce some biases that minority families are reluctant to communicate with school personnel. If minority families suggest some changes or begin to criticize the school and/or its practices, these become real opportunities to reach out to minority families and listen as mentors to their concerns (Berger, 2000). ESL mentors also find ways of getting suggestions. One way is by leaving Suggestion Boxes in various locations in the school building with paper and pencils available with requests for suggestions in native language/s.

Gestwicki (2004) linked uncomfortable feelings with appearances of busy-ness of school staff and showing by deed or word that they have o time for communication with minority families. For school personnel the appearances of busy-ness may only be a reflection of mainstream value systems for values of time and work ethics, but for some minority families this mainstream behavior is perceived as interrupting school staff while they are busy is an impolite and rude behavior. Therefore, minority families decide not to attempt to communicate with school personnel.

Negative Schooling

Many adults in minority families have associated schools with negative experiences. They have experienced the effects of negative schooling while they attended schools in their native countries. When teachers and administrators extend invitations to meetings, and other events and activities to minority families, they are reluctant to accept because of prior negative experiences with schools. And, this factor produces communication barriers such as intimidation, fear and mistrust of the minority families and desires to communicate with school personnel diminish substantially. The unfamiliarity with institutional hierarchy and structure of the American schools leads minority families to confusions on how to communicate and navigate in these mainstream cultural institutions (Chavkin, 1989). With this communication barrier, Yawkey (in preparation) notes that schools are perceived by minority families as "subtractive" institutions; because they are perceived to take away human character, roles, dignity, trust, relations, and personality in their children.

As ESL Mentors

As mediator and cultural broker, the ESL teacher can attempt to turn the "subtractive" into additive factors. For example, helping to expand services to minority families and children is one role of the ESL teacher that needs to be examined thoroughly. Expanding services in the role of the ESL teacher as a mentor means providing or expanding family support services or areas that are needed in health services. For example, by using the avenues of providing minority families with health support services, the communication between school and minority families are strengthened. In a sense, what occurs before school and what occurs after school impacts the learning of ESL students and the capacities to communicate positively with these families over mutual interests and concerns and needs (Flaxman & Unger, 1992).

Differential Treatment

Minority families may see clear examples of unequal treatment by school personnel to themselves and/or their children. Differential treatment may be perceived by minority families as lack of respect or rejection of their culture and language, resulting in feelings of discrimination and unequal treatment in the school. Communication barriers and differential treatment can also result from minority families perceiving school personnel not been able to communicate well and work with them. Thus, there is also a great need for ESL educators to represent the best interest of minority families and their children by showing respect and developing trustworthy relations.

As ESL Mentors

As mediators, ESL teachers can reach out to minority families by developing trust and encouraging pride in diversity of languages and cultures. This reaching out process can begin by visiting one or two minority families. Showing interest, respect, trust and positive interactions with minority families help develop the roles of cultural broker through this reaching out processes.

In addition, and as ESL mentors, we need to reinforce continually with our colleagues that teaching ESL students L2 is *all* teachers responsibilities. It is common experience to see new ESL students coming into the building and to classrooms throughout the U.S. Within a pluralistic and mentoring perspective, these newcomers must *not* be considered students of ESL teachers because they do not speak English. This differential treatment or what Berger (2000) called indifference to ESL students from regular classroom teachers needs changing. Because it is the responsibility of *all* school staff to serve minority families and not the exclusive role of only the ESL staff.

Life Constraints

The world of work and employment for one, both or many family members in the household, often with long work hours and multiple employments may erect barriers, unintentionally. With work coupled with economics and other factors in life constraints including large families, necessities of work and money become premium in the demands of every day living, learning and earning. Therefore, minority families become reluctant to communicate with school personnel or attend school events including parent-teacher conferences due to time constraints.

As ESL Mentors

In roles of mentor, the ESL teacher finds ways of negotiating these life constraints to assist minority families to communicate and to assist as best as possible in school life activities. Perhaps providing for transportation to school where 12th Grade students serve as tutors and sitters begins to pave ways to greater communications. For critical meetings where minority families cannot attend, ESL teachers can make home visits or make phone calls to share critical information as it impacts them and their families. For example, in a former Title VII Preschool through Primary Grade Project, called P.I.A.G.E.T. (Promoting Intellectual Adaptation Given Experiential Transformations), minority family members walked to one neighbor house or nearby school having a safe neighborhood, and project personnel shared and discussed in native language/s the critical news of the schools and community (Yawkey, in preparation).

Epstein Family Involvement Model: Some Procedures and Practices for ESL Teachers

Epstein approach to Family Involvement (Epstein & Dauber, 1991; Epstein, 1995; 1996) is based on the principles developed by Bronfenbrenner and Vygotsky. As previously noted, family involvement has tremendous influences on children's academic achievement in schools (U.S. Department of Education, 1994; Ziegler, 1987). Furthermore, Zill (1996) surveyed research studies that show that family encouragement, reinforcement, and support are better indicators of success than socio-economic status. In addition, increased school attendance, greater amounts of completed homework, and better grades are examples of outcomes of family involvement in schools (Zill, 1996).

Therefore, it is very important for school to involve minority families in and make them a part of school endeavors. In this regard, Epstein has taken a fresh approach to family involvement because she views involvement as the responsibility of the schools and *all* families including minority families. In the following section, Epstein approach is first examined. Then, we present a description of the six types of family involvement, followed by mentoring phases and examples. The six types of family involvement included below are: parenting, communicating, volunteering, learning at home, engaging in decision making, and collaborating with the community.

First Type of Family Involvement: Parenting

Epstein (Epstein & Dauber, 1991; Epstein, 1995; 1996) felt that families are responsible for securing the health and safety of their children, two major factors contributing to the academic achievement and development. The family environment is central for development and academic achievement, not only because of providing basic needs such as health and safety, but also because of its critical role in stimulating children acting in socially and culturally appropriate manners. In this type of family involvement, the schools obligations are to give training to family members so that they better understand and are able to show support for their children growth, development and learning. In undertaking this responsibility, schools give information and demonstrate how to support growth and learning. In a sense, training family members for educational support services at home gives the school a further edge on teaching and learning.

ESL Mentoring for the First Type of Family Involvement

As part of the ESL and *all* teachers roles for minority family mentoring, in this initial type of family involvement, face to face conversations and demonstrations are personal and highly effective ways to develop communication and trust, and to share information about "the hows" of supporting their children's learning in home settings. Ideally, a person from the minority community can demonstrate these support activities and have family members practice them with their children. Native language usage is ideal for these sessions. When minority families bring their child to school, pick them up from school, or during short conversation while training, mentors can get ideas of how the families are helping and supporting their children learning. In addition, a sense of familiarity and trust arise which increases potentials for communication between home and school and to the establishment of parenting and mentoring relations (Gestwicki, 2004).

For ESL teacher mentors, these settings are ideal for gathering information about and coming to understand cultures. In this beginning form of family involvement, the ESL mentors should begin to examine and self-reflect about their own personal attitudes toward minority families, and even write down several leading stereotypes in which they believe. Strong and sound mentoring must begin with these self-examinations and reflections. In turn, teacher mentors must begin with these self-examinations and reflections. In turn teacher mentors can talk with their peers and school colleagues so that they accept diverse cultures (Prager, 2000).

Second Type of Family Involvement: Communicating

In communicating to minority and *all* families, Epstein focused on the schools responsibility to develop and send information to families about their child progress as well as school functions. There are many ways to communicate to minority families. Some of these ways include: family conferences, newsletters, home visits, telephone calls, report cards and so forth. In examining ways to communicate, the best and most effective forms are the ones the families understand and are family friendly.

The forms or ways of communicating are critical especially when ESL mentoring is built into this communicating model. For example, Berger (1994) perceived one-way communication as the traditional, most common method of providing information to parents. This is simply telling families about events and situations happening in the school community. One-way communication is formal and not necessarily family friendly. The other method is two-way communication that encourages minority family interaction and discussion with family members actively responding to the information (Gestwicki, 2004). This approach is informal and time consuming, but rewarding for both teachers and parents.

In communicating, deciding about the importance of the message and linking or matching it with either one-way or two-way forms needs to be thoroughly examined by ESL mentors trying to build minority family trust and communication. Examples of functions of one-way communication include: sending home newsletters for informing parents of school functions, and sending homework for extending school to home learning activities. Bulletin boards in school halls are super for families, who according to Powell (1978) viewed themselves as independent or minority families who really do not wish to talk directly with school personnel. For minority families, native languages in multilingual formats need to be used.

Telephoning is another way of communicating that offers more opportunities for two-way communications. But, telephone talk is best in native languages. Otherwise, if English is used the effectiveness of this mode of communicating is a function of the families levels of English language fluency and therefore questionable for meaningful understanding (Yawkey, in preparation). For traditional cultures that prefer oral, rather than written, forms of communication (such as the case of Hispanic families), a face-to-face interaction between a home visitor and the minority family members may be more appropriate. The school visitor can be an individual from the same minority community, who is knowledgeable of both the native culture and language of the children and their family. In addition, Gestwicki (2004) said that with telephone calls with minority and *all* families, neither speakers nor listeners can see non-verbal body language which carries much of the meaning and understanding. Another mode toward more two-way communication is electronic media such as E-mail. This mode with many minority families may prove effective because they can interact as well as read narrative and meaningfully understand especially if the narrative is written in native languages. However, the number of minority families who have mail capacity may be limited. Surveys are more one way than two-way communication but ideal for getting minority families suggestions, opinions and thoughts especially in initiating ESL mentoring relations.

Second Type of Family Involvement:ESL Mentoring

In deciding to match the communication mode with the importance of the message plus ESL mentoring, the home visit may be the *most effective* method of communicating about school functions, events, and important affairs in the education community. In addition, the minority family members get opportunities to discuss ideas and better understand their impacts and functions on themselves and their families, which represent the oral preferred communication mode of traditional cultures, such as the case of Hispanic families.

Also important is for the ESL mentor to invite some minority family members to classrooms and show them the importance and impact of school information, changes or other urgent school communication. The mentor is also in a sound position to explain the importance and impacts of this information with the minority families. Here, like during home visits, there are greater opportunities to understand each other through an oral mode of communication.

From Prager (2000) perspectives, linking with minority gatekeepers of the community are ideal ways of communicating school information to minority families. For Title VII Project P.I.A.G.E.T, one of the primary methods of sharing school information was using gatekeepers of the minority communities who are native speakers and trusted by the families. In one of our Hispanic P.I.A.G.E.T. communities, we worked with Puerto Rican and Mexican gatekeepers who were restaurant owners and significant contributors to Hispanic cultural events in the community. With our Asian P.I.A.G.E.T. based project, we used Cambodian gatekeepers who were family liaisons to the school systems. And, the Cambodian leaders in their respective communities were key players outside the schools in social services and in entertainment. In volunteering for social services, the Cambodian families frequently interacted with these leaders on the weekends and selected evenings of each week. In entertainment, the gatekeepers lead and played in Cambodian bands on the weekends. Gatekeepers in service of ESL mentors are highly effective in communicat-

ing school information and identifying potential problems of misunder-
standing and miscommunication (Yawkey, in preparation).

In this regard, the National Education Association (1998) recommended
breaking down the size of the school and community. In addition, having
teams for serving each of these sub-communities proved extremely effective
in mentoring minority families and providing them with opportunities for
receiving information in two-way discussion forms (Cassity & Harris,
2000). Each teaching team might have one minority family member and one
teacher. Another approach for mentoring is the use of family centers within
schools that might involve all family members. Here, communication about
school information is given in these special places. Title VII Project P.I.
A.G.E.T. maintained school based family centers at selected sites in Florida
and South Carolina. They were extremely effective in providing mentoring
and communicating school information in family friendly ways (Yawkey,
in preparation).

Third Type of Family Involvement:
Volunteering

In volunteering, minority and *all* families offer their help and services
without charge to the school system or community agency. These volunteering responsibilities are with families who wish to make contributions to
their minority communities and schools and agencies. For example, Head
Start Programs have many thousands of volunteers who share information
about Head Start services throughout communities nationwide. These
volunteers are extremely effective as well in providing minority and *all*
families with empowerment and ownership of their education and direction
of the services that are provided to them. Indeed, because volunteering is
grass roots, it is an extremely powerful and very effective approach for
building mentoring and providing information about schooling functions
throughout the communities.

Third Type of Family Involvement: ESL Mentoring.

Within the Epstein model, volunteering is extremely effective in
developing minority community, and for establishing and expanding
mentoring opportunities. Whether examples are used, as described above,
or modifications are made on them, volunteering is a very viable mode of
communicating and mentoring minority families. Here, discussion uses

minority families' native languages and provides levels of language that are easily understood and clearly meaningful (Center for Family, 1986). And, with easily understood language and speech, volunteering recognizes family feelings and presents two-way communication in a natural format.

Fourth Type of Family Involvement: Learning at Home

A key characteristic of the Epstein perspective is that the best teachers of their children are the members of the family in which they live. With assistance and support, family members play effective roles in encouraging their children and supporting their learning in home settings and can become children's best teachers. This family support includes attention and support for homework assignments. Although there are varieties of activities under this umbrella of volunteering, the central ones include parents and other family members supporting their children at home with homework assignments and other curriculum oriented activities. And, some of these activities can be extensions of learning done originally in school but expanded at home. In addition, minority families can play roles of monitoring and supervising progress of their children in supportive home settings.

Fourth Type of Family Involvement: ESL Mentoring

Understanding the many ways that family members contribute to their children learning in home settings is the key to establish collaborations between minority families and ESL teachers through ESL mentoring strategies. This means building positive rapport with minority family members and avoiding confrontational and negative positions. The Family Literacy Programs funded by the United States Department of Education focus primarily on developing family member abilities to work with and extend learning activities to homes from schools such as public schools, preschools and kindergartens or home care programs offered throughout the communities (Cassity & Harris, 2000). This mentoring idea engages family members in education of their children. These mentoring opportunities are also done using partnerships with religions groups who offer tutoring and other home based education help in neighborhoods (ibid).

These partnerships provide times for family members to meet and talk about home learning and ways in which they support their children learning and teaching. And, from these partnerships and mentoring relations, family members ask questions about their family and schooling

Concerns, such as: disciplining their children, ways to develop more understanding and respect for Hispanic and/or Asian cultures with school personnel, and so forth. As home learning is expanded within a mentoring relationship, this focus provides for many opportunities to explore related areas of home learning. These include: building literacy rich home environments, monitoring of television watching and home work, participating in family and child joint learning activities, and so on.

Fifth Type of Family Involvement: Decision Making

The idea behind this type of family involvement is getting more voices on school decision making and responsibilities. Within minority communities, this fifth type may be extremely difficult to accomplish in the beginning of ESL mentoring. Many minority families come from cultural backgrounds where schools and governments develop and enforce rules, policies and regulations. A democratic or participatory decision making perspective is a very different approach for it involves actual discussions and debates among parents and other stake-holders of education in our communities. This new perspective on the decision-making process in our minority communities is learned over periods of time.

Showing respect for each others' ideas is a significant factor for establishing a two-way communication style. Areas in decision making that need minority family representation include: school-based management committees, school district level committees or councils, planning committees for particular issues concerning education and schools, and so forth. In addition, and to nurture this type of family involvement, school and minority leaders need to understand that all information needs to be shared openly and equally. In other words, the philosophy of the participatory perspective can be summarized by the following sayings: "the more people involve in the decision-making process the better," and "more heads think better than one." Here, this perspective avoids a few people, and always the same people, being involved in school activities and school decisions.

Fifth Type of Family Involvement: ESL Mentoring

Perhaps one initial way of many to begin the mentoring process with this minority family involvement is to use and expand groups currently in operation. For example, using the Parent Teacher Association or Organization can help increase minority family members, and their active participation at meetings. Smaller support groups might also function as a support for mentoring and providing opportunities to develop this family involvement initiative. Said differently, developing decision-making abilities takes time and requires much trust between mentors and minority family members. Remember to be patient. Changes are made over time and beginning in small scale, and change is spread slowly over groups of people, resulting in making effective changes in attitudes and willingness to voice opinions and thoughts (Prager, 2000). In addition, ESL mentors need to be persistent. Making slow progress in developing decision-making abilities among minority family members is better that making a rapid push for this type of involvement.

Sixth Type of Family Involvement: Collaboration With the Community

Collaborating between schools, agencies, social services, religions groups, literacy committees and others offer minority families with many opportunities to receive support for their educational endeavors. These agencies are varied and numerous and examples include: Head Start, Women Infants and Children (WIC), After School Programs, and a host of other support units are also available. Understanding how minority families can access services provided by these agencies and organizations is a primary need. These outreach activities to the community become minority family resources and at the same time strengthen the family and school collaboration, resulting in increasing children's learning, development, and academic achievement in both family and school settings.

Sixth Type of Family Involvement: ESL Mentoring.

Taking advantage of establishing school collaboration with minority families and their communities integrates and strengthens families, schools, and communities. ESL mentoring can provide minority families with opportunities to demonstrate and live their cultures; and make contributions to themselves, their communities and their schools. Martinez (2000) noted that the interplay of these factors with cultural perspectives has the potential of dramatically impacting the development of the family, and type/level of involvement. Mentoring and mediating within this form of family involvement becomes community wide. It must meet the needs of minority families and could include areas such as preparation of taxes, studying for taking the written exam for obtaining a driver's license, solving problems in workplaces, and other common concerns that minority families face. Therefore, mentors can help minority parents relate with their daily needs and solve real-life problems they face by increasing their understandings of how to access the community and society at large in positive, productive, and beneficial ways.

Conclusions

The second Chapter focused on mentoring of ESL and all teachers for minority families and students. Overall, three sections of the article point to and provided many potential applications of mentoring and cultural mediating. Some of these applications include: perspectives of family involvement and its benefits, potentials of minority family involvement, and examples of teachers serving as mentors using Epstein family involvement perspectives.

Within the section on potentials of family involvement, Bronfenbrenner and Vygotsky views are detailed. Emphases were on explaining selected principles, and then showing how these principles can be used by ESL teachers who are working to establish and expand their roles as cultural mediators and mentors. In addition, research foundations demonstrate effectively processes that are used to nurture positive impacts of families and to explain the contemporary significance of family involvement to our society.

In the next section, numerous examples of the potentials of mentoring and cultural mediation activities were provided to demonstrate the applications of these approaches with minority populations. For purposes of discussion, the mentoring applications are based on and framed upon well-known perspectives, such as Vygotsky's and Epstein's perspectives. These perspectives demonstrated the practicality and the potentials of both mentoring and mediating using a contemporary family involvement program.

Chapter 2 pointed out the potentials for ESL mentors to increase their understanding of other cultures in order to develop rapport with minority populations. These understandings included: recognizing minority family concerns and feelings, discussions of issues of concern to minority families about school and community involvement activities, and family education originating from and based on the needs and interests of minority families. Bridging gaps between school and minority families through genuine involvement in a variety of ways can increase tremendously the potentials of family, school, and community for learning and teaching of ESL students.

References

Ariza, E.N. (2002). Cultural considerations: Immigrant parent involvement. *Kappa Delta Pi Record, 38* (3), 134-137.

Aronson, J. Z. (1996). How schools can recruit hard-to-reach parents. *Educational Leadership, 53*(8) 58-60.

Berger, A. (2000). *Parents as partners in education* (5th ed.). NJ: Prentice-Hall.

Center for Family. (1986). *Building family strengths: A manual for facilitators.* Lincoln, NE: University of Nebraska Press.

Bronfenbrenner, U. (1979). *The ecology of human development: Experiments by nature and design.* Cambridge, MA: Harvard University Press.

Brown, H. D. (2000). *Principles of language learning and teaching.* New York: Addison-Wesley.

Brown, H.D. (1992). Sociocultural factors in teaching language minority students. In P. A. Richard-Amoto & M. A. Snow (Eds.). *The multicultural classroom: Readings for content-area teachers* (pp. 73-92). New York: Addison-Wesley.

Cassity, J., & Harris, S. L. (2000). Parents of ESL students. A study of parental involvement. *NASSP Bulletin, 84*(619), 55-62.

Chavkin, N. (1990). Debunking the myth about minority parents. *Educational Horizons, 67*(4), 119-123.

Chavkin, N., & Gonzalez, D. L. (1995). *Forging partnerships between Mexican-American Parents and schools.* Office of Educational Research and Improvement. (ERIC Document Reproduction Service No. ED 384 028).

Coleman, M. (1991). *Planning for parent participation in schools for young children.* Urbana, IL: ERIC Clearinghouse on Elementary and Early Childhood Education.

Couchenour, D.. & Chrisman, K. (2000). *Families, schools and communities: Together for young children.* Albany, NY: Thomson Learning.

Cassity, J., & Harris, S.L. (2000). Parents of ESL students: A study of parental involvement. *NASSP Bulletin, 84,* 55-62.

Department of Education (2005). *Education Secretary Designate Margaret Spellings opening statement at Senate Confirmation Hearing.* Retrieved March 2, 2005 from Web site: http://www.ed.gov/news/speeches/2005/01/01062005.html.

Edwards, A., & Warin, J. (1999). Parent involvement in raising the achievement of primary school pupils: Why bother? *Oxford Review of Education, 25*(3), 325-340.

Epstein, J.L., & Dauber, S.L. (1991). School programs and teacher practices of parent involvement in inner-city elementary and middle schools. *Elementary School Journal, 91*(3), 289-305.

Epstein, J.L. (1995). School/family/community partnerships: Caring for the children we share. *Phi Delta Kappan, 76*(9), 701-712.

Epstein, J.L. (1996). Perspective and previews on research and policy for school, family, and community partnerships. In A. Booth & J. F. Dunn (Eds.), *Family-school links: How do we affect educational outcomes* (pp. 209-246). Mahwah, NJ: Lawrence Erlbaum Associates.

Flaxman, E., & Unger, E. (1992). Parents and schooling in the 1990s. *Education Digest, 57*(9), 3-7.

Floyd, L. (1998). Joining hands: A parental involvement program. *Urban Education ,33*(1), 123-135.

Gamble, K., & Gamble, M. (1982). *Contacts: Communicating interpersonally.* New York: Random House.

Gibson, M. (1984). Approaches to multicultural education in the United States. *Anthropology and Education Quarterly, 15*(1), 94-119.

Geenen, S., Powers, L., & Lopez-Vasquez, A. (2002). Multicultural aspects of parent involvement in transition planning. *Exceptional Children, 67*(2), 256-258.

Gestwicki, C. (2004). *Home, school, and community relations* (5th Ed.). Clifton Park NY: Delmar Learning.

Gettinger, M., & Guetschow, G.W. (1998). Parent involvement in schools: Parent and teacher perceptions of roles, efficacy, and opportunities. *Journal of Research and Development in Education, 32*(1), 38-51.

Gonzalez,V., Brusca-Vega, R., & Yawkey, T.D. (1997). *Assessment and instruction of culturally and linguistically diverse students with or at-risk of learning problems: From theory to practice.* Boston: Allyn & Bacon.

Grab, W., & Stoller, F. L. (1997). Content-based instruction: Research foundations. In D. A. Snow & D. M. Brinton (Eds.) *Content-based classroom: Perspective on integrating language and content* (pp.73-92). N.Y.: Longman.

Karther, D., & Lowden, F. (1997). Fostering effective parent involvement. *Contemporary Education, 69*(1), 41-44.

Keyes, C. R. (2000). Parent-teacher partnerships: A theoretical approach for teachers. Retrieved Oct. 31, 2003 from University of Illinois at Urbana-Champaign Web site: http://ecap.crc.uiuc.edu/pubs/katzsym/keyes.html.

Marshall, P.L. (2002). *Cultural diversity in our school.* CA: Wadsworth.

Martinez, Y.G., & Velázquez, J.A. (2000). Involving migrant families in education. *ERIC Clearinghouse on Rural Education and Small Schools,* EDO-RC-00-4.

Merriam-Webster, Inc. (2003). *Merriam-Webster On-Line.* Retrieved November 21, 2003 from Web site: http://www.m-w.com/cgi-bin/dictionary?book' Dictionary&va'communication

National Education Association (1998). Parent involvement: More than kid's play. *NEA Today, 16*(5), 15.

Pape, B. (1999). Involving parents lets students and teachers win. *Education Digest, 64*(6), 47-51.

Powell, D. (1989). *Families and early children education.* Washington, DC: National Association for the Education of Young Children.

Powell, D. R. (1978). Personal relationship between parents and caregivers in day car settings. *American Journal of Orthopsychiatry, 48(*4), 680-689.

Prager, S. (2000). Representing ESL students in social community. Retrieved November 21, 2003 from *ESL Magazine* Website: http://www.eslmag.com/ modules.php?name'News&file'article&sid'23

Rader, D., & Sitting, L.H. (2003). *New kid in school: Using literature to help children in transition.* New York, NY: Teachers College Press.

Rosenthal, D., & Sawyers, J. (1996). Building successful home/school partnerships. *Childhood Education, 72* (4), 194-200.

Schinke-Llano, L. (1993). On the value of a Vygotskian framework for SLA theory. *Language Learning, 43*(1), 121-129.

TESOL (1997). *ESL standards for pre-K-12 students.* TESOL: Washington, D.C.

U.S. Department of Education. (1994, September). Strong families, strong schools: Building community partnerships for learning. Washington, D.C.

Useem, R. H. (Ed.). (1999). *A third culture kid bibliography* (2nd ed.) (Available from Dr. Ruth Hill Useem, Berkey Hall, Dept. of Sociology, Michigan State University, E. Lansing, MI 48824-1111).

Vygotsky, L. (1968). *Mind in society: The development of higher psychological processes.* Cambridge, MA: Harvard University Press.

Vygotsky, L. (1962). *Thought and language.* Cambridge, MA: MIT Press.

Walqui,.A. (2000). *Scaffolding subject matter instruction for English language learners.* Paper presented at Improving America Schools Conference. NABE and OBEMLA Sponsored Institute, Washington, D.C., December.

Wheeler, P. (1992). Promoting parent involvement in secondary schools. *NASSP Bulletin , 76* (546), 28-35.

Woodlief, L. (2002). The high-quality learning conditions needed to support students of color and immigrants at California community colleges. *California Tomorrow.* Retrieved Oct. 31, 2003 from Web site: http://www.sen.ca. gov/masterplan/ 020307SLCALIFTOMORROWTESTIMONY.HTM.

Yawkey, T.D.(in preparation). Retraining of in-service teachers for culturally and linguistically diverse ESL and all students. [Research Monograph]. University Park, Pennsylvania: The Pennsylvania State University.

Yawkey, T.D., Jackson, A., Wang, L-H., & Chuang, C. P.(2003). Examining program impacts in the training of in-service graduate-level teachers of culturally and linguistically diverse (MINORITY) students; *Adelante* perspectives. *Multicultural Perspectives, 5*(4), 31-37.

Ziegler, S. (1987). The effects of parent involvement on children's achievement: The significance of home/school links. In A.T. Henderson & N. Berla (Eds.), *A new generation of evidence: The family is critical to student achievement* (pp. 151-152). Washington, D.C.: Center for Law and Education.

Zill, N. (1996). Family change and student achievement: What we have learned, what it means for school. In A. Booth & J. F. Dunn, *Family-school links How do we affect educational outcomes* (pp. 209-246). Mahwah, NJ: Lawrence Erlbaum Associates.

Part II

AN ALTERNATIVE RESEARCH VIEW TO THE STUDY OF DEVELOPMENT AND ACADEMIC ACHIEVEMENT IN MINORITY AND MAINSTREAM CHILDREN

3

CULTURAL AND LINGUISTIC GIFTEDNESS IN HISPANIC KINDERGARTNERS: ANALYIZING THE VALIDITY OF ALTERNATIVE AND STANDARDIZED ASSESSMENTS

℘∞℘

*Virginia Gonzalez, Patricia Bauerle
and Ellen Riojas Clark*

Introduction

Chapter 3 starts Part II of the book on applying the Ethnic Research alternative paradigm to the study of development and achievement in language-minority and majority children. This Chapter presents alternative methodologies for more accurately assessing development and academic achievement in Hispanic young learners.

More specifically, Chapter 3 presents a research study that illustrates the effect of developmental, and cultural and linguistic factors on young minority children's giftedness, as measured by both alternative and standardized assessments. The objective of this study was to test empirically an assessment model that can identify giftedness in young Hispanic children when using measures that represent cultural and linguistic factors.

Three research questions guided the statistical data analysis: (1) Are there different patterns of the children's performance in alternative (the

Qualitative Use of English and Spanish Tasks—QUEST, the Cartoon Conservation Scales—CCS, Parents' and Teachers' Ratings) and standardized (Language Assessment Scales—LAS, the Test of Nonverbal Intelligence—TONI) measures when comparing cultural and linguistic giftedness?, (2) Which alternative (QUEST, CCS, Parents' and Teachers' Ratings) or standardized measures (LAS, TONI) are better predictors of giftedness in language-minority children?, and (3) Can QUEST predict the children's performance on other alternative (CCS, Parents' and Teachers' Ratings) and standardized (TONI, LAS) measures?

The first research question was tested using a multiple factor analysis model, and the second and third questions were analyzed using a regression model. Thirty bilingual Hispanic kindergartners, 1st-2nd-and-3rd generation Mexican-Americans, from low socioeconomic backgrounds participated in this study. Results showed that alternative assessments revealed new dimensions of minority children's giftedness: (1) culturally-linguistically loaded cognitive domains, and (2) universal and non-verbal cognitive domains. Moreover, alternative assessments are good predictors of minority children's giftedness, especially when these valid instruments use: (1) developmental ages as guidelines for assessing cognitive and linguistic processes; and (2) verbal and non-verbal tasks that are developmentally, culturally, and linguistically adequate to bilingual minority-children's characteristics.

Objectives

The main objective of this research study was to present evidence supporting our argument that cognitive giftedness in young Hispanic children can be identified when using measures that represent cultural and linguistic developmental factors. Then, the main purpose of this study was to uncover patterns or profiles of cognitive and language development when comparing: (1) non-verbal and verbal performances in culturally and linguistically gifted children; (2) standardized and alternative methods of cognitive and language development; and (3) reports of different informants including parents, teachers, and evaluators.

The second objective was to test empirically an identification and assessment model that offers several advantages over traditional assessment approaches when used with young language-minority children, because it: (1) is developmentally adequate; (2) differentiates verbal from non-verbal cognitive processes; (3) represents cultural minority factors in its stimuli and tasks; (4) uses dominant language administration representing both the minority and mainstream dominant languages; and (5) includes parents, teachers, and bilingual/bicultural evaluators as multiple informants across home and school environments representing both the minority and mainstream cultures.

Theoretical Framework

The theoretical framework for the model for identifying gifted Hispanic children endorses developmental, Constructivistic, and ecological perspectives derived from contemporary cognitive psychology theory (i.e., the constraint approach, e.g., Markman, 1984) and neo-Piagetian approaches (e.g., Lewis, 1991; Matarazzo, 1992). The model based on which the two developmental assessment methods used were constructed (the Qualitative Use of English and Spanish Tasks—QUEST, Gonzalez, 1991, 1994, 1995; and the Cartoon Conservation Scales—CCS, De Avila, 1976) represents cultural, linguistic, and developmental variables affecting cognition and language in minority young children. Within this assessment model multiple alternative developmental measures including different informants and contexts (i.e., parents' and teachers' ratings of the children's cognitive development), and verbal and non-verbal tasks were used for the identification of giftedness in Hispanic kindergartners.

The critical literature review presented below represents the variables studied in the analysis of the characteristics of verbal and non-verbal conceptual development in monolingual and bilingual children. In the first section, studies conducted with monolingual children are presented, from two perspectives: (1) a traditional framework encompassing Chomsky' s, Piaget's, and the Sapir-Whorf hypotheses; and (2) a more contemporary perspective represented by the constraint approach. In a second section, studies conducted with bilingual children are presented, emphasizing the advantages of bilingualism for children's cognitive development.

Characteristics of Verbal and Non-Verbal Conceptual Development in Monolingual and Bilingual Children

As this literature review attests, most studies have been either conducted on monolingual or bilingual children, but very few have compared both populations using the same methodology. Even though most of the studies conducted with monolingual children take a psychological, developmental perspective; there is yet scarcity of developmental studies discovering the process of verbal and non-verbal concept formation in bilingual children.

Then, in this section an effort is made to present some traditional and contemporary perspectives derived from the study of mainstream populations, and compare them with contemporary research findings with bilingual children.

Studies Conducted with Monolingual Children

Most studies on the relation between cognition and language have been conducted with monolingual children, trying to uncover the developmental processes underlying mapping non-verbal concepts onto linguistic forms, which represent a cultural convention. Three major theoretical approaches within mainstream psychological theories will be discussed briefly below (for an extended review of this topic see Gonzalez & Schallert, 1999). The first three are traditional theories, including Chomsky's theory of syntactic acquisition, Piagetian conceptual developmental theory, and the Sapir-Whorf hypotheses. The first two traditional perspectives were incorporated into a more contemporary interaction view, the constraint approach. This interaction view proposes a relation between semantic constraints and cognitive and cultural factors surrounding the process of mapping non-verbal conceptual structures onto linguistic forms and meanings.

Thus, these different theoretical perspectives applied to monolingual children also represent diversity: (1) in the behavioral processes studied, measured, and analyzed; and also (2) in the derived interpretations of behavioral expressions of underlying psychological processes of cognitive and language development. These findings can be considered as a general framework from which to understand how language can affect the cognitive development of minority children, who are bilingual and bicultural. These developmental studies conducted with monolingual children can provide some reference for generating heuristic research on how changing the linguistic, cultural, and SES background of children can also affect their psychological developmental performance. The urgent need area where mostly innovative research needs to be undertaken is the cognitive and linguistic development of language-minority, or limited English proficient children, from low SES backgrounds.

Traditional Perspectives: Chomsky, Piaget, and Sapir-Whorf

Chomsky introduced the concept of constraint during the 1950's, proposing the presence of a Language Acquisition Device (LAD) in children's brains, a highly abstract innate linguistic structure that imposes constraints in the acquisition of syntax in young children. That is, biological factors, the genetic endowment, would guide the brain maturation and the unfolding of automatic developmental processes for language acquisition. Then, according to Chomsky's generative grammar theory, an innate predisposition would explain how very young children are able to learn and master syntax in their native language.

Whereas Chomsky studied language acquisition from a linguistic perspective, with a focus on syntactic processes underlying language acquisition and use; Piaget (1967, 1968) conducted pioneer work in the area of cognitive development. Piaget used language as a symbolic window to the complex conceptual systems of the children's minds. Piaget wanted to uncover the origin of knowledge by studying logical operations and intelligence processes in young children. Piaget invented the clinical-critical method, which became a major breakthrough allowing for the first time to study the complexity of conceptual structures using verbal and non-verbal representations.

Piaget (1967, 1968) used language only as a tool for uncovering the abstract, non-verbal, logical operations that were the focus of his interest. He considered that language was a semiotic function, a vehicle for abstract non-verbal thinking or intelligence to become integrated into simultaneous systems of interdependent transformations or logical operations. However, genuine intelligence or abstract thinking was non-verbal in nature; and language was a necessary, but not sufficient, condition needed only for the construction of logical operations. That is, language was a semiotic function when labels would be connected with concepts or logical operations (e.g., classification, seriation, conservation, number, time, space, causality, etc.). But, labels could also be learned only as signs with no conceptual meanings attached, such as a string of numbers with no underlying non-verbal concepts. That is, according to Piaget how linguistic meanings are mapped onto non-verbal concepts would depend on the non-verbal cognitive developmental level achieved by the child.

On the other hand, according to Piaget (1967, 1968), intelligence would be independent and would precede language acquisition in young children.

However, the onset of language would permit individuals to socially regulate their thinking processes. That is, language provides a symbolic tool and vehicle for children to articulate their ideas and engage into cooperative and interpersonal exchanges. Then, according to Piagetian theory, there are three possibilities for the relation of thought and language: (1) thought can take a non-verbal form, which is more abstract and is called *intelligence*; (2) thought can take a verbal form as it intersects with conceptual use of language and is called *semantic development*; and (3) language can be used in a non-conceptual form called *speech*. Thus, the original Piagetian position defended a *cognitive determinism* perspective, also known as the *strong cognition hypothesis*.

Later on, during the 1970's Sinclair proposed the *weak cognition hypothesis*, acknowledging the reciprocal effect of language on cognitive development, since new labels or linguistic forms could also trigger the formation of new verbal and non-verbal concepts in cognition. Within a more contemporary approach, Nelson (1988) suggested that language represents the social construction of meaning which evolve dynamically in the daily interactions occurring in a society across multiple contexts. She has also proposed that meanings also evolve within the individual in relation to his/her level of world knowledge, acquired within a particular sociocultural environment. Thus, this neo-Piagetian perspective proposes a triple interaction among cognitive, linguistic, and sociocultural factors influencing verbal and non-verbal conceptual formation processes in young children. That is, semantic development is influenced by internal cognitive factors, as well as by external learning factors including the social interaction of the individual with real-world experiences.

The idea of language influencing cognition was not a new Piagetian perspective, but it had been present in the literature since the 1920's with its original author Sapir, and further elaborated afterwards by Whorf during the 1950s. Both Sapir (1929) and Whorf (1956) proposed that linguistic forms, especially labels and grammatical structures (i.e., lexical, morphological, syntactic, and cultural habitual verbal behavior), influence how individuals think and form semantic and conceptual categories. This approach was called *linguistic relativity* because grammatical patterns and cultural, habitual, verbal behaviors acquired by the learner as a native language would unconsciously shape his/her mental and sensory interpretations or perceptions of reality, and ultimately the underlying conceptual systems formed.

Linguistic relativity considers that certain abstract representations constructed by the culture surrounding the native language learner are mediated solely by linguistic symbols, and not by direct or immediate real-life experiences. For instance, the concept of time (e.g., days of the week, scheduling, etc.) is a cultural abstraction, which is acquired by the child in his/her native language through linguistic structures and cultural habitual behaviors. For instance, the first day of the week for Spanish speakers socialized within the Hispanic culture is considered to be Monday (represented as a common noun in the Spanish language). In contrast, for English speakers, socialized within the American mainstream culture, the first day of the week is Sunday (linguistically a proper noun that needs to be capitalized in English). Thus, as this example illustrates, according to the Sapir-Whorf hypothesis of *linguistic relativity*, languages would provide cultural ways of categorizing world experiences; instead of innate predisposition or constraints originating language acquisition, as proposed by Chomsky and later on incorporated by the constraint approach.

Whorf called this cultural ways of categorizing verbal concepts that are represented in linguistic forms a *pattern-system*, which was later incorporated by Keil (1986), and Gelman and Coley (1991) as a *naive theory*. These contemporary developmental psychologists proposed that theories guide the acquisition of concepts and language. According to this naive theory view, naming is used by young children to restructure concepts. Keil (1986) proposed that relations among concepts signal differences between kinds of concepts in reference to their underlying conceptual structure (*nominal concepts* defined by a single criterion—triangle, even number; *natural concepts* that form classes based on nature's laws—lions, tigers; and *artifact concepts* formed by man-made objects—chairs, tables). Keil assumed that different word learning and conceptual processes would be used by the same learner for acquiring these different kinds of concepts. Thus, within a traditional perspective, cognitive influences language (*strong cognition hypothesis* within a Piagetian view); and at the same time language brings new cultural representations influencing cognition (*weak cognition hypothesis*, proposed by neo-Pagetians).

The Constraint Approach

The construct of an innate predisposition or constraint, proposed by Chomsky in relation to syntactic developmental processes, has been applied to the explanation of the process of semantic development in children by contemporary developmental psychologists, who endorsed the constrain approach. However, according to Byrnes and Gelman (1991), "currently there are few programs of research examining semantic and conceptual development from a cross-linguistic perspective [that could] address questions of universality and relativity" (p. 22-23).

Thus, many more research studies examining the relation of thought and language with cultural representations in language-minority children from a low socioeconomic status background are needed. Bilingual children can become a *virtual laboratory* for the interaction of: (1) linguistic experiences, (2) verbal and non-verbal thinking processes, and (3) living experiences within different cultural environments. The alternative assessment method used in this study (QUEST, Gonzalez, 1991, 1994, 1995) represents such an effort, trying to tap bilingual children's semantic and conceptual developmental performance in both the Spanish and the English languages and cultures.

Contemporary researchers, endorsing the constraint approach, study conceptual and semantic systems. These researchers are interested in studying how young monolingual children map non-verbal concepts onto linguistic forms and meanings. Then, they study the relation between cognitive and language development at a process level, trying to uncover how young children think with language. The constraint approach assumes a bi-directional relation between thought and language, with the specific characteristics of language structures influencing and, at the same time, representing verbally the complexities of non-verbal conceptual learning. These developmental psychologists try to uncover what *conceptual* and *pragmatic constraints* are present among young children, and from those which are universal or language-specific conventions representing the surrounding cultural environment.

Several researchers have represented this contemporary constraint approach, among them Clark (1973), Markman (1984), and Waxman (1990). According to Clark (1973), *conceptual categories* help young children figure out the meaning of words, and prag*matic principles* help them shape these concepts into verbal forms following cultural conventions. Markman (1984) has studied the *taxonomic assumption*, leading young children to think that labels refer to objects of the same taxonomic kind, encompassing basic and non-basic objects. Basic objects are defined as every day labels for objects, such as the label "chair." Intermediate labels include subcategories of objects, such as the label "bedroom furniture." Whereas super-ordinate non-basic labels represent classes or categories of objects (such as the category label "furniture"). Finally, subordinate non-basic labels represent sub-categories of objects (such as the label "rocking chair"). Markam's argument is that basic-level categories are universal, and are common across languages and cultures. That is, Markman (1984) proposed that non-basic labels at the super-ordinate and subordinate levels are different across languages and cultures. A the same time, the way in which these conceptual categories are marked linguistically show young children at what basic or non-basic level they should be represented (e.g., novel adjectives would mark subordinate categories, versus novel nouns would mark taxonomic categories).

Some influence of the original ideas of Sapir and Whorf is also seen in Waxman's (1990) and Markman's (1984) research work within the constraint approach. That is, a weak form of *linguistic determinism* can be identified in the taxonomic constraint assumed by Waxman, which would make young children more attentive to basic and non-basic labels, rather than to other semantic relations between verbal and non-verbal concepts. For example: (1) thematic relations (i. e., scripts for narrating experiences such as going to a restaurant); (2) functional relations (i.e., things that are used for activities such as things for cooking); (3) relational similarity (i.e., people associated by kinship such as mother and baby); and (4) metaphorical relations (i.e., a comparison used for interpreting connected meanings in different conceptual categories such as "mother earth").

Markam (1991) also proposed the *mutual exclusivity assumption* in which young children would assume that each object has only one label; and the *whole-object assumption*, which will make young children assume that a label refers to the whole object and not to its parts. Waxman (1990) proposed an interaction between conceptual and linguistic forms done by the young bilingual child through the use of *implicit biases* when learning new words.

Within the constraint approach, Gelman and Coley (1991) proposed that language characteristics and structure influence children's formation of non-verbal and verbal categories. These authors take the perspective that language is a vehicle for the human mind to explain the world, and to draw inferences about the unknown, and ultimately to develop *theories* (mental explanations) of how to restructure mental categories, that modify perceptual similarity, into deeper predictive abstract properties. In addition, Gelman and Coley (1991) opposed the perspective that language reflects natural categories present in the physical environment, which are perceived in naturally correlated attributes of objects. This latter explanation represents the *realist position* defended by the *characteristic attribute approach* proposed by Rosch and colleagues in the 1970s and 1980s (see e.g., Mervis & Rosch, 1981; Rosh, 1978).

Gelman and Coley (1991) opposed a *nominalist position* (defended in the 1950s by Bruner, Goodnow, & Austin, 1956). Instead Gelman and Coley (1991) proposed that categories are just arbitrary mental concepts imposed on the world, completely arbitrary and unrelated to natural characteristics of objects. These authors proposed a *theory-laden categories* approach, proposing that language as a cultural product *invents* classification systems, which need to be consistent with constraints or natural patterns present in the environment, but are not limited by perceptual salient features (contrary to the realist position).

That is, as explained by Gelman and Coley (1991), "theory-laden categories encourage us to discover more similarities among the objects being classified than we would ever discover otherwise" (p. 151). They proposed that there are six properties of theory-laden categories, including (1) rich inductive potential; (2) bases for making non-obvious inferences (capture deep similarities not always based on perceptual attributes); (3) an essence or unique underlying property (psychological essentialism) that explains universals among natural categories; (4) existence of anomalies that differ from the category prototype at a perceptual or surface level, but share deeper attributes to belong to the category; (5) division of linguistic labor, in relation to experts that can make a distinction between more unique or abstract categories and its members; and (6) corrigibility so that categories are dynamic and open to historical change due to previous error or incompleteness. As Gelman and Coley (1991) explained, "Attention to different attributes could lead to different categories, [and thus] categorization is an inventive act" (p. 149).

According to Gelman and Coley (1991), non-theory-laden categories are distinct, and form artificial systems of classification, which are constructed for practical functions (e.g., white things, classification that goes across many natural categories). That is, "the class of blue circles is merely a grouping based on perceptual attributes; it does not capture non-obvious similarities, nor does it draw on richer sorts of knowledge children have about the worlds" (Gelman & Coley, 1991, p. 161). These authors propose that children can acquire natural kind categories well before the onset of formal schooling and prior knowledge about science in general and scientific domains in particular.

Gelman and Coley (1991) presented some research evidence showing that including natural categories and probing deeper understanding in children (ages 2 and a half to 5 years) provides them an opportunity to demonstrate their ability to use categories for (1) making inductive inferences across items with dissimilar appearances, (2) identifying shared non-obvious properties that do not always correspond to explicit perceptual attributes, and (3) including anomalous members in categories. It is also interesting to note that hearing a label helped the preschool children to draw correct inferences about natural kind category membership, which were expressed through verbal justifications of properties of objects (and thus much more than pointing or using a label was needed for considering that the child had learned a conceptual category). Moreover, as concluded by Gelman and Coley (1991), when children form natural kind categories, language can help them classify or reclassify objects, provided that the category learned is coherent and the new word provided maps onto a natural kind. Children have a natural assumption, called *linguistic transparency* by Gelman and Coley (1991) that names convey natural kind categories, providing clues for making inferences based on familiar category labels, and modifying their conceptions about objects.

Thus, as pinpointed by Gelman and Coley (1991), "conceptual grasp of the category being named, and not just the label itself, influences children's expectations about a label" (p. 186). These authors proposed that language can help young children overcome limitations of relying only on perceptual similarities, enabling them to determine which categories are coherent based on: (1) language form (e.g., nouns, adjectives) or linguistic structure of the input that can give children clues of whether the category named is theory-laden; (2) parental input or naming strategies based on the linguistic form in which a word is embedded, the context of social interaction, such as variations in how objects are labeled and map out into categories; and (3) prototypes that can have functional utility for introducing and assimilating new categories.

Language and labels are also a major socialization tool used by adults and parents, because as stated by Gelman and Coley (1991), "our natural kinds are passed down to the children through the language we speak. The cultural naming practices are fundamental to the content of our natural kinds" (p. 184). Thus, language learning influences cognition within the context of real world sociocultural experiences. As explained by Gelman and Coley (1991), "language helps structure children's categories, but the influence is subtle and works within the context of children's nonlinguistic understanding" (p. 189). According to Gelman and Coley the most important function of language is to encode theories of natural kind categories, encode them symbolically, and then use verbal communication to transmit knowledge and cultural beliefs and values to youngsters. As explained by Gelman and Coley (1991), based on these theory-laden linguistic categories, young children's cognition is stimulated to: (1)

discover higher knowledge levels; and (2) learn about the world by making inferences, searching for non-obvious similarities (other than perceptual), and go beyond what is explicitly taught to them in formal and informal educational contexts (school and home).

Then, preschool children use natural kind category labels to make inferences about underlying properties of objects. For instance, several researchers (Dolgin & Behrend, 1984; Masey & Gelman, 1988; Richards & Siegle, 1986) have demonstrated that 3-and-4-year-old children could differentiate conceptually animate from inanimate objects, based on subtle cues rather than overall similarity. Other researchers have shown that children can understand conceptually the non-obvious, such as differentiating between internal thoughts or mental and emotional states, behaviors, and objects (Wellman & Estes, 1986; Wellman & Gelman, 1988), and have used their beliefs to predict behavior (Winner & Perner, 1983). Research evidence (Gelman & Coley, 1991; Keil, 1986) has also shown that young children use *psychological essentialism*, believing that deeper properties are more important than superficial or perceptual ones for forming categories. Preschoolers use these essential properties (e.g., innate factors, intrinsic nature, and growth) more often for natural kind categories than for artificial categories when explaining the reason why members share attributes, and when justifying verbally properties of objects and categories.

Other researchers, such as Mandler (1989), have made developmental distinctions to the taxonomic assumption studied further by Markman and Waxman. Mandler found that 1 and 2 year-old children could only distinguish conceptual categories at the global level, and could not differentiate many basic-level categories. Moreover, Mandler (1989) differentiated super-ordinate from global categories, as he stated, "early conceptual categories may be more appropriately described as global in nature, rather than as either basic level or super-ordinate" (p. 134). Mandler (1989) proposed that in order to be able to form basic-level categories as an abstraction, children need to go though an initial "global characterization to successively finer distinctions process that is also called foundation for conceptual theory building" (p. 136).

Mandler (1989) conducted an experimental study in which object-manipulation tasks were presented to young, pre-verbal children. The child was placed in front of two categories of objects, and the spontaneous sequential touching of the child was considered the "grouping" of the items that the child made. Control for random touching is made by comparing the child's "responses [with chance, and] above-chance performance indicates that the response to the objects is not random" (Mandler, 1989, p. 132).

Interestingly, knowing the label did not make a difference in children's responses, as Mandler explained, "children who labeled objects were no more or less likely to categorize the objects than those who were silent... [and] over-extension of a term for one basic-level category from the same super-ordinate [category] was also unrelated to correct categorization" (p. 137).

Moreover, Mandler also explained the case that young children can also under-extend the use of labels, and may be forming global categories that are not used by their cultural and linguistic models (e.g., animals that walk). That is, language use may not reflect the actual underlying verbal and non-verbal conceptual categories formed by young children. These experimental findings presented by Mandler, go counter the developmental expectation that more perceptual attributes are represented by basic level objects, versus more abstract attributes are represented by non-basic categories or classes of objects. These kinds of experimental studies, conducted within a contemporary developmental perspective, are very useful to improve our understanding of semantic development. Mandler's study certainly opens up some light on what is the role of language on non-verbal conceptual formation in pre-linguistic children.

Mandler (1989) defended that "perceptual similarity is not a necessary condition for categorization" (p. 133); since young, pre-verbal children's "basic-level categories...may be either broader or narrower than those of the adult, and can even overlap several adult-basic categories that come from different super-ordinate classes" (p. 131). In fact, given the conditions of the task and age of the children studied by Mandler (1989), it seems that *spatio-temporal relatedness* (i.e., "objects that are associated by virtue of being found in the same place or used in the same activities," p. 132) is a more valid bases for categorization for young, pre-verbal children; rather than perceptual similarity. Moreover, Mandler (1989) also makes a very interesting point relating cognitive, cultural, and linguistic factors in how verbal and non-verbal concepts are acquired by young children. Mandler (1989) stated, "a basic-level category is said to be dependent not only on correlated clusters of attributes in the world, but also on the culture and level of expertise of the perceiver" (p. 131).

Thus, linguistic labels, whether basic or non-basic, also carry underly-ing cultural representations that filter the child's experiences of the world; and influence how the child maps linguistic forms carrying cultural connotations and conventions onto non-verbal and verbal concepts. These contemporary developmental psychologists also consider other factors influencing the process of mapping non-verbal concepts into verbal meanings. Besides semantic constraints inspired in Chomskyan's generative grammar theory, the constraint approach has several other assumptions: (1) the dynamic interaction between an innate predisposition in young children and their world knowledge (proposed by Waxman), (2) the language community (proposed by Clark, 1973; and Waxman, 1990), (3) a general cognitive predisposition (proposed by Markman, 1984), and (4) cultural representations filtering mapping verbal onto non-verbal concepts (proposed by Mandler, 1989). As very nicely explained by Gelman and Coley (1991), "children's understanding of natural kinds is both linguistically and conceptually based. Rather, children have certain expectations about categories and how they are named. These expectations together influence the nature of the categories a child constructs"(p. 182-183). Thus, all these authors acknowledged the complexity of underlying non-verbal conceptual systems, which were not considered, or oversimplified, by the Chomskyan theory that focused only on innate constraints used for acquiring syntactic linguistic structures.

Studies Conducted with Bilingual Children

During the last 40 years research studies have provided evidence for the advantages of bilingualism on cognitive development, such as in problem-solving skills, creativity, flexibility of thinking, concept formation, and metalinguistic awareness (see Gonzalez, 1999, 2002; for a more detailed review of the literature). The faster developmental pace found in bilinguals in a number of studies, can be explained as the result of having access to two symbolic representational systems, which can be expressed through a variety of explicit metalinguistic behaviors.

For instance, Galambos and Goldin-Meadow (1990) studied the effect of bilingualism on cognitive development, in relation to metalinguistic skills in four to 8 year-old children. They found that the developmental sequence was similar when comparing bilingual with monolingual children's ability to detect, to correct, and to explain grammatical errors; making progress from a content-based to a form-based orientation to language (from implicit to explicit knowledge levels). However, the specific types of grammatical constructions that bilinguals and monolinguals could master were different, with bilinguals showing a faster speed of transitioning from content to a form-based approach towards language when detecting and correcting errors. So, as concluded by Galambos and Goldin-Meadow (1990), "the experience of learning two languages hastens the development of certain metalinguistic skills in young children, but does not alter the course of that development" (p. 2).

As explained by Galambos and Goldin-Meadow (1990), it seems that there are multiple levels of implicit and explicit knowledge of language with "a developmental continuum based on the explicitedness of awareness, the end point being overt verbalized metalinguistic judgments" (p. 5). For instance, evidence of the influence of bilingualism on thinking processes can be found in the study of a number of verbal behaviors. For instance, spontaneous translations between languages, asking for names of objects or properties of objects (e.g., the child may ask, What is the color of this?) in both languages, change of language code in relation to audience and/or social or experiential context, change of language to match vocabulary knowledge, asking for the meaning of words, asking about the meaning of print (e.g., What does it say here?), and so forth. Another example is that whether or not bilingual children mix both languages, and use code switching and/or code mixing, would depend on the social language models they are exposed to, the needs of their environments, and also on their individual psychological or developmental characteristics. Moreover, as proposed by Galambos and Goldin-Meadow (1990) "different experiences with language promote metalinguistic awareness at one level of explicitness but not at other levels" (p. 5).

There are also psychological factors, such as individual differences across bilinguals influencing their cognitive development. For instance, it is generally expected that children would separate the syntactic and grammatical features of both languages by the age of 3 or 4, due to the metalinguistic awareness that they speak two languages. However this realization may happen earlier or later, depending on the idiosyncratic developmental characteristics of children. Furthermore, there are also developmental factors affecting cognitive development in bilinguals. For instance, there may be an expected developmental progression on the children's ability to explicitly detect and correct grammatical errors, as an overt metalinguistic behavior. Galambos and Goldin-Meadow (1990) found that preschool bilingual children could detect only a limited number of grammatical errors, and when they intended to correct them content-oriented explanations were used. Bilingual kindergartners could already provide grammatical or form-oriented explanations, which increase in number and degree of sophistication significantly in bilingual first graders.

Another example of the effect of developmental factors will be the interaction across cognitive and affective domains, as well as the effect of external factors (i.e., such as socioeconomic status—SES). For example, when studying mental processes, it is interesting to observe how bilingualism enhances cognitive development, resulting in more complex interactions between cognitive and affective processes in learning and academic achievement. For instance, Bochner (1996) compared monolingual and bilingual adolescents' learning strategies and styles, controlling for some individual differences including first-and-second language proficiency levels, SES, intelligence, achievement, and educational opportunities and teaching environments. He studied the effect of these independent variables on the learning strategies used by 14 and 16 year-old students in Sydney, Australia; about half were from an Asian background, and the other half were from a European background. All the students were highly proficient in English, and were attending a highly selective high school. As explained by Bochner (1996), "in Australia, bilingual usually means a second generation immigrant and being bicultural" (p. 92).

Then, the fact of being bilingual also carries with it a bicultural component; resulting in a double interaction between language, culture with cognitive processes (e.g., the learning styles studied by Bochner). Moreover, other factors are also acting as mediational variables on the effect of bilingualism on cognitive processes, such as ethnicity, SES, and socialization practices. An instance of this mediational effect is illustrated by Bochner's suggestion that the typical superior academic achievement of Asian students in the Western schools, may be due to the fact of being bilingual, rather than to primarily cultural factors or socialization practices supporting educational achievement, or predominantly middle SES backgrounds. However, I would think that all these external family structure, cultural, and SES factors interact with bilingualism; rather than confound the positive effect of the presence of two languages.

Learning style is defined by Bochner as "how a student approaches the task of acquiring new knowledge" (p. 83), with the presence of individual differences and enduring traits within individuals. Bochner measured two separate, but congruent, components in students' learning styles: (1) motives (surface, intrinsic, and achieving), and (2) learning strategies (reproductive, deeply focused on meaning, and achieving). He considers that learning style is less affected by external confounding variables, such as culture; in comparison to other psychological constructs such as intelligence. Bochner (1996) also expected that schools with more emphasis on formal academic achievement will stimulate students to have more surface motivation and learning strategies; whereas schools stimulating students' autonomy and offering a supportive teaching environment would result in deeper approaches towards learning.

Bochner (1996), tested a hypothesis stating that "bilingualism will have a positive effect, but only on children who are above average in intelligence, and who function in a stimulating intellectual environment, both at home and at school." (p. 84). However, Bochner also state that "bilingualism will have a negative effect on children who are less gifted, and less exposed to intellectual stimulation" (p. 84). He also expected "bright bilinguals [to] respond differently than monolinguals to educational influences" (p. 92). Thus, there would be a double interaction between internal cognitive ability factors and external schooling factors, as "findings showed that bilingualism has a positive effect on gifted, intellectually stimulated children" (Bochner, 1996, p. 83). When comparing the motives, strategies, and approaches of the bilinguals with the monolinguals, both groups showed the same surface level processes; but having a second language positively influenced the capacity to have a "deeper" learning style (i.e., achieving motives and leaning style, both focused on meaning).

Bochner found that bilinguals had a more positive perception of learning, showing intrinsic motivation and deriving positive self-esteem from their academic accomplishments; using more appropriate strategies to attain their goals. Bilinguals could also integrate prior with new knowledge in a more advanced manner, and were more systematic in organizing the physical and temporal conditions for studying. Thus, Bochner's study illustrates the trend in contemporary research studies showing the complex interaction between internal psychological differences (e.g., intelligence levels, motivational and affective factors) and external environmental factors (e.g., quality and degree of stimulation in the home and school).

Even though, some continuities or universals are present when comparing the results of studies conducted with monolinguals and bilinguals, results also show some cultural specifics introduced by the presence of a second language. Thus, leading researchers still need to discover what are the effects of bilingualism and biculturalism on the cognitive development in language-minority children (or lack of proficiency in either first or second language thereof), and to compare it with mainstream children using the same methodology. However, as attested by this critical review of contemporary studies, studies conducted with mainstream monolingual children use traditional methodology, versus studies conducted with language-minority children tend to use alternative methodologies. The use of different methodological paradigms makes this comparison problematic, generating many apparent developmental discontinuities.

Methodology

Research Questions

The three research questions stated are linked to the objectives and purposes of this study, and were analyzed using factors analysis tests. These three research questions aim to the identification of patterns or profiles of cognitive and language development in potentially gifted, Hispanic Kindergartners as measured by standardized and alternative measures, and by different informants. It is our objective to present evidence that cognitive giftedness in language-minority children can be identified when using alternative measures that represent the interaction of cultural and linguistic factors. Moreover, these three research questions also test the construct validity, and concurrent or criterion-referenced validity of alternative measures (parents' and teacher's ratings of children's Spanish and English proficiency levels, and the Qualitative Use of English and Spanish Tasks—QUEST) and of a standardized test (Language Assessment Scales. LAS) for the identification of cultural and linguistic giftedness in Hispanic Kindergartners.

Thus, through this data analysis, it is our objective to test empirically an identification and assessment model that can identify patterns or profiles of cognitive and language development that predict potential giftedness in Hispanic young children. These three research questions are:

1. What are the patterns of first-and-second language development that emerge when potentially gifted, Hispanic children are assessed by a standardized test (LAS) and alternative measures (teachers' ratings, parents' ratings)?

2. What are the patterns of cognitive or non-verbal development that emerge when potentially gifted, Hispanic children are assessed by the Cartoon Conservation Scales (CCS)?

3. What are the patterns of cognitive or non-verbal and linguistic or verbal development that emerge when potentially gifted, Hispanic children are assessed by QUEST?

Subjects

Thirty language-minority Hispanic Kindergartners participated in this study. They were 1st-2nd-and-3rd generation Mexican-Americans, attending public schools in low SES neighborhoods in the central Texas and south Arizona areas. The average age of the children was 6 years, with ages ranging from 7 years to 5 years and 6 months. In this study, the language dominance and degree of language proficiency in Spanish and/or English in children, represents the reality of Hispanic children in the public school system in the US. In this sample, some of the children were monolingual Spanish, others were monolingual English, and some had no command of English and/or Spanish. Then, it is also important to note that some of these Hispanic children may not be proficient in either language. Information on the children's language proficiency levels in Spanish and English was obtained from their school files, based on their Language Assessment Scales (De Avila & Duncan, 1986, LAS) scores administered by the school. From these 30 children, 8 were considered English dominant and fluent speakers by the Arizona school district, and therefore no LAS scores were available for them.

From the available LAS scores, the following information can be obtained: (1) 6 children in the Texas sample, and 5 children in the Arizona sample were monolingual Spanish; (2) 8 children in the Arizona sample were English dominant and fluent, and (3) the other 16 children had some degree of language proficiency in both Spanish and English, and thus had some degree of bilingualism. The LAS scores for the third cluster of 16 children indicated intermediate and balanced proficiency levels in both English and Spanish (with a group mean in the LAS scores of 3.307 in English and 3.461 in Spanish).

In order to obtain some information regarding the overall cognitive developmental levels of the participating children, the Test of Nonverbal Intelligence (TONI, Brown, Sherbenou, & Dollard, 1982), was administered in this study. The TONI was selected because it offers a non-verbal procedure that can screen, in a short administration time, the children's conceptual processes in relation to spatial and temporal relations. Due to some time constraints in parental permissions provided, TONI scores were available for 19 children, indicating an average mean of intelligence quotient (mean of 99.89, with a mode of 82, and scores than ranged between 136 and 74; with 50% of the sample obtaining a score of 95 or above). That is the reason why, due to incomplete data in the sample, TONI scores could only be used for descriptive purposes, and not for data analysis procedures.

Subjects were selected based on two referral procedures for potential giftedness including: (1) a Home Language Survey (Gonzalez, 1991, 1994), and (2) a teachers' and parents' rating scale of giftedness that was designed by the authors in collaboration with school district personnel. The LAS scores, or the categorization by the school district as dominant and fluent English speaker, were used for deciding in which language the children would be administered the two alternative assessments (QUEST and CCS). Then, either lack of proficiency in more than one language, or lack of evidence of proficiency in Spanish (for the English dominant children with no LAS scores in Spanish and English) prompted us to administer the alternative assessments in only one language (the dominant one, for which evidence was available).

A t test was used for attempting to separate the subjects into monolingual and bilingual groups based on their LAS scores in Spanish and/or English. For this case no significant difference was found in the children in relation to their Spanish and English proficiency levels. In addition, a t test was also used for testing whether the Arizona and Texas sample showed any significant difference in their Spanish and English proficiency levels attained in the LAS test. For this second case also no significant difference was found in the subjects in relation to their Spanish proficiency levels; but there was a difference between the Arizona and Texas samples in relation to their English language proficiency levels.

Then, the existence of one group was confirmed, empirically supporting the decision of analyzing the data as one single sample. In addition, these results also supported the decision to enter only language dominance as a variable for data analysis, because there was a difference in the English dominant children in the Arizona and Texas samples (they had different English language proficiency levels). Thus, since there was no complete information for language proficiency levels in all subjects, the variable of language proficiency was confounded in this study; but the variable of language dominance remained as a significant source of variance in the sample.

It is also important to note that using only the children's performances in alternative assessments (QUEST and CCS) in their dominant language may have increased their developmental levels attained. In previous studies conducted with QUEST (e.g., Gonzalez, 1991, 1994, 1995; Gonzalez, Bauerle, & Felix-Holt, 1996), language-minority children's performances in both Spanish and English were compared. This practice followed in earlier studies may have resulted in lower developmental levels in either language, but control for individual differences in Spanish and English performances was also achieved. However, in this study only language dominance was controlled, entering only one language administration per child. Then, in this study there is no control of individual differences in the comparison of Spanish and English language performance in QUEST administrations. Thus, some information may have been lost by not comparing the same child's performance in both Spanish and English QUEST administrations. But, the reality of the sample pointed to the need to administer QUEST only in the language in which they were proficient enough to respond. This practice may have resulted in new information brought out by this study due to the children's higher levels of command of the dominant language in which QUEST was administered.

Instruments

Four qualitative, alternative measures were used for data collection. The first one is the Teachers' and Parents' Ratings of the child's first-and-second language proficiency levels (Gonzalez, 1991, 1994) that consists of Likert scales. These surveys were used for data analysis purposes, as they measured the cultural variable of the child's first-and-second-language proficiency levels. The second qualitative measure is the Teacher's and Parents' Rating Scale of Giftedness (TPRSG) that consists of seven open-ended questions eliciting respondents to describe the child's linguistic, problem-solving, and individual and group working and playing abilities at home and school. This second instrument was only used for sample selection purposes, as a referral criteria for potentially gifted language-minority children.

The third alternative instrument is the Qualitative Use of English and Spanish Tasks (QUEST) developed by Gonzalez (1991, 1994, 1995). QUEST is a developmental method that includes verbal (labeling, defining, and verbal justification of sorting) and non-verbal (sorting and category clue) classification tasks. These problem-solving tasks are designed to assess bilingual children's general and linguistic-gender conceptual processes for two different abstract, symbolic and linguistic semantic categories represented by animals (animate) and food (inanimate) objects. These stimuli used for the five classification tasks are represented by plastic full-color objects representing 14 groupings reflecting the interaction of cognitive, cultural, and linguistic factors. Stimuli groupings were validated using judges for assuring construct validity and three pilot tests for assuring content validity (Gonzalez, 1991, 1994, 1995).

The scoring system was also empirically validated during the construction of the model and instrument (internal validity— i.e., construct validity; see e.g., Gonzalez, 1991, 1994, 1995). The scoring system is divided into five point assignment areas including language development, verbal and non-verbal general, and verbal and non-verbal gender areas. Based on these five point assignment areas, children's responses were categorized into eight developmental categories: (1) no classification , (2) pre-conceptual: perceptual, (3) pre-conceptual: functional, (4) symbolic representations (expression of semantic or verbal and non-verbal cultural knowledge, showing internalization of cultural knowledge, such as storytelling, gestures, onomatopoeic sounds, cultural scripts—narratives of "going shopping," "making a salad," "going to the circus," "ordering at a restaurant," acting out behaviors such as role playing, etc.), (5) analogical reasoning (comparison of similarities and differences among subjects that resemble in different perceptual or semantic features, e.g., "This apple is like a ball, it bounces too"), (6) concrete, (7) creativity (children's behaviors showing flexibility of thinking through responses expressing mental transformations of representations—re-instantiations of concepts, evidence of using multiple dimensions of categorizations, evidence of uncommon or unique responses; e.g., "This is a tortilla, it is flat, but it can also be a rug, and if you look at it from here it looks like a penguin"), and (8) metalinguistic. Some of these developmental categories are adapted from neo-Piagetian theory, others (symbolic representations, analogical reasoning, and creativity) were developed by the authors based on the actual patterns found in bilingual children's responses. Thus, this study differed from previous studies conducted with QUEST, because it added three more developmental categories to the qualitative data coding of QUEST, as well as subdividing the Category Clue task into two portions for data analysis (the Sorting and the Verbal Justification of Sorting portions).

Moreover, this study also differed from previous ones, because the criterion for reaching any developmental stage for the Category Clue task was more rigid. With the advise of a expert in probabilistic theory, it was established that the child had independent trails for sorting the 8 stimuli in the Category Clue task into feminine and masculine groupings, which is a case of "Repeated Bernulli Trials." Based on the application of this probabilistic procedure, it was established that the child had a 39% probability of guessing the "correct" sorting of all the 8 items correctly into feminine and masculine groupings. Since we wanted to avoid by chance "correct" categorizations into this feminine and masculine groupings, the child needed to classify consistently at least 6 out of the 8 stimuli presented; which only has a 10.9% probability of guessing "correctly" by chance.

The fourth alternative measure is the Cartoon Conservation Scales (CCS, De Avila, 1976), a measure of intellectual development derived from the theory of Jean Piaget. It is based upon the universality of conceptual tasks including length, number, substance, distance, egocentricity, horizontality, volume, and probability.

In addition, data for two other standardized tests was collected. The first one is the Language Assessment Scales (LAS, De Avila & Duncan, 1986), for which scores were provided by the school district. These scores were used for determining the language proficiency of the children in Spanish and English, as well as their language dominance. The LAS scores were used for data analysis as well as for sample description purposes. The second standardized test was the TONI, which was only used for sample description purposes due to incomplete data files.

Procedure. Classroom teachers were asked to nominate bilingual children, who were potentially gifted. Parents who gave consent for the children's participation in the study, completed surveys (the parents' rating scale of the child's first-and-second-language proficiency levels, and potential cognitive giftedness). Teachers of these children also completed the teachers' ratings scales of the child's first-and-second- language proficiency levels. Trained bilingual graduate students of school psychology and bilingual education assessed the children individually. In the Arizona and Texas sites of data collection, graduate students received a 10 hour training workshop using previous studies conducted with QUEST, videotapes, and manuals as materials for assuring reliability in coding and diagnosing procedures. Students worked in pairs for both the training sessions as well as in the actual administration sessions, in order to assure reliability of data by comparing coding results of both evaluators. In each pair of evaluators, at least one person was bilingual, with good command of the Spanish language. Three administration sessions were conducted in the child's dominant language (Spanish or English), one for each of the three measures used (QUEST, CCS, and TONI). These administrations took place in the child's school, as much as possible in a quiet room (counselor's office, principal's office, teacher's lounge, cafeteria, auditorium; all when not in use).

Data Source

The qualitative data collected using the alternative measures (QUEST and CCS) was coded using nominal categories representing developmental scoring systems. In addition, these two alternative measured and the standardized test used (LAS) were analyzed with statistical factor analysis tests. When using the scoring systems, children's responses were assigned nominal categories that described their verbal and non-verbal conceptual developmental level achieved across classification and conservation tasks. This elaborated qualitative analysis of data resulted in nominal categories, which facilitated the insightful interpretation of the results generated by the factor analysis tests.

Three sets of factor analysis tests were run, in which control for children's language dominance was maintained. The factor analyses tests run resulted in linear combinations of loadings, with possible correlation among factors. That is, the resulting factors may interface in some common measures that load in more than one factor. We controlled this correlational problem by conducting Varimax rotations, so that each factor would tend to load high on a smaller number of variables, and low or very low on other variables (orthogonal or uncorrelated factors). In this way, interpretation of results would be easier. Correlation values for the three sets of factor analysis tests run were from high to moderate, with a cut off score of .5.

In these three sets of factor analysis tests, children's language proficiency levels in Spanish and English were confounded though, with language dominance remaining as a variable, as explained in the subjects section above. The factor analysis tests were used to discover patterns or profiles of cognitive and language development in potentially gifted Hispanic children; as measured by standardized and alternative measures, and by different informants. A factor analysis model was used for testing the three research questions of this study, representing the purposes and objectives of this research project: to present evidence that cultural and linguistic giftedness in Hispanic children can be identified when using alternative, valid, and reliable measures.

The first set of factor analysis tests run included the teacher's and parents' rating of the child's language proficiency levels in Spanish and English, and the LAS scores also in both Spanish and English. Four factors were found in this first set. The second set of factor analysis tests run included the eight scales of the CCS, an alternative measure of cognitive development. Two factors were found in this second set.

The third set of factor analysis procedures encompassed the children's responses to QUEST in their dominant language. In this first set, QUEST data was separated by 6 tasks variables: (1) labeling, (2) defining, (3) sorting, (4) verbal justification of sorting, (5) category clue—sorting portion, and (6) category clue—verbal justification of sorting portion; by 2 cultural factors variables: (1) animate object referents (animals), and (2) inanimate object referents (food); and by 2 linguistic variables: (1) linguistic-gender assignment scoring system, and (2) general classification scoring system. Thus, the third set of factor analysis procedures run had a 6 X 2 X 2 research design; representing 24 subcategories of measures for each child.

Results and Discussion

Results are reported in relation to the three research questions stated, that were analyzed using factors analysis tests. These three questions aim to the identification of patterns or profiles of cognitive and language development in potentially gifted, Hispanic, young children.

First research question: What are the patterns of first-and-second language development that emerge when potentially gifted, Hispanic children are assessed by a standardized test (LAS) and alternative measures (teachers' and parents' ratings)? Results from a Principal Component Analysis run with Varimax rotations showed a first set of four orthogonal factors when entering 3 independent measures in Spanish and English: the teachers' and parents' ratings, and LAS scores. This first set of factor analysis procedures was run for determining the number and nature of constructs underlying these different alternative and standardized measures of English and Spanish language proficiency, also representing different informants and contexts of evaluation. The emerging constructs can also help to identify patterns or profiles of language development in Spanish and English in potentially gifted, young, Hispanic children. Table 3.1. shows the factor analysis results for this first set.

For the first set, results show four factors. We labeled the first factor "School Spanish," and the second factor "School English" because the LAS scores correlated very highly with the teacher's ratings of different areas of language development in the child (i.e., phonology, vocabulary, syntax and grammar, and academic and social language). It seems that the child's command of the Spanish and English languages at school, as perceived by the teacher, correlates moderately with the child's scores in Spanish and

English in the LAS (which loading is .58 in this first factor for Spanish, and .55 for the second factor in English). In contrast, all the teacher's ratings correlated very highly (factor loadings ranged between .89 to .93 for Spanish in the first factor, and between .88 to .92 for English in the second factor). These results indicate that the teacher's ratings across all areas in both Spanish and English languages were highly consistent. In addition, the teachers' ratings open new dimensions to the child's Spanish and English language proficiency levels, other than the ones represented and assessed by the LAS test (since the correlation between LAS and the teachers' ratings were only moderate). Moreover, bringing in the teacher as another informant may have introduced another variation or window in how the child's Spanish and English language proficiency levels were perceived.

The third factor was labeled as "Home Spanish" because it is a bipolar factor with a very high positive loading of the parents' ratings of the child's Spanish language proficiency (with a correlation coefficient of .96). This third bipolar factor also carries negative, moderate loadings of the LAS scores in English; and negative, very low loadings of the teachers' ratings of the child's language proficiency in English across areas (phonology, vocabulary, syntax and grammar, and academic and social language). This third factor indicates that the higher the parents rated the child's Spanish proficiency, there was a good probability that the lower the child's scores were in the LAS English; and there was also a very low probability that the lower were the teachers' ratings of the child's language proficiency in English. Results show that the three sources of information (i.e., the parents' ratings, the standardized test, and the teacher's ratings) differed markedly in their measurements of the child's Spanish and English language proficiency levels.

The fourth factor was labeled "Home English," because the parents' ratings of the child's language proficiency in English loaded highly on this factor (with a correlation coefficient of .81). In addition, this factor was bipolar because it had negative, moderate loadings of the LAS Spanish scores; and also negative, very low loadings of the teachers' ratings of the English social language only. This fourth factor reveals that the higher were the parents' ratings of the child's English language proficiency, there was a moderate probability that the lower were the LAS Spanish scores, and there was also a low probability that the lower were the teachers' ratings of the social language ability of the child in English.

Second research question: What are the patterns of cognitive or non-verbal development that emerge when potentially gifted, Hispanic children are assessed by the Cartoon Conservation Scales (CCS)? For the second set of factor analysis procedures, all the eight scales of the CCS were entered, and only one principal factor emerged. This factor showed moderate factor loadings of the number and length scales (with a correlation of .59661 and .68268). Then, it seems that the CCS measures primarily one construct, and that children's responses were consistent for the number and length scales.

Third research question: What are the patterns of cognitive or non-verbal and linguistic or verbal development that emerge when potentially gifted, Hispanic children are assessed by QUEST? For the third set of factor analysis procedures, all the 6 verbal and non-verbal tasks of QUEST were entered separately by 2 cultural factors (animate and inanimate objects—animals and food items), and also by 2 linguistic factors (linguistic gender and general scoring criteria). Then, this 6 X 2 X 2 design resulted in 24 measures for QUEST, which were entered together for determining the number of underlying constructs. This was a confirmatory factor analysis, matching the three objectives of this research study: (1) to generate more evidence of the construct validity of QUEST; (2) to uncover some developmental patterns or profiles emerging from potentially gifted, Hispanic, young children; and (3) to develop a model of identification of potentially gifted, Hispanic, young children. Four factors were found ranging from strong to moderate factor loadings, with two bipolar factors (as shown in Table 3.2.).

The first factor is labeled "Verbal and Non-Verbal Universal Conceptual Development for Animates and Inanimates: Cultural and Linguistic Commonalties," because the five sub-tasks that loaded were: (1) Labeling for animals at the linguistic-gender level (encompassing naming animals according to their physical gender, a verbal task), (2) Labeling for food at the general level (encompassing naming food according to general characteristics, a verbal task), (3) Category Clue for food at the general level (Sorting portion, asking the child to categorize food items based on a general criteria, a non-verbal task), (4) Category Clue for food at the general level (Verbal Justification of Sorting portion, requiring the child to explain the categorization of food items based on a general criteria, a verbal task), and (5) Sorting for animals at the linguistic-gender level (requiring the child to group animal items according to linguistic and cultural conventions representing physical gender, common to Spanish and English, non-verbal task, negative loading).

Because the last sub-task showed a negative loading, with all the other four sub-tasks showing positive loadings, this first factor is bipolar. The last negative loading indicates that the child's ability to sort animate objects based on linguistic-gender criteria was independent of his or her ability to form verbal and non-verbal concepts following universal or general criteria. That is, it seems that Hispanic children form independent representational processes for culturally and linguistically loaded concepts (which may or may not be common between their first and second languages), and for general or more universal concepts. All these four sub-tasks loading on this first factor represent an underlying construct of commonalties or universals present in verbal and non-verbal concepts in the Spanish and English languages and cultures.

The second factor is called "Verbal and Non-Verbal Conceptual Development for Inanimates: Cultural Commonalties and Unique Linguistic Conventions in Spanish," because the 4 sub-tasks that showed high to moderate loadings represented verbal and non-verbal concept formation processes in relation to food items only. These four sub-task were: (1) Labeling for food objects at the general level (requiring the child to name the food items in relation to general characteristics, verbal task, common to Spanish and English languages and cultures), (2) Sorting for food objects at the general level (asking the child to categorize objects based on general characteristics, non-verbal task, common to Spanish and English languages and cultures), (3) Verbal Justification of Sorting for food objects at the linguistic-gender level (asking the child to explain the categorization of objects based on linguistic convention criteria, verbal task, unique to the Spanish language), and (4) Category Clue for food objects at the linguistic-gender level (Verbal Justification of Sorting portion requiring the child to explain the categorization of food items based on linguistic convention criteria, verbal task, unique to the Spanish language).

The underlying construct for this second factor represented both: (1) cultural commonalties, and (2) unique linguistic conventions of the Spanish language; when constructing verbal and non-verbal concepts for inanimates. It seems that Hispanic children used general concepts, common to both Spanish and English, when labeling and sorting the food items. In addition, Hispanic children also used unique cultural and linguistic concepts when verbally justifying their groupings of food items. It is interesting to note that this verbal justification may have occurred in either Spanish or English, since only the first (and dominant) language of administration was considered in the data analysis. Even though the English language does not show linguistic markers for gender, at the cultural level some children did use some cultural conventions related to gender for their categorization criteria. For instance, a child may verbally justify his or her groupings by saying: "This is for my mommy and these others are for my daddy." And then, when prompted to further explain the underlying reasons for his or her groupings, the child may reply: "The small food is for my mommy, and the large things are for my daddy. My daddy eats a lot..."

The third factor had three sub-tasks loadings, and was called "Universal Verbal and Non-Verbal Conceptual Development for Animates: Cultural and Linguistic Commonalties." These three sub-tasks were: (1) Labeling for animals at the general level (requiring the child to name animals, using the general label independent of their particular physical gender, a verbal task), (2) Verbal Justification of Sorting for animals t the general level (asking the child to explain the categorization of animals using general criteria, a verbal task), and (3) Category Clue for animals at the linguistic-gender level (Sorting portion, requiring the child to group animals according to their physical gender as marked by linguistic conventions, a non-verbal task). The underlying construct of this factor is verbal and non-verbal concept formation processes in relation to a particular category of objects: animates showing commonalties in their cultural and linguistic representations in the Spanish and English cultures and languages.

The fourth factor has four sub-tasks with both positive and negative loadings, representing a bipolar factor. This fourth factor is called "Universal Verbal Conceptual Development for Animates and Inanimates: Cultural Commonalties." These four sub-tasks were: (1) Defining for animals at the general level (encompassing providing a description of animal objects, pointing to general characteristics, verbal task), (2) Defining for food at the general level (requires the child to provide a description of food items, pointing to general characteristics, verbal task), (3) Sorting for food at the linguistic-gender level (requires the child to group food items following linguistic conventions present in Spanish only, non-verbal task, with a moderate negative loading), and (4) Category Clue for food items at the linguistic gender level (Sorting portion that requires the child to group food items following linguistic conventions present in Spanish only, non-verbal task, with a rather high negative loading).

The underlying construct represented in this fourth factor indicates that: (1) verbal concept formation processes for both animates and inanimates share universal cultural and linguistic commonalties between Spanish and English; and (2) that this construct negatively correlates with the child's ability to form non-verbal concepts for inanimates in relation to linguistic conventions unique to the Spanish language. That is, there is a separation in how Hispanic children represent verbal and non-verbal concepts, and specifically when they represent non-verbal concepts for inanimate objects that are unique to the Spanish culture and language.

Conclusions

It is interesting to note that this study generated a revised model of cognitive and language development in bilingual children, when cultural and linguistic factors are represented in alternative measures. The emerging constructs in this revised model can help us identify patterns or profiles of language development in Spanish and English in potentially gifted, young, Hispanic children. This study expanded the original model constructed with QUEST (see Gonzalez, 1991, 1994, 1995) because: (1) it included other developmental stages in the qualitative data coding; (2) it also separated the Category Clue sub-task into its verbal and non-verbal portions (separating Sorting from Verbal Justification of Sorting aspects); (3) it used a more strict criteria for avoiding correct classification based on linguistic or physical gender (feminine and masculine groupings) just by chance; (4) it included only one measure of QUEST administered in the child's dominant language (eliminating the Spanish and English language of administration variable); and (5) in some previous studies a Principal Component Analysis was conducted resulting in uncorrelated linear combinations, whereas in this study factor analysis was conducted resulting in linear combinations that are correlated). Then, even though this study introduced some methodological changes in the qualitative analysis of QUEST data, the resulting patterns or factors still have some structural similarities with the original model found.

More recently, a series of sequential studies have been conducted for proving the external validity of QUEST; and for empirically validating the construct and criterion-related validity of a more complex, revised, multidimensional, interactional model including cognitive, linguistic, developmental (age), cultural, socioeconomic, family structure, schooling, and assessment factors (see e.g., Felix-Holt & Gonzalez, 1999; Gonzalez et al., 1996; Gonzalez, 2005; Oviedo & Gonzalez, 1999). The study conducted by Gonzalez and collaborators (1999) also provided empirical support for a revised model comparing monolingual (Spanish and English) and bilingual children (English/Spanish with different degrees of language proficiencies in both languages, and different language dominance). Results of this former study (Gonzalez et al., 1999) showed that the process of verbal and non-verbal concept construction is related to the cultural and/or linguistic nature of the representations.

The major contribution of this series of studies is the validation of a data-driven model explaining why and how bilingualism affects cognition, taking into account the interaction of multidimensional internal and external factors. In fact, two new ways of representing verbal concepts and word knowledge were found in bilinguals, when compared with monolingual counterparts of similar or different low or mid-high SES backgrounds. Thus, this series of studies have proven that regardless of degree of language proficiency in first and second language, bilingual children (even the so considered limited English proficient) show advantages in how they construct verbal and non-verbal concepts.

Then, for this first set all four rotated factors clustered by school or home language contexts, with a positive correlation between school culture measures and informants for the English language (LAS scores and teachers' ratings), and a negative correlation between home language (in Spanish or English) and the measures of school culture (in English or Spanish correspondingly). Thus, these four factors represent the underlying four independent constructs of home language and school language, for both Spanish and English languages. Thus, these results seem to indicate the presence of four emerging patterns of language development in Spanish and English in potentially gifted, young children: (1) school Spanish language proficiency, (2) school English language proficiency, (3) home Spanish language proficiency, and (4) home English language proficiency. These four patterns also indicate that the ratings of different informants (parents and teachers) are only moderately correlated with standardized measures of both Spanish and English proficiency levels (LAS). More importantly, these four patterns also indicated that teachers' and parents' ratings loaded into independent factors, representing independent constructs of language proficiency separated by context (home and school).

Similarities found between this revised model and previous studies of the construction and validation of the model (see e.g., Gonzalez, 1991, 1994, 1995; Gonzalez, et. al, 1996) indicate the presence of cultural and linguistic factors affecting the verbal and non-verbal concept formation process in Hispanic young children. More specifically, cultural factors (animate and inanimate categories), and linguistic factors (general criteria or linguistic-gender categorizations) still showed to affect whether Hispanic children would form common or unique verbal and non-verbal representations or concepts.

In addition, this revised model also expands the findings into more specific developmental profiles in light of new data and more complex coding systems. Actually this new revised model opens new windows to how potentially gifted Hispanic children form concepts in their dominant languages.

A factor analysis of the first research question revealed the presence of three patterns: (1) a first factor showing a relation between children's knowledge of symbolic sociocultural meanings conveyed in Spanish (as measured by QUEST) and their *non-verbal* concept formation ability (as measured by QUEST, TONI, and CCS), (2) a second factors showing a relation between children's content knowledge in Spanish and English (as measured by QUEST) and their *non-verbal* concept formation ability (as measured by QUEST, TONI, and CCS) and (3) a third factor showing a relation between children's content knowledge in Spanish and English (as measured by QUEST) and their *verbal* concept formation ability (as measured by QUEST, LAS, and Teachers' and Parents' Ratings). Regression analysis of the second research question revealed that developmental age (as measured by the classification verbal and non-verbal tasks of QUEST, and the conservation non-verbal tasks of CCS) was the best predictor of giftedness in language minority children. Results of the regression test of the third research question show that the children's performance on the verbal and non-verbal classification tasks of the QUEST significantly predicted their performance on other alternative and standardized measures.

In summary, we can conclude in light of findings from this study, that the language-minority children represent knowledge in: (1) symbolic culturally loaded forms, unique to Spanish, which are related to their non-verbal concept formation abilities; and (2) universal forms shared by both their first-and-second languages, which are related to their non-verbal and verbal concept formation abilities. Then, alternative assessments revealed new dimensions of minority children's giftedness: (1) culturally-linguistically loaded cognitive domains, and (2) universal and non-verbal cognitive domains. Moreover, alternative assessments are good predictors of minority children's giftedness, especially when these valid instruments use: (1) developmental ages as guidelines for assessing cognitive and linguistic processes; and (2) verbal and non-verbal tasks that re developmentally, culturally, and linguistically adequate to language-minority children's characteristics.

Theoretical and Practical Significance of the Study

This study offers a contribution to the fields of bilingual education, special education, and school psychology in the form of theoretical and practical implications of using alternative assessments for accurately measuring language-minority children's cognitive and language development. Alternative assessments used in this study show construct and criterion-referenced validity, because they include: (1) different informants, (2) verbal and non-verbal tasks representing the children's minority culture, and (3) administrations in the dominant language of the children. This evidence contributes to the need for developing successful alternative methods for the identification of giftedness in young language-minority children.

References

Bochner, S. (1996). The learning strategies of bilingual versus monolingual students. *British Journal of Educational Psychology, 66,* 33-93.

Brown, L, Sherbenou, R. J., Dollard, S. (1982). *Test of Nonverbal Intelligence (TONI).* Austin, TX: Pro-Ed.

Bruner, J. S., Goodnow, J. J., & Austin, G. A. (1956). *A study of thinking.* New York: Wiley.

Clark, E. V. (1973). What's in a word? On the child's acquisition of semantics in his first language. In T. Moore (Ed*.), Cognitive development and the acquisition of language* (pp. 65-110). New York: Academic Press.

Clark, E. R., & Gonzalez, V., (1998). *Voces* and voices: Cultural and linguistic giftedness. *Educational Horizons, 77*(1), 41-47.

De Avila, E. A. (1976). *Cartoon Conservation Scales (CCS).* San Antonio, TX: Stephen Jackson & Associates.

De Avila, E. A. , & Duncan, S. E. (1986). *The Language Assessment Scales.* Monterey, CA: CTB/McGraw-Hill.

Dolgin, K., & Behrend, D. (1984). Children's knowledge about animates and inanimates. *Child Development, 55,* 1646-1650.

Felix-Holt, M., & Gonzalez, V. (1999). Alternative assessment models of language-minority children: Is there a match with teachers' attitudes and instruction? In V. Gonzalez (Vol. Ed.), *Language and cognitive development in second language learning: Educational implications for children and adults* (pp. 190-226). Needham Heights, MA: Allyn & Bacon.

Galambos, S. J., & Goldin-Meadow, S. (1990). The effects of learning two languages on levels of metalinguistic awareness. *Cognition, 34,* 1-56.

Gelman, S. A., & Coley, J. D. (1991). Language and categorization: The acquisition of natural kind terms. In J. P. Byrnes & S. A. Gelman (Eds). *Perspectives on language and thought: Interrelations in development* (pp. 146-197). New York: Cambridge University Press.

Gonzalez, V. (1991). *A model of cognitive, cultural, and linguistic variables affecting bilingual Spanish/English children's development of concepts and language.* Doctoral Dissertation. Austin, Texas: The University of Texas at Austin. (ERIC Document Reproduction Service No. ED 345 562).

Gonzalez, V. (1994). A model of cognitive, cultural, and linguistic variables affecting bilingual Hispanic children's development of concepts and language. *Hispanic Journal of Behavioral Sciences, 16* (4), 396-421.

Gonzalez, V. (1995). *Cognition, culture, and language in bilingual children: Conceptual and semantic development.* Bethesda, MD: Austin & Winfield.

Gonzalez, V. (2002). Advanced cognitive development and bilingualism: Methodological flaws and suggestions for measuring first-and-second-language proficiency, language dominance, and intelligence in minority children. In J. A. Castellano and E. Diaz (Eds.), *Reaching new horizons: Gifted and talented education for culturally and linguistically diverse students,* pp. 47-75. Needham Heights, MA: Allyn & Bacon.

Gonzalez, V., (2005). Cultural, linguistic, and socioeconomic factors influencing monolingual and bilingual children's cognitive development. In Gonzalez, V., & Tinajero, J.V. (Co-Editors). *National Association for Bilingual Education (NABE) Review of Research & Practice,* Vol. 3 (pp. 67-104). Lawrence Erlbaum Associates (LEA): Mahwah, NJ.

Gonzalez, V., & Schallert, D. L. (1999). An integrative analysis of cognition, language, and culture: Implications for bilingual children's conceptual and semantic development. In V. Gonzalez (Vol. Ed.), *Language and cognitive development in second language learning: Educational implications for children and adults* (pp. 19-55). Needham Heights, MA: Allyn & Bacon.

Gonzalez, V., Bauerle, P, & Felix-Holt, M. (1996). Theoretical and practical implications of assessing cognitive and language development in bilingual children with qualitative methods. *Bilingual Research Journal, 20* (1), 93-131.

Keil, F. C. (1986). The acquisition of natural kind and artifact terms. In W. Demopoulos & A. Marras (Eds.), *Language learning and concept acquisition (*pp. 133-153). Norwood, NJ: Ablex.

Lewis, J. (1991). Innovative approaches in assessment. In R. J. Samuda, S. L. Kong, J. Cummins. J. Lewis, & J. Pascual-Leone, *Assessment and placement of minority students,* (pp. 123-142). C. J. Hogrefe: Toronto, Ontario, Canada.

Mandler, J. M. (1989). Categorization in infancy and early childhood. In M. A. Luszcz & T. Nettelbeck (Eds.). *Psychological development: Perspectives Across the Life-Span* (pp. 127-139). North-Holland: Elsevier Science Publishers.

Markman, E. M. (1984). The acquisition of hierarchical organization of categories by children. In C. Sophian (Ed.). *Origin in cognitive skills.* The 18th Annual Carnegie Symposium on Cognition (pp. 376-406). Hillsdale, NJ: Lawrence Erlbaum.

Massey, C. M., & Gelman, R. (1988). Preschoolers' ability to decide whether a photographed unfamiliar object can move itself. *Developmental Psychology, 24,* 307-317.

Matarazzo, J. D. (1992). Psychological testing and assessment in the 21st century. *American Psychologist, 46* (8), 1007-1018.

Mervis, C. B., & Rosch, E. (1981). Categorization of natural objects. *Annual Review of Psychology, 32,* 89-115.

Nelson, K. (1988). Constraints in word learning? *Cognitive Development 3,* 221-246.

Oviedo, M. D., & Gonzalez, V. (1999). Standardized and alternative assessments: Diagnosis accuracy in minority children referred for special education assessment. In V. Gonzalez (Vol. Ed.), *Language and cognitive development in second language learning: Educational implications for children and adults* (pp. 227-269). Needham Heights, MA: Allyn & Bacon.

Piaget, J. (1967). Piaget's theory. In P. H. Mussen (Ed.), *Carmichael's manual of child psychology,* Vol. I , (pp. 703-732). New York: John Wiley.

Piaget, J. (1968). *Six psychological studies.* New York: Vintage Books.

Richards, D. D., & Siegler, R. S. (1986). Children's understanding of the attributes of life. *Journal of Experimental child Psychology, 42,* 1-22.

Rosch, E. (1978). Principles of categorization. In E. Rosch & B. B. Lloyd (Eds.), *Cognition and categorization* (pp. 27-48). Hillsdale, NJ: Erlbaum.

Sapir, E. (1929). The status of linguistics as a science. *Language, 5,* 207-214.

Waxman, S. R. (1990). Linking language and conceptual development: Linguistic cues and the construction of conceptual hierarchies. *The Genetic Epistemologist, 17,*13-20.

Wellman, H. M., & Estes, D. (1986). Early understanding of mental entities: A re-examination of childhood realism. *Child Development, 57,* 910-923.

Wellman, H. M., & Gelman, S. A. (1988). Children's understanding of the non-obvious. In R. J. Sternberg (Ed.), *Advances in psychology of human intelligence* (Vol. 4, pp. 99-135). Hillsdale, NJ: Erlbaum.

Whorf, B. L. (1956). *Language, thought, and reality.* Cambridge, MA: MIT Press.

Wimmer, H., & Perner, J. (1983). Beliefs about beliefs: Representation and constraining function of wrong beliefs in young children's understanding of deception. *Cognition, 13,* 103-128.

Table 3.1.

Factor Loadings for the Teachers' and Parents' Ratings and LAS Scores of the Children's

Language Proficiency Levels in Spanish and English

| | | Factors | | |
Measure	1 School Spanish	2 School English	3 Home Spanish	4 Home English
• LAS Scores: Spanish	.586811			-.04988
• LAS Scores: English		.55079	-.62644	
• Parents' Ratings: Spanish			.96364	
• Parents' Ratings: English			.81559	
• Teachers' Ratings: Spanish				
Spanish phonology	.93372			
Spanish vocabulary	.93372			
Spanish syntax & grammar	.93418			
Spanish academic language	.89394			
Spanish social language	.92815			
• Teachers' Ratings: English				
English phonology		.91746	-.15000	
English vocabulary		.92219	-.05703	
English syntax & grammar		.92468	-.14483	
English academic language		.89973	-.13078	
English social language		.88740	-.20093	-.01452

Table 3.2.

Factor Loadings for the Qualitative Use of English and Spanish Tasks (QUEST) in the Children's Dominant Language

QUEST Sub-Tasks	Conceptual development Factors			
	1 Universal Ani. & Ina. Cul. & Lin. Com Ver. & Non-Ver.	**2** Ling. Unique Ina. Cult. Com. Ver. & Non-Ver.	**3** Universal Ani. Cul. & Lin. Com. Ver. & Non-Ver.	**4** Universal Ani. & Ina. Cul. Com. Ver
• Labeling				
Animals general	.90786			
Animals linguistic-gender	.83669			
Food general			.73009	
Food linguistic-gender		.50649		
• Defining				
Animals general				
Animals linguistic-gender				
Food general		.81351		
Food linguistic-gender				.50013
• Sorting				
Animals general				
Animals linguistic-gender	-.50578			
Food general		.59790		
Food linguistic-gender				-.53875

. . . continued

... Table 2 continued ...

QUEST Sub-Tasks	Conceptual development Factors			
	1 Universal Ani. & Ina. Cul. & Lin. Com Ver. & Non-Ver.	2 Ling. Unique Ina. Cult. Com. Ver. & Non-Ver.	3 Universal Ani. Cul. & Lin. Com. Ver. & Non-Ver. Ver	4 Universal Ani. & Ina. Cul. Com.
• Verbal Justification for Sorting				
Animals general				
Animals linguistic-gender				
Food general		.89882		
Food linguistic-gender			.71538	
• Category Clue (Sorting portion)				
Animals general				
Animals linguistic-gender	.62623			
Food general			.74312	
Food linguistic-gender			-.78463	
• Category Clue (Verbal Justification of Sorting portion)				
Animals general				
Animals linguistic-gender				
Food general	.62303			
Food linguistic-gender		.81226		

4

RELATIONSHIP OF FAMILY STRUCTURE FACTORS TO GIFTED, HISPANIC POOR CHILDREN'S COGNITIVE AND LINGUISTIC DEVELOPMENT

ഇന്ദ്ര

Virginia Gonzalez

Introduction

C hapter 4 continues with Part II of the book on applying the Ethnic Research alternative paradigm to the study of development and achievement in language-minority and majority children. Chapter 4 brings in the topic of studying family structure as central factors on the development and academic achievement in Hispanic young learners. More specifically, Chapter 4 presents a quasi-experimental study with the purpose of studying the relationship of some family structure factors (as measured by a Home Language Survey) to Hispanic, low socioeconomic (SES) children's cognitive and language developmental performance (as measured by an alternative assessment, the Qualitative Use of English and Spanish Tasks, QUEST; Gonzalez, 1991, 1994, 1995). Eight research questions were tested, in relation to the relationship of seven family structure factors (independent variables) to the children's performance in QUEST (dependent variable). Each of the eight family structure factors was tested by a research question: (1) language use at home by the child, parents, and siblings; (2) parents' self-rated, and parents' ratings of child's language proficiency in Spanish and English; (3) parental perceptions of the effect of schooling on the child's Spanish and English language proficiency; (4) use of code mixing and code switching at home; (5) mother's and father's educational levels and occupations; (6) number of siblings; (7) birth order of child; and (8) parents' number of years of residence in the US.

Sixty Hispanic (Mexican-American) kindergartners and first graders, nominated by their parents and/or teachers for possible cognitive and linguistic giftedness, participated in this study. Parents and teachers were asked to fill out an open-ended survey constructed by the authors, about their perceptions of the child's potential for cognitive and linguistic giftedness. The nominated children were attending either regular or bilingual classrooms in a large cosmopolitan school district, located in a Hispanic low SES "barrio" in the Southwest region of the US. As rated by their parents and teachers, these children were either monolingual Spanish (N=50), or bilingual (N=10) with Spanish as a first language in most children.

QUEST consists of a set of verbal and non-verbal classification tasks, representing the bicultural and bilingual sociocultural reality of Hispanic children. It controls for methodological variables affecting the Hispanic children's performance in cognitive and linguistic measures, including the confounding effects of language and culture. Thus, in addition to study the effect of family structure variables, other mediational variables were also controlled for by the valid and reliable alternative measure of cognitive and language development used.

Frequencies, percentages, and Pearson correlation analyses were used as descriptive data. In addition, one-way ANOVA tests were conducted for analyzing the relationship of the seven family structure variables, measured by the Home Language Survey, to the children's performance in QUEST tasks. Putting together the descriptive data, the patterns obtained from the Pearson correlation tests, and the results of the one-way ANOVA tests, two conclusions can be derived in relation to the research questions. First, in order to understand verbal and non-verbal classifications problems posed at the highest metalinguistic level, children needed to have a certain degree of Spanish language proficiency. In turn, children's proficiency levels attained in Spanish were also found to be related to their: (1) parents' and siblings' home language, (2) use of code mixing and code switching, (3) birth order, (4) parents' educational levels and occupation, and (5) parents' number of years of US residence (Research Questions 1, 4, 5, 6, 7, and 8). Second, having English as a home language was found to be related to the children's: (1) and their parents' higher English language proficiency levels, (2) number of siblings, and (3) birth order. In addition, the child's higher English language proficiency levels (as rated by parents) was found in turn related to the child's ability to form non-verbal classifications (Research Questions 1, 6, and 7).

This study presents some evidence of the importance of including parents in the referral process, and of gathering information on family structure factors when evaluating language-minority, low SES children, who are potentially gifted. Educational implications derived from the study refer to the importance of using alternative assessments for screening and evaluating young children from a Hispanic, low SES background. These alternative assessments need to represent cultural and linguistic factors affecting verbal and non-verbal conceptual development.

Purpose and Objective

This quasi-experimental study has the purpose of investigating the relationship of some family structure factors to the performance of Hispanic (Mexican-American), young, low socioeconomic status (SES) children on an alternative measure of cognitive and language development (the Qualitative Use of English and Spanish Tasks, QUEST, Gonzalez, 1991, 1994, 1995). More specifically, our purpose was to study the relationship of eight major family structure factors to the verbal and non-verbal concept formation processes and developmental levels achieved by Hispanic children. These eight family structure factors were measured by a Home Language Survey (Gonzalez, 1991, 1995), and included: (1) language use at home by the child, parents, and siblings; (2) parents' self-rated, and parents' ratings of child's language proficiency in Spanish and English; (3) parental perceptions of the effect of schooling on the child's Spanish and English language proficiency; (4) use of code mixing and code switching at home; (5) mother and father's educational levels and occupations; (6) number of siblings; (7) birth order of child; and (8) parents' number of years of residence in the US.

Theoretical Framework

The Role of Family Structure Factors on Young, Hispanic, Low SES Children's Cognitive Development

This study complements a series of validation studies on the alternative assessment of cognitive and language development in young, Hispanic, low SES children conducted previously (see e.g., Clark & Gonzalez, 1998; Felix-Holt & Gonzalez, 1999; Gonzalez, Bauerle, & Felix-Holt, 1994, 1996; Gonzalez, Bauerle, Black, & Felix-Holt, 1999; Gonzalez, Brusca-Vega, & Yawkey, 1997; Gonzalez & Clark, 1999; Oviedo & Gonzalez, 1999). This study also contributes to the understanding of the influence of mediational variables present in the home environment of Hispanic children (i.e., family structure factors) on their cognitive and language development. These family structure factors, represented in this study as independent variables, were measured by a Home Language Survey (Gonzalez, 1991).

These mediational variables have been considered by previous ethnographic and quasi-experimental studies conducted with Hispanic children as important family structure factors affecting socialization and acculturation processes (see e.g., Cocking, 1994; Delgado Gaitan, 1994; Harrison, Wilson, Pine, Chan, & Buriel, 1990; Shatz, 1991). Therefore, ecological variables affecting the quality of the family structure factors can also in turn affect the language-minority children's higher or lower cognitive and language developmental levels attained. The family structure is comprised of multiple linguistic, sociocultural, and SES factors affecting the degree of acculturation attained by language-minority parents and their children. According to Delgado Gaitan (1994), the degree of acculturation will be related to the number of years of residency in the US and the language used at home, all factors affecting their degree of access to opportunities for social mobility within mainstream institutions, such as the US public school system.

More specifically, socialization has been defined by Harrison and colleagues (1990) as "the processes by which individuals become distinctive and actively functioning members of the society in which they live" (p. 354). The most important mechanisms used by parents to socialize children are common to majority and minority groups, and include principles of classic and social learning theories (e.g., imitation, reinforcement, role modeling, and identification). However, the particular ethnic background of families will also bring important cultural components into the socialization process. As Phinney and Rotheram (1987, cited in Harrison et al., 1990) have pointed out, the impact of cultural factors in families results in "group patterns of values, social customs, perceptions, behavioral roles, language use, and rules of social interactions that group members share in both obvious and subtle ways" (p. 297). Thus, the particular socialization goals, child-rearing techniques, and adaptive strategies will be directly connected to the cultural background of ethnic families, which can be sharply different than the mainstream US socialization processes. For instance, traditional values of modesty and respect for elders among Hispanic families contrast with the assertiveness and value of youth present in the US mainstream society.

In the two sections below, each of these mediational home environmental variables will be analyzed critically in relation to relevant contemporary studies, resulting in a theoretical framework for understanding the methodology and findings of this study. These two sections examine the role of home language and culture, and of SES factors in Hispanic children's development.

The Role of Home Language and Culture on Hispanic Children's Development.

This section discusses the importance of understanding the impact of the minority family degree of acculturation on the children's cognitive and language development, and ultimately on their achievement levels attained in school. This section discusses how language and cultural practices at home relate to the degree of acculturation of parents and children, which are reflected on their bicultural or minority identities. Depending on the degree of acculturation of minority families, some discontinuity or continuity approaches can be taken for explaining the underachievement problems, or the resilience or potential giftedness present in minority children. Thus, the review of this literature becomes key for understanding what effect family structure factors (e.g., home language use, degree of acculturation) had on the cognitive and language development of potentially gifted, young children from low SES backgrounds.

Several authors (see e.g., Delgado Gaitan, 1994; Ogbu, 1982; Suarez-Orozco, 1989) have studied the impact of language used at home by parents in the socialization process of minority children. These authors support the contemporary view that language is used as a major tool to transmit implicitly cultural values to children. Thus, the way in which language is used at home by parents also reflects different cultural ways of socializing children, called by Shatz (1991) "communicative modes" or styles related to cultural content transmitted. For instance, some socialization practices transmit cultural patterns of social and linguistic interactions among individuals as well as in relation to social institutions. Moreover, Ochs and Schiefellin (1984) concluded that how language was used by adults also carried implicitly information about how to function within a particular social system. Given that the US public school system is also a social institution, then the continuity or discontinuity of language and cultural practices at home and school may be an explanation for the degree of adaptation present in minority parents and their children.

Different patterns of home language use present among different generation Hispanic families also reflect a variation in degrees of acculturation. In the case of Hispanic (Mexican-American) immigrant parents, the primary use of Spanish by children does affect positively the family structure and quality of communication with parents. In contrast, first generation Hispanic, Mexican-American parents participating in Delgado Gaitan's (1994) study spoke English as their primary language, with Spanish spoken only with relatives who were monolingual Spanish (typically of a previous immigrant generation such as grandparents). As Delgado Gaitan (1994) observed "not only had English become the first language in one generation but Spanish language loss was significant in most cases..." (p. 79).

Interestingly, even though language loss occurs only after one generation, the traditional Hispanic (Mexican-American) values survive across intergenerational socialization practices even when using English, but only in relation to the context of interpersonal family relations (Delgado Gaitan, 1994). For instance, the practice of traditional Mexican-American values such as respect for elders, was observed by Delgado Gaitan (1994) in how parents ask their children "not to interrupt" when adults chat among themselves. All the children participating in this study were from a Mexican-American background, and thus these findings are relevant for this population. However, it is important to note that these language and cultural patterns studied among Mexican-American, low SES families may be different among other Hispanic sub-groups (i.e., Puerto Ricans, Cubans, central and South Americans) representing other SES levels. Ethnic groups, such as Hispanics, tend to be very heterogeneous in racial, SES, cultural, and linguistic characteristics.

Thus, the more traditional view of considering language the only tool for the transmission of cultural values to children (e.g., see Ochs & Schiefellin, 1984) is too simplistic. There is need to consider that even monolingual English first generation parents can transmit the duality of traditional Hispanic values as well as mainstream cultural values, even though they are using only English and/or Spanish as a communication and socialization tool. Then, native speakers of English, who come from a minority background, can use the mainstream language with minority modes of communication. For instance, parents using *code mixing* and *code switching* and culturally appropriate Hispanic non-verbal behaviors at home may transmit implicitly minority cultural values to their children. That is, in reality mainstream English and culture is not modeled by parents within the family environment, but a new bicultural identity is created within a minority family with a specific degree of acculturation.

Thus, Hispanic families trying to integrate two cultural systems also stimulate in their children a greater cognitive and social flexibility, which may result in potential for giftedness. Then, bicultural children can also adapt to the discontinuities of home and school cultures, since they can successfully accomplish situational problem-solving processes. Finally, as discussed below, to the extent that ethnicity and sociocultural adaptive strategies are independent from SES, the fact of being poor should be an independent factor on the quality of the home structure.

The Role of Socioeconomic Satus (SES) on Hispanic Children's Development.

Most minority children are at-risk of suffering from developmental delays and underachievement because of the negative impact of poverty on their cognitive and language development. The sample of this study is an exception to this trend due to the mediational role of quality family structure factors that positively impacted the Hispanic children's cognitive and language development. Thus, in this second section we will present a discussion of the interaction of low SES factors, and the protective mechanisms present in the family, supporting minority children's cognitive and language development.

Demographic statistic information in reference to poverty suffered by young children is alarming. As Hill and Sandfort (1995) recommended, "the fact that the child poverty rate in the US is now double that of other industrialized countries requires us to act quickly to help the children of our nation" (p. 122). Based on demographic statistics from the US Bureau of the Census (1996), as of 1994, 22% of American children lived in families with cash incomes below the poverty threshold. In addition, as reported by Bronfenbrenner, McClelland, Wethington, Moen, and Ceci (1996; cited in McLoyd, 1998), the level of poverty has also increased, with 47% of poor families living with incomes 50% below the poverty threshold in 1993 (in comparison to 32% in 1975). Moreover, as noted by Bronfenbrenner and collaborators (1996; cited in McLoyd, 1998), poverty tends to occur more often during early childhood, under the age of 6, primarily because of the higher likelihood of having younger parents with lower wages.

It is also the case that minority children are at a higher risk of being below poverty level, in comparison to mainstream children. As reported by the US Bureau of the Census (1994), by 1992, one in three American children under the age of 5 was an ethnic minority (66% non-Latino Whites, 15% African Americans, 14% Latinos, 4% Asians or Pacific Islanders, and 1% American Indians).

As defined by McLoyd (1998), "unlike poverty status, SES signifies an individual's, a family's, or a group's ranking on a hierarchy according to its access to or control over some combination of valued commodities such as wealth, power, and social status" (p. 188). Many parental characteristics such as occupation, educational level, prestige, power, and lifestyle denote a multidimensionality of mediational factors associated with SES, that affect children's development. For instance, the parents' SES strongly affects their behaviors and child rearing practices, through some mediational variables such as parental educational levels and occupational attainments, and therefore home language use in relation to academic or literacy activities stimulated at home. It is important to note that these environmental factors can vary its mediational effects with age, gender, race, and ethnicity; and thus findings with majority populations cannot be generalized to minority groups. Even further, as mentioned in the previous section, there is also diversity within minority groups, so the effect of ecological factors needs to be analyzed in light of the confounding effect of race, ethnicity, SES, cultural, and linguistic factors.

However, the presence of poverty does not mean that the cultural background of parents and children is also deprived or diminished. As discussed above, in many instances minority cultural values and goals are preserved within a bicultural identity, and help to maintain high educational aspirations of parents for their children. As any other family, minority, low SES parents can stimulate successfully the development of their children by providing socio-emotional nurturance within a well structure family environment. Even though parents may be poor and have low levels of formal education, they maintain for their children a stable and well structure environment, which provides strong moral values and ethnic pride in their children, helping to promote even gifted development (Clark & Gonzalez, 1998).

In addition, the parents' SES is also related to the number of years of residency in the US, and therefore to whether they are immigrants or first, second, third generation Hispanics in the US. Then, the level of acculturation can interact with the presence of poverty, which is also related to the parental stress and difficulty levels present, and whether or not they are able to access mainstream resources and be able to become fully-fledged participants within the mainstream society. For instance, Wang (1993) studied Hispanic (first-and-second generation Caribbean families—i.e., Cuban, Puerto Rican, or Costa Rican), African-American, and Anglo second-grade children from low and middle-class SES backgrounds, living in Orlando, Florida. Wang found that cultural familial factors (e.g., family structure such as family size, child's birth order, parents' marital status, parental divorce and separation, and language spoken at home; and parent-child interactions such as whether parents assisted in their child 's homework) related to SES were better predictors of the child's metacognitive developmental skills; rather than the child 's ethnicity. Thus, Wang concluded that "SES supersedes ethnicity as a predictor for a child's metacognitive development" (p. 87). Similar findings were also reported by Walker, Greenwood, Hart, and Carta (1994), who showed that differences found between Hispanic and African-American children from low SES backgrounds were attributable to their SES-related factors (the home, community, and school environments), rather than to their minority background.

Furthermore, some authors have found that household characteristics related to small family size can enable parents to develop higher quality home environments and influence more positively their children's development (Blake, 1989; Zuravin, 1988; both cited in Garrett, P., Ng'andu, N., & Ferron, J., 1994). Then, some household characteristics can impact the child's development outcome. For instance, the low SES family composition can have an effect on number of siblings and the presence or absence of mother/father companion, and other adults (e.g., extended family member).

Thus, poverty can be a high-risk factor for child development, and could have a negative impact when significant mediational processes for successful adaptation are damaged, such as the quality of the attachment between parents and child. The presence of committed, involved, caring, and competent parents is a crucial and powerful adaptive system that protects the child's development. Well adapted parents, or any other committed and effective adults, can function as scaffolds to provide opportunities, protective mechanisms, and emotional support for children exposed to at-risk ecological factors (such as poverty) to develop resilience. Masten and Coatsworth (1998) highlighted the importance of providing at-risk children (due to poverty factors) with a protective ecological environment, especially during infancy and early childhood because "there is no such a thing as an invulnerable child" (p. 216). Thus, studying the dynamic way in which developmental and ecological factors influence adaptive, resilient processes in at-risk children is challenging, especially because of the complex role of culture and language. This study tries to shed some light on understanding how this dynamic interaction of family structure factors positively influences cognitive and language development in potentially gifted, Hispanic, young children from low SES backgrounds.

Method

Research Questions

1. What is the relationship of the language used at home by the child, parents, and siblings to the child's performance in QUEST?

2. What is the relationship of the parents' self-rated Spanish and English proficiency to the child's performance in QUEST?

3. What is the relationship of the child's use of code mixing and code switching to his/her performance in QUEST?

4. What is the relationship of the number of siblings to the child's performance in QUEST?

5. What is the relationship of the child's birth order to his/her performance in QUEST?

6. What is the relationship of the parents' occupations and educational levels to the child's performance in QUEST?

7. What is the relationship of the parents' number of years of residency in the US to the child's performance in QUEST?

Participants

Thirty kindergarten and thirty first grade children, who were nominated by their parents and/or classroom teachers for giftedness potential participated in this study. Parents and teachers used an open-ended survey, created by the authors, for describing qualitatively their perceptions of the child's potential for cognitive and linguistic giftedness. The sixty children comprising this sample were selected from a larger pool of completed surveys. These sixty children were selected for further evaluation because they were screened as potentially gifted by the authors, based on the qualitative descriptions gathered in the parents' and teachers' survey. All the sixty children were from a Hispanic ethnic background (Mexican-American), most of them first-generation, and attended public elementary schools located in low SES abarrios of a medium size cosmopolitan area in the Southwest region of the US.

Information about the language proficiency and dominance of the children was gathered form the school district files, based on surveys completed by parents as well as Language Assessment Scales (LAS, DeAvila & Duncan, 1986) administered by school personnel. This information was complemented by the Home Language Survey filled out by parents of the children participating in this study. Fifty of these children were monolingual, with an equal percentage of English and Spanish proficient speakers, who were attending either monolingual English or bilingual classrooms correspondingly. Only 10 children had some degree of additive bilingualism, with Spanish as a first and proficient language, and an intermediate proficiency of English. This information was coincident with their parents' and teachers' qualitative ratings, based on which these children were rated as either monolingual Spanish (N=50), or bilingual (N=10, with Spanish as a first language in most children).

Instruments

Teacher's and parents' survey. This survey was designed by Gonzalez (1991) for the purpose of eliciting referrals from parents and teachers for potential cognitive and linguistic giftedness in Hispanic children. It consists of seven open-ended questions eliciting respondents to describe qualitatively their perceptions about the child's linguistic, problem-solving, and individual and group working and playing behaviors and abilities at home and at school. Finally, parents and teachers were asked to circle descriptors that they perceived better described the child's behaviors and abilities, and write additional comments. This instrument has been validated since its construction in 1991 in several studies with minority and mainstream children (see e.g., Felix-Holt & Gonzalez, 1999; Gonzalez, et al., 1994, 1996; Gonzalez & Clark, 1999).

Home Language Survey. It was developed by Gonzalez (1991) and consists of open-ended questions and Likert scales asking parents to: (1) rate the frequency of use at home of Spanish and English by parents, siblings, and the child; (2) self-rate their Spanish and English proficiency; (3) rate their child's Spanish and English proficiency; (4) rate the effect of schooling on the child's Spanish and English proficiency levels; (5) report the frequency of use of code mixing and code switching by the child; (6) provide information on their educational levels; (7) provide information on their occupations; (8) provide the number of siblings in the home; (9) provide the birth order of the child; and (10) provide the number of years of US residency of both parents.

*Qualitative Use of English and Spanish Tasks (QUEST).*Gonzalez's (1991, 1994) developed a model of concept formation in bilingual children; which identifies two knowledge representational systems depending on the particular cognitive, linguistic, and cultural characteristics of the content learned. The first conceptual representational system is abstract, universal, and non-verbal; and the second one is semantic, verbal, and culturally-linguistically bound. Cognitive factors were considered abstract knowledge representations instantiated in cultural symbolic conventions and in linguistic structures and markers. Cultural and linguistic factors were selected because Spanish assigns linguistic gender for both animate and inanimate abstract conceptual categories, corresponding to culturally important symbolic distinctions, that are expressed through linguistic rules and markers. In contrast, English only assigns linguistic gender to some animate conceptual abstract categories.

The model from which the classification tasks were derived was based partially on Piagetian theory (Piaget, 1967) and on the constraint model (Markman & Hutchinson, 1984; Waxman, 1990), and it was found to have construct validity as shown by parametric and non-parametric tests (Gonzalez, 1991). The derived verbal and non-verbal classification tasks were designed to assess bilingual children's general and linguistic gender conceptual processes for two different abstract, symbolic and linguistic semantic categories represented by animals (animate) and food (inanimate) objects. Stimuli used for the five classification tasks were plastic full-color objects representing 14 groupings reflecting the interaction of cognitive, cultural, and linguistic factors. Stimuli groupings were validated using judges for assuring construct validity and three pilot tests for assuring content validity (Gonzalez, 1991, 1994). Moreover, internal validity and reliability of the classification tasks was demonstrated by using Pearson chi-square association tests (Gonzalez, Bauerle, & Felix-Holt, 1996).

Three of these five classification tasks are verbal including labeling, defining, and verbal justification of sorting; and two tasks are non-verbal including sorting and category clue. Tasks will be described following the pre-established order of administration (for a more complete description of tasks see Gonzalez, 1991, 1995). For the labeling task, the child is presented plastic objects and asked to name them (What *do you call this?*), while giving her one item at a time, followed by the defining task at the production level in which the child is asked four different probes to elicit a description of the object(s) (*What is a ___?*; *What is a ___ like?*, *Tell me something about a ___*, and *What does a ___ look like?*). After, for tapping the comprehension level of the defining task, the child is given a definition that points to verbal and non-verbal clues for class inclusion categories of objects (taxonomic categories: superordinate, intermediate, and subcategories). This definition is repeated three times, and after the child is asked to define three different kinds of items. For the sorting task, the child is asked to group the objects by linguistic gender; followed by the verbal justification of sorting task in which the child is asked to explain the order imposed on the objects, and she is presented with metalinguistic counterexamples that change groupings and labels. Finally, for the category clue task, the child is provided with a model of how to group objects by linguistic gender using two pictures of identical dolls; and then she is asked to sort the objects following the model provided, to explain her groupings, and to answer metalinguistic counter-examples that change groupings and labels.

The scoring system is divided into five point assignment areas including language development, verbal and non-verbal general, and verbal and non-verbal gender areas; based on which children are diagnosed on conceptual development (for an extended description of scoring see Gonzalez, 1991, 1995). See Table 4.1. for a description of the double scoring classification system for tasks, for the general and gender-based criteria.

General areas include any valid criteria that the child uses for classification (e.g., color, functions, subcategories, etc.). Gender areas include classification criteria based on physical gender for animates, linguistic gender assignment for inanimates, or functional use for both animates and inanimates. The language development area includes only the labeling task. The verbal general and gender-based areas include defining and verbal justification of sorting tasks, and the non-verbal general and gender-based areas include sorting and category clue tasks. Thus, children's responses to the five tasks administered in both languages were scored twice, assigning points for both general and gender areas. The language development area was categorized into three levels: (a) low (0-2 points), (b) moderate (3-5 points), and (c) high (6-8 points); according to the number of labels produced by the child.

For the other four areas children's responses were categorized into five stages based partially on Piaget's theory (1965): (1) no classification (affective responses, juxtaposed groupings and graphic collections), (2) pre-conceptual: perceptual (extralinguistic features—color, size, shape, parts of objects), (3) pre-conceptual: functional (thematic relations), (4) concrete (taxonomic categories showing class-inclusion), and (5) metalinguistic (taxonomic semantic categories). Attaining the fifth metalinguistic developmental level is considered to be very advanced (or potentially gifted) cognitive and language development in kindergartners and first graders. Tables 4.2. and 4.3. show the double scoring system, and also provide examples of the actual children's responses for the defining, sorting, verbal justification of sorting, and category clues tasks. In order to be diagnosed in any of these five developmental stages for any of the five verbal and non-verbal tasks, children's responses needed to be at that level at least for three out of the eight items that were included in the tasks.

Procedure

A large Southwest metropolitan school district with 50% of minority students adopted QUEST as an alternative individualized procedure for selecting and placing bilingual Hispanic students in gifted education. Both parent and teachers were invited to refer children for possible giftedness evaluation. For participation in this study it was sufficient to have only one referral, either from a parent or a teacher; according to information obtained from the Home Language Survey, as well as their LAS scores available from their permanent records.

Children were individually assessed in their first language by evaluators trained in the administration of QUEST. Fourteen graduate students majoring in educational psychology, who were completing a course on testing of minorities served as evaluators. They received 10 hours of training in administering QUEST, including watching 3 administration videos, and hands-on practice sessions where pairs of students administered the assessment to each other and scored protocols. Two pairs of evaluators were trained in Spanish, each consisting of a native Spanish speaker who administered QUEST, and a non-native Spanish speaker who served as the recorder. The other five pairs of evaluators were trained in English, each consisting of two monolingual English speakers who served as administrators and recorders. Each pair assessed two children, recorded responses in protocols, made an assessment decision on the children's verbal and non-verbal conceptual developmental levels, and wrote a summary report. Evaluators and children were allowed to use code mixing and/or code switching for administering or responding to QUEST. The second co-author of this paper conducted a reliability check of the coding of children's responses reviewing both videotapes of the administration sessions as well as the summary reports and protocols, including assessment and placement decisions.

Description of Data Analysis

Non-parametric analysis of data includes frequencies and percentages for describing the family structure factors examined in the Home Language Survey. As described above in the instruments section, ten areas of information were gathered using Likert-Scale and close-and-open-ended questions. When using the scoring system, children's responses were assigned nominal categories that described their verbal and non-verbal conceptual development achieved across classification tasks (as explained in the section above, and as described in Tables 4.1., 4.2., and 4.3). The frequencies obtained from the Home Language Survey were used as the independent factors, and the nominal categories of QUEST were used as the dependent variables for conducting one-way ANOVA tests.

For both parametric tests, a significance level of .05 was set as a minimum, and only significant tests at the .05 or higher are included. Since a series of previous studies have showed different developmental levels achieved by children for the non-verbal and verbal tasks, the two different scoring systems (general and linguistic gender), and for the animate and inanimate object referents; they were treated separately in the analyses. Moreover, because not all students were assessed in both languages, resulting in unequal numbers for each language, only the first administration in the child's first language was entered in both parametric tests. When the administration of QUEST was conducted twice in the same language, the first administration was used for statistical analysis. However, when the first assessment had missing data, the second complete assessment was used. These data reflects the reality faced by evaluators when assessing bilingual children who are not fully proficient in both languages, and who do not have either a language dominance.

Results and Discussion

First the descriptive information on the family structure factors gathered through the Home Language Survey will be reported. The ten areas comprised by this instrument will be described and explained using frequencies and percentages (see Table 4.4. for a summary of this descriptive data). Second, we will report and discuss the Pearson correlation for the Home Language Survey information on the family structure factors reported by the parents. Third, five sets of one-way ANOVA tests will be reported, with a discussion of the interpretation of results. Fourth, a summary of all the results will be presented in relation to the research questions posed.

Description of Family Structure Factors

Language Use at Home.

Most mothers (N=41, 68.5%) and fathers (N=44, 73.5%) used Spanish at home, with about one third of parents using English at home (mothers, N=19, 31.5%, and fathers, N=16, 26,5%). The number of children who used English or Spanish at home was almost equal, with 28 children using English (46.5%), and 32 children (53.5%) using Spanish at home. The same balance between siblings using Spanish or English at home was found, with 31 siblings using English (51.5%) and 29 siblings (48.5%) using Spanish. Thus, the use of Spanish and English at home was almost equal for mothers, fathers, as well as for siblings.

Parent's Proficiency in Spanish and English

From the Spanish speaking mothers, most self-rated their Spanish proficiency as not quite adequate (N=12, 20%), with a smaller portion considering their Spanish as adequate (N=5, 3.8%), or above average (N=3, 5%). Thus, about one third of the mothers considered themselves as Spanish speakers to some degree. However, most mothers considered themselves as not Spanish speakers.

Similarly, from the about 40% of Spanish speaking fathers, most self-rated their Spanish proficiency as not quite adequate (N=17, 28.3%), with only some considering their Spanish proficiency as either adequate (N=6, 10%) or above average (N=2. 3.3%). However, about one third of the fathers self-rated as not Spanish speakers.

From the English speaking mothers, one fourth considered their English proficiency as adequate (N=15, 25%), in contrast to fewer considering their English proficiency as above average (N=5, 8.4%) or not quite adequate (N=11. 18.4%). In addition, half of the mothers considered themselves as not English speakers (N=30. 50%).

From the English speaking fathers, most self-rated their English proficiency as not quite adequate (N=17, 28.5%), with some considering their English proficiency as adequate (N=10, 16.6%), and only a few as above average (N=2, 3.3%). A large portion of fathers (N=31, 51.6%) considered themselves as not English speakers.

Thus, in general comparing the mothers and fathers' English and Spanish proficiency levels, two patterns emerged. First, about half reported having English as their first language (30 mothers and 29 fathers) with a difference in the levels at which they rated their English skills. Mothers were inclined to rate their English proficiency skills as adequate or above adequate more often than fathers (N=15 for mothers in comparison to N=10 for fathers). Second, more fathers had Spanish as their first language (N=25) than mothers (N ' 20), with no actual difference in the levels at which they rated their Spanish language skills. Thus, according to the survey results about 10 mothers and 6 fathers were bilingual, with some degree of proficiency of Spanish and English.

Child's Proficiency in Spanish and English

The majority of children's language proficiency was rated by their parents as not quite adequate (N=21, 35% for Spanish, and N=24, 40% for English), with some as adequate (N=9, 15% for both Spanish and English), and few for above average (N=6, 10% in Spanish, and N=1, 1.6% for English). About the same number of children spoke Spanish (N=36) and/or English (N=34) to some degree; with 10 bilingual children with some degree of Spanish and English proficiency levels.

Effect of Schooling on Children's Spanish and English Proficiency Levels

Parents reported that the effect of schooling on their children's language proficiency had either increased the use of English (N=25, 41.6%) or had not resulted on a noticeable change (N=29, 48.5%). Only few parents reported that schooling had increased the use of Spanish (N=4, 6.6%) or had decreased the use of English (N=2, 3.3%).

Use of Code Mixing and Code Switching

Most parents reported that their children did not use code mixing or code switching (N=38, 63.5%). However, about one third of the parents reported that their children used that communication mode (N=22, 36.5%).

Educational Level of Parents

Most parents reported that they had finished their high school education (N=38, 63.4% for mothers, and N=42, 70.2% for fathers). Similarly, 20% of mothers and fathers hold a bachelors degree (N=12), with only very few holding a masters degree (N=4 for mothers and N=1 for fathers). Only very few parents had attended college for 1-2 years (N=3, 5% for both mothers and fathers) or for more than 3 years (N=3, 5% for mothers, and N=1, 1.6% for fathers).

Occupation of Parents

Most mothers were homemakers (N=38, 63.5%), with about one third working in blue collar jobs (N=17, 28.3%), and only few working as professionals (N=4, 6.6%) or in white collar jobs (N=1, 1.6%). Most fathers worked in blue collar occupations (N=44, 73.5%), with some working as professionals (N=10, 16.5%) and only few working in white collar jobs (N=3, 5%) or staying at home unemployed (N=3, 5%).

Number of Siblings and Child's Birth Order

Most children had either one sibling (N=22, 36.6%) or two (N=16, 26.6%), or 3 (N=11, 18.5%); with only few being the only child (N=6, 10%) or having more than 3 siblings (N=5, 8.3%). Most children were either the first born (N=24, 40%) or the second born (N=22, 36.6%). Only few children were either the third or fourth child (N=5, 8.5% correspondingly), or the fifth or seventh (N=2, 3.3% correspondingly).

Thus, most families had between one and three children with the majority of families being composed of two children (N=22, 36.6%), followed by families with three or four children (N=27, 45%). Thus, still among low SES Hispanic families, there is a tendency for having and raising a rather large number of off-springs. Since the majority of children participating in this study were the first or second born, then most of their siblings were preschoolers or younger. Thus, these were young families with their older children in primary school and their younger children were either young toddlers or infants. Thus, it was very likely that these children would continue two have newer additions to their families, resulting in large families of three or four or more siblings.

Parents' Number of Years of Us Residency

Most parents had 16 or more years of residence in the US (N=36, 60%) with one fourth of parents (N=15, 25%) having arrived to the US between 6- to 10 years ago, and very few having arrived to the US either 11- to 15 years ago (N=4, 66%) or 1 to 5 years ago (N=5, 8.4%).

Pearson Correlation of the Home Language Survey Information Reported by Parents

Pearson correlation tests conducted across the family structure factors indicated a number of interesting associations, all reported in Table 4.5. Only the associations significant at the .05 level or higher will be discussed here. For the first set of home language factors, there was a strong association between the language that the mother, the father, the siblings, and the child spoke at home. That is, it seems that mothers and fathers who had the same first language tended to get married (r=.459, p < .01) and to use their dominant language for communication with their children at home. Another interesting piece of information is that the number of years of US residence of the mothers and fathers was also associated (r=.887, p < .01), so that it seems that the couples tended to immigrate to the US during the same period of time.

More specifically, the first language of the mother had a stronger association to the child's first language (r=.657, p < .01) and to the siblings first language (r=.666, p < .01), than to the first language of the father (r=.590 for the child and r=.602 for the siblings, p < .01), even though the level of significance was the same. There was also a very strong association between the home or first language of the child and the home language of his or her siblings (r=.897, p < .01), the child's proficiency in Spanish and the home language of siblings (r=.641, p < .01), and a negative correlation between the child's English language proficiency and the home language of siblings (r=.502, p < .05). That is, the higher the children's Spanish language proficiency, the more likely it was for their siblings to speak Spanish at home; and vice versa for the case of English.

Moreover, the mother's and the father's self-rated proficiency in English was negatively correlated with the home language of the child (r=.675, p < .01, r=.387, p < .05 correspondingly) and of the siblings (r=.721, r=.486, p < .01, correspondingly); and the mother's and father's self-rated Spanish language proficiency was positively associated with the home language of the child (r=.396, r=.382, p < .05, correspondingly), and of the siblings (r=.486, p < .01 for the father only). That is, all these correlation coefficients point to the higher likelihood for the children's and their siblings' first language to be influenced by the home language of their parents, with a stronger probability for parents to speak Spanish at home. However, there were also several negative correlation coefficients between the home language of both parents, and the home language of the child and siblings and the number of years of US residence of both parents (all significant at p < .05 level, see Table 4.5.). These negative associations point to the fact that the fewer number of years the parents had spent in the US, the less association was found between what language the children and the parents used most often at home.

In addition, there was an association between the mother's and father's proficiency in Spanish and their home language use (r=.575, r=.548, p <. 01 correspondingly); and a negative correlation between the parents' proficiency in English and their home language (r=.666, p < .01 for the mothers, and r=.353, p <. 05 for the fathers). These results indicate the presence of two patterns: (1) the higher the parents self-rated their proficiency in Spanish, the more likely it was that they used Spanish at home; and (2) the lower the parents self-rated their English proficiency, the less likely it was that they used English at home. Furthermore, the mother's, the father's, and the child's proficiency in English was positively associated with the number of years of US residence (r=.689, p < .01, r=.625, p < .01, and r=.282, p < .05 correspondingly); but not for the Spanish language. Interestingly, the number of years of US residence for both parents' was negatively correlated with the child's proficiency in Spanish (significant at the p < .01 level, see Table 4.5.).

One-Way ANOVA Tests in Relation to the Research Questions Stated

Eight sets of one-way ANOVA tests were run, with the Home Language Survey eight areas measuring the family structure factors as the dependent variables, and the child's performance in QUEST by sub-tasks as the dependent variables. An independent ANOVA test was run for each of the variables measured, with a total of 21 tests run clustered into eight sets by content. These eight sets of ANOVA tests examine the research questions posed. The first set of three tests examines the relationship of the home language use by the mother, father, and siblings to the child's performance in QUEST. The second set of four tests examines the relationship of the mother's and father's Spanish and English proficiency levels to the child's performance in QUEST.

The third set of two tests examines the relationship of the child's Spanish and English proficiency levels (as rated by their parents) to the child's performance in QUEST. The fourth set of two tests studies the relationship of the number of siblings and birth order to the child's performance in QUEST. The fifth set of two tests examines the relationship of schooling on the child's Spanish and English proficiency levels to the child's performance in QUEST. The sixth set of two tests examines the relationship of the use of code mixing and code switching at home to the child's performance in QUEST. The seventh set of four tests examines the relationship of the parents' educational levels and occupations to the child's performance in QUEST. The eight set of two tests examines the relationship of the parents' number of years of US residency to the child's performance in QUEST. See Table 4.6. for a summary of the significant tests across sets.

First and Fifth Sets of Tests

The first (relationship the home language use by the child, mother, and sibling), fifth (relationship of schooling to the first-and-second-language proficiency levels of the child), and sixth set of tests (use of code mixing and code switching by the child) were significantly related to the child's verbal performance on QUEST. It is interesting to note that the father's home language did not show a significant relationship to the child's performance in QUEST. More specifically, these three sets of factors were significantly related to the child's language development for: (1) vocabulary learning for inanimate object referents (food), in relation to linguistic gender (represented by the labeling task); and (2) the formation of verbal concepts for food, at the linguistic gender level (represented by the defining task). These two abilities tap cultural conventions present in the Spanish language only, and also require higher levels of understanding of linguistic structures and cultural symbolic representations at the abstract or metalinguistic level. That is, there is no correspondence between the intra-linguistic features of linguistic gender and the extra-linguistic real-life characteristics of the inanimate object referents (i.e., food that does not have a corresponding physical gender, but the speaker just follows social symbolic conventions).

In contrast, the relationship of these three sets of factors was significant only in very few verbal tasks in relation to animate object referents (animals) at the general classification level. These kinds of tasks have shown to be easier developmentally for children (see e.g., Gonzalez, 1991, 1994, 1995; Gonzalez, et al., 1996) because there is a correspondence between the intra-linguistic features and the extra-linguistic reality for animals (i.e., physical gender corresponding to the linguistic gender representations, and these symbols can be also transferred more frequently between Spanish and English).

At the non-verbal conceptual developmental level, the relationship of these three sets of factors was significant only for the category clue task for inanimate object referents (food) at the linguistic gender level. Again, as for the verbal tasks, this particular task requires the child to perform at higher non-verbal concept developmental levels in order to solve successfully the classification problems posed. That is, children need to understand the relation between intra-linguistic characteristics and the social symbolic conventions in Spanish, requiring an abstract or metalinguistic ability.

Second and Eight Set of Tests

The second set of tests (the mother's Spanish and English language proficiency, the father's proficiency in English only) and the eight set of tests (the parents' number of years of US residence) was significantly related to the child's performance in QUEST. More specifically, the mother's and father's proficiency in English, and the number of years of US residence of both parents showed a significant relationship to nonverbal conceptual developmental levels achieved by the child. Particularly, the child's conceptual development for the sorting and category clue tasks in relation to animate and inanimate object referents (animals and food, primarily at the general level). That is, these tasks require children to be able to understand verbal instructions (sorting) for the model presented (category clue), and its underlying abstract classification system, even when forming general level classes or groupings. The parents' English proficiency level showed to be related for the children's conceptual ability because most youngsters with adequate English proficiency levels could perform at adequate developmental levels (even if they did not have Spanish proficiency).

In addition, the parents' number of years of US residence also was significantly related to the children's verbal conceptual developmental levels for animate and inanimate object referents (animals and food, in relation to linguistic gender classifications only). Again, as explained before this type of symbolic cultural classification requires in children the ability to understand vocabulary (labeling task) at a higher developmental level, in which they need to relate intra-linguistic knowledge with extra-linguistic real-life knowledge for animals (i.e., linguistic gender assignments with physical gender characteristics), or just to form abstract and metalinguistic concepts in Spanish for inanimate object referents.

Third Set of Tests

The third set of two tests examines the relationship of the child's Spanish and English proficiency levels (as rated by their parents) to the child's performance in QUEST. Results were only significant for two of the Spanish sub-tasks of QUEST. More specifically, the children's proficiency level in Spanish did were significantly related to their non-verbal conceptual ability in relation to the sorting and category clue tasks only, and only for inanimate object referents (food) for linguistic gender classifications. That is, in order to form abstract and metalinguistic classes that represent the intra-linguistic features of symbolic gender, children needed to have some degree of Spanish proficiency, or some knowledge of linguistic and cultural conventions.

Fourth Set of Tests

The fourth set of two tests examines the relationship among the number of siblings and birth order to the child's performance in QUEST. The children's birth order and number of siblings were mostly related to their non-verbal performance, particularly at the general classification level for animals, which has been shown by past research to be the easiest type of tasks (see e.g., Gonzalez, 1991, 1994, 1995; Gonzalez et al., 1996). Similarly, the children's verbal performance was also significantly related to the child's vocabulary developmental level attained for animals at the general level. Thus, it seems that the number of siblings and the child's birth order was significantly related to their non-verbal and verbal developmental level achieved, both for their performance on the hardest and the easiest types of classification tasks.

Seventh Set of Tests

The seventh set of four tests examines the relationship of the mother's and father's educational levels and occupations to the child's performance in QUEST. Only for few tasks, the parents' occupation and educational levels was significantly related to the children's performance. This positive relationship mostly appeared for verbal tasks associated with linguistic gender categorizations of animate and inanimate (animals and food) object referents. These particular tasks offer a higher level of difficulty, requiring children to perform at higher developmental levels (mostly metalinguistic) in order to successfully solve the verbal classification problems present to them. These verbal tasks dealt with labeling and defining food and animal objects. These verbal tasks represent the children's language development (mostly vocabulary) and verbal conceptual ability to describe objects and form verbal conceptual classes of objects (at the general classification or scoring system level). These verbal tasks also measure the child's ability to think symbolically with language, and to relate extra-linguistic real-life characteristics of objects (e.g., animates have two physical genders) with its linguistic gender representation in a label or in a verbal description. For example, a child might say, "This is the mommy cow and this is the daddy cow, or this is the cow and this is the bull."

At the non-verbal level, the parents' occupation and educational levels was significantly related to the children's performance at the linguistic gender assignment level for both animate or inanimate object referents (animals or food). Again, only for the hardest problem-solving classification tasks to solve, which require the children to understand the linguistic gender assignment and to be able to do a non-verbal metalinguistic classification (sorting task). These classification tasks represented cultural conventions of the Spanish language for linguistic gender assignments for food (verbal justification of sorting), or required the child to follow a model that represented and related extra-linguistic (physical gender of animals) and intra-linguistic gender representations (category clue task).

Summary of Results and Conclusions

Descriptive data provided information about the family structure factors present in the daily lives of the children participating in the study. Parents reported that Spanish and English were used at home almost equally by mothers, fathers, siblings, and the children. By comparing the mothers and fathers' English and Spanish proficiency levels, two patterns emerged. The first pattern showed that about half of the mothers and fathers reported having English as their first language, with mothers rating their English proficiency skills at higher levels than fathers. The second pattern showed that more fathers than mothers had Spanish as their first language, with no actual difference in the levels at which they rated their Spanish language skills. Thus, about 10 mothers and 6 fathers were bilingual, with some degree of proficiency of Spanish and English.

In reference to educational levels, most parents reported that they had finished their high school education. Most mothers were homemakers, with about one third working in blue-collar jobs; whereas most fathers worked in blue-collar occupations. The majority of parents had 16 plus years of residence in the US, with one fourth of parents having arrived to the US between 6 to 10 years ago.

Parents reported that about half of the children spoke Spanish and/or English to some degree; with 10 bilingual children with some degree of Spanish and English proficiency levels. About half of the parents reported that the effect of schooling on their children's language proficiency had either increased the use of English or had not resulted on a noticeable change. Most parents reported that their children did not use code mixing or code switching. However, about one third of the parents reported that their children used code switching and code mixing as a communication mode. Most families had between one and three children with the majority of families being composed of two children, followed by families with three or four children.

Pearson correlation tests conducted across the family structure factors indicated a number of interesting associations, indicating eight patterns of language use at home. The first emerging pattern indicated that the children's and their siblings' first language was influenced by the home language of their parents, with a stronger probability for parents to speak Spanish at home. The second pattern indicated that the higher the children's Spanish language proficiency, the more likely for their siblings to speak Spanish at home; and vice versa for the case of English.

The third pattern indicated that the higher the parents self-rated their proficiency in Spanish, the higher the likelihood that they used Spanish at home. And vice versa, the fourth pattern indicated that the lower the parents self-rated their English proficiency, the less likelihood that they used English at home. However, the fifth pattern indicated that the fewer number of years the parents had spent in the US, the less association was found between what language the children and the parents used most often at home. Relatedly, the sixth pattern showed that the mother's, the father's, and the child's proficiency in English was positively associated with the number of years of US residence. Moreover, the seventh pattern showed that the number of years of US residence for both parents was negatively correlated with the child's proficiency in Spanish. Finally, the eight emerging pattern showed that the number of years of US residence reported by mothers and fathers was highly associated.

Eight sets of one-way ANOVA tests were conducted, with the eight areas of the Home Language Survey measuring the family structure factors as the dependent variables, and the child's performance in QUEST by sub-tasks as the dependent variables. An independent ANOVA test was run for each of the variables measured, with a total of 21 tests run clustered into eight sets by content. These eight sets of ANOVA tests examine the research questions posed, and results showed significant relations of three sets of independent variables on the child's verbal performance on QUEST: (1) the first set of the effect of the home language use by the child, mother, and sibling; (2) the fifth set of the effect of schooling on the first-and-second-language proficiency levels of the child; and (3) the sixth set of tests regarding the child's use of code mixing and code switching. More specifically, these three sets of factors had a significant effect on the children's understanding of linguistic gender for food present in the Spanish language only, represented in the following abilities: (1) vocabulary learning in the labeling task, (2) verbal concept formation in the defining task, and (3) non-verbal concept formation in the category clue task.

In addition, the parents' occupation and educational levels (seventh set of tests) was significantly related to the children's verbal and non-verbal concept formation for linguistic gender categorizations of animals and food (represented in the labeling and defining tasks). Moreover, the parents' number of years of US residence (eight set of tests) had a significant effect on the children's verbal conceptual developmental levels for animals and food in relation to linguistic gender classifications. In order to solve these classification problems, children needed to understand abstract concepts, requiring a metalinguistic ability. More importantly, the children's proficiency level in Spanish (as rated by their parents, third set of tests) had a significant effect on their non-verbal conceptual ability in relation to the sorting and category clue tasks for food for linguistic gender classifications. That is, in order to form abstract and metalinguistic classes, children needed to understand the relation between intra-linguistic characteristics and the social symbolic conventions in Spanish, but they also needed to have some degree of Spanish proficiency, or some knowledge of linguistic and cultural conventions.

In addition, other family structure factors were related to the children's non-verbal concept formation at the general classification level: (1) the mother's and father's proficiency in English (second set of tests) was significantly related to the non-verbal conceptual developmental levels for animals and food, and (2) the children's birth order and number of siblings (fourth set of tests) was related to the children's vocabulary development and non-verbal concept formation for animals. These non-verbal tasks require children to be able to understand verbal instructions (sorting) or the model presented (category clue), and its underlying abstract classification system, even when forming general level classes or groupings. Thus, when forming general classes, the children's degree of English language proficiency (which was in turn indirectly related to their parents and siblings' English language use and degrees of proficiency), was directly related to their ability to understand and form general non-verbal conceptual classifications at higher levels (i.e., classes or groupings of objects at the concrete or abstract levels).

Putting together the descriptive data, the patterns obtained from the Pearson correlation tests, and the results of the one-way ANOVA test, two conclusions can be derived in relation to the research questions:

1. *Research Questions 1, 4, 5, 6, 7, and 8.* The language used at home by parents, siblings, and the child; and the use of code mixing and code switching done by the child were significantly related to the developmental levels attained by children. More specifically, these family structure factors were related to the children's ability for vocabulary learning and non-verbal concept formation (i.e., linguistic gender for food in Spanish). That is, children who performed at higher levels in non-verbal classification tasks, also used Spanish at home, and had siblings who were also Spanish speakers. Moreover, the children's birth order, their parents educational levels and occupation, and their parents' number of years of US residence were re-

lated to the children's verbal and non-verbal conceptual developmental levels attained (i.e., for linguistic gender classifications for food in Spanish). Thus, in order to understand the higher level metalinguistic and abstract verbal and non-verbal classifications problems posed, children needed to have a certain degree of Spanish language proficiency (in turn related to their parents' and siblings' home language, their birth order, and to their parents' educational levels and occupation).

In sum, this study demonstrated that all these family structure factors (and more specifically the home language of parents and children, and the parents' number of years of US residence) were related to the *degree of acculturation* present in the language-minority parents and their children.

2. *Research Questions 1, 6, and 7.* The parents' self-rated degree of English language proficiency levels, the number of siblings, and the child's birth order were significantly related to the non-verbal conceptual developmental level attained by the child, in relation general classifications for animals and food. That is, the higher the parents' English proficiency levels, the more likely it was that English was used at home by parents and siblings, and thus also by the child. Having English as a home language also resulted in the child's higher English language proficiency levels (as rated by parents), language dominance that was reflected in the child's ability to form non-verbal general classifications.

Theoretical and Practical Implications of the Study

The most important theoretical implication is that this study provides some evidence for the significant relation between ecological variables and the cognitive and language development of Hispanic, young, low SES children. More specifically, family structure factors (i.e., home language of parents and siblings, the parents' Spanish and English language proficiency levels, the parents' educational levels and occupations, the number of siblings, and the child's birth order) were significantly related to the child's cognitive and language developmental level attained. When alternative assessments methodologically control for conceptual differences introduced by cultural and linguistic factors, the significant relation of family structure factors can also be demonstrated in language-minority, low SES children's conceptual development.

Thus, when alternative assessments are used, such as QUEST, which represent the cultural and linguistic factors affecting cognitive and language development in minority children, the advantages of bilingualism or of speaking a minority language can be shown. The children who had some level of proficiency in Spanish were able to perform at a metalinguistic or abstract developmental level when forming non-verbal and verbal concepts related to the cultural conventions and symbolic and verbal representations of the Spanish language (see the first conclusion above). In contrast, children exhibited a different performance level when forming non-verbal and verbal concepts related to general classification systems, common to cultural conventions and symbolic representations of the Spanish and English languages (see the second conclusion above).

In terms of practical educational implications, this study presents some empirical evidence for the importance of involving parents in the referral process of potentially gifted, language-minority children, who come from low SES backgrounds. Information provided by parents on family structure factors becomes key for evaluators to understand how ecological variables are related to first-and-second-language learning process, and to cognitive development in bilingual, low SES children. Furthermore, further research studies need to be conducted on the relationship between cultural and linguistic factors and the minority parents' beliefs about giftedness, and cognitive and language development (see Williams & Gonzalez, in this book for a preliminary study in majority and minority, monolingual, mid-high and low SES children).

Limitations of the Study

This study is limited by the comparison of children's performance in QUEST in only one language administration. However, the sample for this study just represents the actual reality observed in public school settings across the nation. That is, most Hispanic children are proficient in one language, and only fewer are bilinguals who can perform in cognitive measures in both Spanish and English. However, all the children were given the opportunity to use both languages for responding (using one at a time or both together—resulting in code mixing and code switching). In addition, the presence of bilingual evaluators provided children with the freedom to use interchangeably Spanish and English during the administration of QUEST.

Another limitation is that this study only focuses on the relationship of cultural and linguistic factors on verbal and non-verbal concept formation processes (particularly for the case of linguistic gender assignment and classification tasks). Other cognitive processes can be studied in order to encompass a broader range of skills and abilities. In addition, other cultural and linguistic content also needs to be studied beyond the linguistic gender case. The scoring system used in QUEST can also be broaden in order to reflect creativity, symbolic play, flexibility of thinking, and other problem-solving strategies used by children. Finally, the analysis of particular cultural content present in the children's responses can also broaden the scope of the study of concept formation processes in bilingual children.

References

Clark, R. E., & Gonzalez, V. (1998). *Voces* and voices: Cultural and linguistic giftedness. *Educational Horizons, 77* (1), 41-47.

Cocking, R. R. (1994). Ecologically valid frameworks of development: Accounting for continuities and discontinuities across contexts. In P. M. Greenfield & R. R. Cocking (Eds.), *Cross-cultural roots of minority child development* (pp. 393-409). Hillsdale, NJ: Lawrence Erlbaum Associates.

De Avila, E. A., & Duncan, S. E. (1986*). The Language Assessment Scales (LAS).* Monterey, CA: CTB/McGraw-Hill.

Delgado Gaitan, C. (1994). Socializing young children in Mexican-American families: An intergenerational perspective. In P.M. Greenfield & R. R. Cocking (Eds.). *Cross-cultural roots of minority child development* (pp. 55-86). Hillsdale, NJ: Lawrence Erlbaum Associates.

Felix-Holt, M, & Gonzalez, V. (1999). Alternative assessment models of language-minority children: Is there a match with teachers' attitudes and instruction? In V. Gonzalez (Vol. Ed.), *Language and cognitive development in second language learning: Educational implications for children and adults (pp.190-226).* Needham Heights, MA: Allyn & Bacon.

Garrett, P., Ng'andu, N., & Ferron, J. (1994). Poverty experiences of young children and their quality of their home environment. *Child Development, 65,* 331-345.

Gonzalez, V. (1991). *A model of cognitive, cultural, and linguistic variables affecting bilingual Spanish/English children's development of concepts and language.* Doctoral Dissertation. Austin, Texas: The University of Texas at Austin. (ERIC Document Reproduction Service No. ED 345 562).

Gonzalez, V. (1994). A model of cognitive, cultural, and linguistic variables affecting bilingual Hispanic children's development of concepts and language. *Hispanic Journal of Behavioral Sciences, 16*(4), 396-421.

Gonzalez, V. (1995). *Cognition, culture, and language in bilingual children: Conceptual and semantic development.* Bethesda, MD: Austin & Winfield.

Gonzalez, V., Bauerle, P., Black, W., & Felix-Holt, M. (1999). Influence of evaluators' beliefs and cultural-linguistic backgrounds on their diagnostic and placement decisions for language-minority children. In V. Gonzalez (Vol. Ed.), *Language and cognitive development in second language learning: Educational implications for children and adults* (pp. 269-297). Needham Heights, MA: Allyn & Bacon.

Gonzalez, V., Bauerle, P., & Felix-Holt, M. (1994). A qualitative assessment method for accurately diagnosing bilingual gifted children. *NABE Annual Conference Journal 1992-1993, 37*-52. Washington, DC: NABE.

Gonzalez, V., Bauerle, P, & Felix-Holt, M. (1996). Theoretical and practical implications of assessing cognitive and language development in bilingual children with qualitative methods. (*Bilingual Research Journal, 20*(1), 93-131.

Gonzalez, V., Brusca-Vega, R., & Yawkey, T. D. (199*7). Assessment and instruction of culturally and linguistically diverse students with or at-risk of learning problems: From research to practice.* Needham Heights, MA: Allyn & Bacon.

Gonzalez, V., & Clark, E. R. (1999). Folkloric and historic views of giftedness in language-minority children. In V. Gonzalez (Vol. Ed.), *Language and cognitive development in second language learning: Educational implications for children and adults* (pp. 1-18). Needham Heights, MA: Allyn & Bacon.

Harrison, A. O., Wilson, M. N., Pine, C. J., Chan, S. Q., & Buriel, R. (1990). Family ecologies of ethnic minority children. *Child Development, 61,* 347-362.

Hill, M. S., & Sandfort, J. R. (1995). Effects of childhood poverty on productivity later in life: Implications for public policy. *Children & Youth Services Review, 17*(1/2), 91-126.

Masten, A. S., & Coatsworth, J. D. (1998). The development of competence in favorable and unfavorable environments. *American Psychologist, 53*(2), 205-220.

McLoyd, V. C. (1998). Socioceconomic disadvantage and child development. *American Psychologist, 53*(2), 185-204.

Markman, E. M., & Hutchinson, J. E. (1984). Children's sensitivity to constraints on word meaning: Taxonomic vs. thematic relations. *Cognitive Psychology, 16,* 1-27.

Ochs, E., & Schiefellin, B. B. (1984). Language acquisition and socialization: three developmental stories. In R. Shweder & R. LeVine (Eds.) *Culture theory: Essays on mind, self, and emotion* (pp. 276-320). Cambridge University Press.

Ogbu, J. (1982). Cultural discontinuity and schooling. *Anthropology and Education Quarterly, 13*(4), 290-307.

Oviedo, M. D., & Gonzalez, V. (1999). Standardized and alternative assessments: Diagnosis accuracy in minority children referred for special education assessment. In V. Gonzalez (Vol. Ed.), *Language and cognitive development in second language learning: Educational implications for children and adults* (pp. 227-269). Needham Heights, MA: Allyn & Bacon.

Piaget, J. (1967). Piaget's theory. In P. H. Mussen (Ed.), *Carmichael's manual of child psychology,* Vol. I , (pp. 703-732). New York: John Wiley & Sons.

Suarez-Orozco, M. (1989). *Central American refugees and US high schools: A psychological study of motivation and achievement.* Stanford, CA: Stanford University Press.

Shatz, M. (1991). Using cross-cultural research to inform us about the role f language in development: Comparisons of Japanese, Korean, and English, and of German, American English, and British English. In M. H. Bornstein (Ed.), *Cultural approaches to parenting_*(pp.139-153). Hillsdale, NJ: Lawrence Erlbaum Associates.

US Bureau of the Census (1996). *Statistical Abstract of the United States: 1996.* Washington DC: US Government Printing Office.

US Bureau of the Census (1994*). Statistical Abstract of the United States: 1994.* Washington DC: US Government Printing Office.

Wang, A. Y. (1993). Cultural-familial predictors of children's metacognitive and academic performance. *Journal of Research in Childhood Education, 7*(2), 83-90.

Waxman, S. R. (1990). Linking language and conceptual development: Linguistic cues and the construction of conceptual hierarchies. *The Genetic Epistemologist, 17,*13-20.

Table 4.1
Double Scoring Classification System for Tasks:
General and Gender-Based Criteria

	Classification System		
	General	Gender-Based	
Level	**Abstract Categories**	**Semantic Categories**	
No classification			
Pre-conceptual: Perceptual Features	Color Size Parts	*Extralinguistic Features*	in relation to physical gender
Pre-conceptual: Functional	Activities	*Extralinguistic Features*	in relation to functional groups
Concrete	Subcategories	*Extralinguistic & Intralinguistic Features*	in relation to linguistic gender assignment and physical gender
Metalinguistic		*Intralinguistic*	in relation to gender
		Features	linguistic structures and markers

Table 4.2.

Double Scoring Classification System for the Defining Task

Defining Task

General Classification System *Extralinguistic Features*	Gender-Based Classification System *Intralinquist Features*
PERCEPTUAL FEATURES	
(pigs) **Colors**	
"They are black."	"The cow that has more pink on her lips is the mom."
Parts of the Body	
"They have two eyes."	"The dad has a lot of hair."
(dinosaurs)	
Size	"The big one is the daddy, the tiny one is the mommy."
FUNCTIONAL	
(pigs) **Activities**	
"They do noises."	"The dad always sleeps, the mom goes and looks for food."
(birds) "They fly."	
CONCRETE	
Subcategories	
(Cows) "They are mammals."	"Some are women and some are men."
METALINGUISTIC	
"The cow and the bull have different names, but they are the same kind of animals."	"The cats are the same, this can be the daddy or this can be the mommy but you can not exchange the cow & bull, they are the same kind of animal but they look different."

Table 4.3.
Double Scoring Classification System for the Sorting,
Category Clue, and Verbal Justification of Sorting Tasks

Sorting/Category Clue/Verbal Justification of Sorting Tasks

General Classification System	Gender-Based Classification System
PERCEPTUAL FEATURES	By Gender: "The Moms are smaller and the dads are bigger."
Extralinguistic Features Two lines in parallel correspondence or one group with no spatial arrangements No subcategories by color, size, or parts of the body	
FUNCTIONAL	by Gender: "These are for the girls and these are for the boys"
Extralinguistic Features Two parallel lines in correspondence or one group with no spatial arrangements. No subcategories by Activities	
CONCRETE	*Extralinguistic Features* *and Intralinguistic Features* by Gender: "These are men and these are women."
METALINGUISTIC	*Intralinguistic Features* by Gender: "These start with el and these with la."

Table 4.4.
Frequencies and Percentages of Family Demographic Variables
Reported in the Home Language Survey

Variable	Frequencies	Percentage
Language Used at Home		
Mothers Spanish	41	68.5
Fathers Spanish	44	73.5
Children Spanish	32	53.5
Siblings Spanish	29	48.5
Parents' Proficiency in Spanish		
Mothers		
Not quite adequate	12	20.0
Adequate	5	3.8
Above average	3	5.0
Fathers		
Not quite adequate	17	28.3
Adequate	6	10.0
Above average	2	3.3
Parents' Proficiency in English		
Mothers		
Not English speakers	30	50.0
Adequate	15	25.0
Above average	5	8.4
Fathers		
Not English speakers	31	51.6
Not quite adequate	17	28.3
Adequate	10	16.6
Above average	2	3.3
Children's Proficiency in Spanish as Rated by Parents		
Not quite adequate	2	35.0
Adequate	9	15.0
Above average	6	10.0

Table 4.4 continued . . .

Variable	Frequencies	Percentage

Parents' Proficiency in English as Rated by Parents

Not English speakers	24	40.0
Adequate	9	15.0
Above average	1	1.6

Effect of Schooling on Children Spanish & English Proficiency

Increase their Use of Spanish	4	6.6
Increase their Use of English	25	41.6
Increase their Use of English	2	3.3
No Change	29	48.5

Use of Code Mixing and Code Switching

Not Used by Children	38	63.5
Used by Children	22	36.5

Educational Level of Parents

Mothers

Finished High School	38	63.4
Bachelors Degree	12	20.0
Masters Degree	4	6.6
Attended College for 1-2 yrs.	3	5.0
Attended College for 3 yrs. or more	3	5.0

Fathers

Finished High School	42	70.2
Bachelors Degree	12	20.0
Attended College for 1-2 yrs.	3	5.0
Attended College for 3 yrs. or more	1	1.6

Table 4.4 continued . . .

Variable	Frequencies	Percentage
Occupation of Parents		
Mothers		
Homemakers	38	63.5
Blue collar jobs	17	28.3
White collar jobs	1	1.6
Professionals	4	6.6
Fathers		
Unemployed	3	5.0
Blue collar jobs	44	73.5
White collar jobs	3	5.0
Professionals	10	16.5
Number of Siblings		
One sibling	22	36.5
Two siblings	16	26.6
Three siblings	5	8.3
Birth Order		
First born	24	40.0
Second born	22	36.6
Third or Fourth Child	5	8.5
Fifth or Seventh	2	3.3
Parents' Number of Years in the U.S.		
1 to 5 years	5	8.4
6 to 10 years	15	25.0
11-15 years	4	66.0
16 or more years	36	60.0

Table 4.5

Pearson Correlation of the Home Language Survey Information Reported by Parents

Variable	1	2	3	4	5	6	7	8	9	10	11	12
1. Home language of mother	1.00											
2. Home language of father	.459	1.00										
3. Home language of child	.657**	.590	1.00									
4. Home Language of siblings	.666**	.602**	,897**	1.00								
5. Mother's proficiency in Spanish	.575**	.285	.396*	.319	1.00							
6. Father's proficiency in Spanish	-.666**	-.388*	-.675**	-.721**	-.238	1.00						
7. Mother's proficiency in English	.200	.548**	.382*	.300	.080	.003	1.00					
8. Father's proficiency in English	-.353*	-.390*	-.387-	-.486**	-.088	.252-	.243	1.00				
9. Child's proficiency in Spanish	.527**	.537**	.689**	.641**	.491**	-.451**	.249	-.296	1.00			
10. Child's proficiency in English	-.267	-.226	-.397**	-.502**	-.065	.562**	.055	.303	-.124	1.00		
11. Mother's years of US Residence	-.593**	-.389**	-.520**	-.619**	-.288	.689**	-.208	.248	-.428**	.240	1.00	
12. Father's years of US Residence	-.519**	-.411**	-.604**	-.652**	-.187	.625**	-.249	.328*	-.386**	.282*	.887**	1.00

Note ** Correlation is significant at the.01level (2 tailed), p<.01

* Correlation is significant at the.05 level (2 tailed), p<.05

Table 4.6.

One-Way ANOVA Tests for Home Language Survey Information as Independent Variables and Children's Performance in QUEST Sub-Tasks as Dependent Variables

IV/DV

		Sum of Squares	df	Mean Square	F	Sig.
Home Language of Mother						
•Labeling A, Gd	Between Groups	1.626	1	1.626	3.839	.055
	Within Groups	22.022	52	.424		
	Total	23.648	53			
•Defining A, Gd	Between Groups	9.700	1	9.700	6.617	.013
	Within Groups	76.226	52	1.466		
	Total	85.926	53			
•Defining F, Gd	Between Groups	7.900	1	7.900	5.829	.019
	Within Groups	70.471	52	1.355		
	Total	78.370	53			
•Cat. Cl. F, Gd	Between Groups	9.036	1	9.036	5.182	.027
	Within Groups	90.668	52	1.744		
	Total	99.704	53			
Home Language of Child						
•Labeling F, Gd	Between Groups	2.715	1	2.715	7.558	.008
	Within Groups	17.958	50	.359		
	Total	20.673	51			

Table 4.6 continued . . .

		Sum of Squares	df	Mean Square	F	Sig.
•Defining F, Gd	Between Groups	6.055	1	6.055	4.126	.048
	Within Groups	73.387	50	1.468		
	Total	79.442	51			
•Cat. Cl. F, Gd	Between Groups	10.718	1	10.718	6.189	.016
	Within Groups	86.589	50	1.732		
	Total	97.308	51			

Home Language of Siblings

		Sum of Squares	df	Mean Square	F	Sig.
•Labeling F, Gd	Between Groups	1.768	1	1.768	6.321	.016
	Within Groups	10.632	38	.280		
	Total	12.400	39			
•Cat .Cl. F, Gd	Between Groups	6.741	1	6.741	3.901	.056
	Within Groups	65.659	38	1.728		
	Total	72.400	39			

Mother's Spanish Language Proficiency

		Sum of Squares	df	Mean Square	F	Sig.
•Labeling A, Gl	Between Groups	2.222	3	.741	3.223	.032
	Within Groups	9.422	41	.230		
	Total	11.644	44			

Table 4.6 continued . . .

		Sum of Squares	df	Mean Square	F	Sig.
Mother's English Language Proficiency						
•Cat. Cl. F, Gl	Between Groups	18.651	3	6.217	3.659.	020
	Within Groups	69.660	41	1.699		
	Total	88.311	44			
•Cat. Cl. F, Gd	Between Groups	23.096	3	7.699	5.190	.004
	Within Groups	60.815	41	1.483		
	Total	83.911	44			
Father's English Language Proficiency						
•Sorting F, Gl	Between Groups	9.384	3	3.128	2.781	.054
	Within Groups	42.735	38	1.125		
	Total	52.119	41			
•Sorting F, Gd	Between Groups	17.635	3	5.878	3.896	.016
	Within Groups	57.341	38	1.509		
	Total	87.976	41			
Child's Spanish Language Proficiency						
•Sorting F, Gd	Between Groups	18.149	3	6.050	3.369	.025
	Within Groups	98.766	55	1.796		
	Total	116.915	58			

Table 4.6 continued . . .

		Sum of Squares	df	Mean Square	F	Sig.
•Cat Cl F, Gd	Between Groups	15.026	3	5.009	3.067	.035
	Within Groups	89.822	55	1.633		
	Total	104.847	58			

Schooling Effect on Child's Spanish and English Language Proficiency

		Sum of Squares	df	Mean Square	F	Sig.
•Labeling A, Gl	Between Groups	4.394	3	1.465	5.897	.002
	Within Groups	10.184	41	.248		
	Total	4.578	44			
•Defining A, Gl	Between Groups	5.749	3	1.916	3.082	.038
	Within Groups	25.495	41	.622		
	Total	31.244	44			
•VJS. A, Gd	Between Groups	21.548	3	7.183	4.228	.011
	Within Groups	69.652	41	1.699		
	Total	91.299	44			

Code Mixing

		Sum of Squares	df	Mean Square	F	Sig.
•Sorting F, Gl	Between Groups	7.350		7.350	4.611	.036
	Within Groups	94.059	59	1.594		
	Total	101.410	60			

Table 4.6 continued . . .

Number of Siblings

		Sum of Squares	df	Mean Square	F	Sig.
•Labeling A, Gd	Between Groups	6.108	5	1.222	3.501	.007
	Within Groups	22.681	65	.349		
	Total	28.789	70			
•Labeling F, Gd	Between Groups	5.891	5	1.178	3.918	.004
	Within Groups	19.545	65	.301		
	Total	25.437	70			
•Sorting A, Gl	Between Groups	27.171	5	5.434	5.696	.001
	Within Groups	62.012	65	.954		
	Total	89.183	70			
•Sorting A, Gd	Between Groups	25.983	5	5.197	4.701	.001
	Within Groups	71.848	65	1.105		
	Total	97.831	70			

Number of Siblings

		Sum of Squares	df	Mean Square	F	Sig.
•Cat Cl A, Gl	Between Groups	21.206	5	4.241	3.373	.009
	Within Groups	81.724	65	1.257		
	Total	102.930	70			
•Cat Cl A, Gd	Between Groups	31.881	5	6.376	4.534	.001
	Within Groups	91.414	65	1.406		
	Total1	23.296	70			

Table 4.6 continued . . .

		Sum of Squares	df	Mean Square	F	Sig.
Birth Order						
•Sorting A, Gl	Between Groups	15,019	5	3.004	2.633	.031
	Within Groups	74.164	65	1.141		
	Total	89.183	70			
•Sorting A, Gd	Between Groups	20.021	5	4.004	3.345	.009
	Within Groups	77.810	65	1.197		
	Total	97.831	70			
•Cat Cl A, Gl	Between Groups	18.089	5	3.618	2.772	.025
	Within Groups	84.840	65	1.305		
	Total	102.930	70			
Birth Order						
•Cat Cl A, Gd	Between Groups	26.406	5	5.281	3.543	.007
	Within Groups	96.889	65	1.491		
	Total	123.296	70			
Mother's Occupation						
•Cat Cl A, Gd	Between Groups	22.140	3	7.380	4.775	.005
	Within Groups	98.919	64	1.546		
	Total1	21.059	67			

Table 4.6 continued . . .

		Sum of Squares	df	Mean Square	F	Sig.
Father's Occupation						
•Labeling F, Gl	Between Groups	2.728	3	.909	3.170	.031
	Within Groups	16.923	59	.287		
	Total	19.651	62			
•Defining F, Gl	Between Groups	6.234	3	2.078	3.037	.036
	Within Groups	40.369	59	.684		
	Total	46.603	62			
Mother's Educational Level						
•Defining A, Gd	Between Groups	25.865	4	6.466	5.982	.001
	Within Groups	52.969	49	1.081		
	Total	78.833	53			
Mother's Educational Level						
•Defining F, Gd	Between Groups	29.193	4	7.298	7.049	.001
	Within Groups	50.733	49	1.035		
	Total	79.926	53			
•Sorting F, Gd	Between Groups	22.707	4	5.677	3.214	.020
	Within Groups	86.552	49	1.766		
	Total	109.259	53			

Table 4.6 continued . . .

		Sum of Squares	df	Mean Square	F	Sig.
•VJS A, Gd	Between Groups	22.269	4	5.567	3.252	.019
	Within Groups	83.879	49	1.712		
	Total	106.148	53			

Father's Educational Level

•Defining A, Gd	Between Groups	14.885	5	2.977	2.546	.042
	Within Groups	49.115	42	1.169		
	Total	64.000	47			

Mother's Years of U.S. Residence

•Labeling F, Gd	Between Groups	3.991	3	1.330	4.194	.010
	Within Groups	17.129	54	.317		
	Total	21.121	57			
•Defining A, Gd	Between Groups	13.433	3	4.478	3.004	.038
	Within Groups	80.498	54	1.491		
	Total	93.931	57			
•Defining F, Gd	Between Groups	11.516	3	3.839	2.958	.040
	Within Groups	70.071	54	1.298		
	Total	81.586	57			

Table 4.6 continued . . .

		Sum of Squares	df	Mean Square	F	Sig.
•Cat Cl F, Gd	Between Groups	30.860	3	10.287	7.602	.001
	Within Groups	73.071	54	1.353		
	Total	103.931	57			

Father's Number of Years of US Residence

		Sum of Squares	df	Mean Square	F	Sig.
•Labeling F, Gd	Between Groups	4.371	3	1.457	5.125	.004
	Within Groups	13.931	49	.284		
	Total	18.302	52			

Father's Number of Years of U.S. Residence

		Sum of Squares	df	Mean Square	F	Sig.
•Defining A, Gd	Between Groups	16.269	3	5.423	3.893	.014
	Within Groups	68.259	49	1.393		
	Total	84.528	52			
•Cat Cl F, Gd	Between Groups	20.356	3	6.785	4.915	.005
	Within Groups	67.644	49	1.380		
	Total	88.000	52			

Note:
A   Animals
F   Food
Gl   General Scoring System
Gd   Linguistic Gender Scoring System
VJS   Verbal Justification of Sorting Task
Cat Cl Category Clue Task

5

Parents' Perceptions and Home Environmental Factors Influencing Potential Giftedness in Monolingual Low and High Socioeconomic Status (SES) Preschoolers

℘ℑℂℜ

Nina Williams and Virginia Gonzalez

Introduction

C hapter 6 continues with the Part III of the book on an alternative research view to the study of development and academic achievement in language-minority and mainstream children. More specifically, Chapter 6 deals with external home and school environmental similarities and differences affecting low and high socioeconomic status (SES) monolingual children's psychological development, learning processes, and academic performance. Chapter 6 highlights the theme of psychological, developmental, environmental, and SES factors affecting monolingual children's assessment and academic performance. In addition, Chapter 6 highlights other themes of the book by clearly demonstrating the need for an alternative *developmental* view to assessment and academic performance when studying and serving monolingual economically advantaged and disadvantaged young learners.

That is, the study presented in Chapter 6 is used to illustrate the important role of home cultural factors on monolingual advantaged and disadvantaged preschool children's cognitive development, as measured by both standardized and alternative assessments within the mainstream school cultural environment. More specifically this study focuses on the influence of parents' perceptions and home environment on preschoolers' cognitive development before they were identified as gifted. Thirteen high SES and 13 low SES preschool children were referred for giftedness evaluation by their parents and teachers. Most children were mainstream (24 Caucasian), with a small proportion of minority children (1 African-American and 1 Asian-American). All children were monolingual, with an equal representation of females and males in both high and low SES groups.

Parents were surveyed and interviewed and the children were administered two cognitive skills measures:

1. Kaufman Assessment Battery for Children (K-ABC)

2. Qualitative Use of English and Spanish Tasks (QUEST, Gonzalez, 1994, 1995)

Patterns found suggested that:

1. Parental perceptions about giftedness were related to environmental factors, and the children's personality and language development

2. Some home environmental factors (i.e., father's education, number of siblings, mother's work hours, and time parents spend with children) predicted the children's performance on the cognitive measures.

It was concluded that parental perceptions and the home environment are reciprocal external factors influencing children's cognitive development before giftedness identification.

Objectives and Purposes

The purpose of the study is to explore the influence of two major external factors, parental perceptions about cognitive development and home environment, on children's potential giftedness *before* the identification process is initiated. This study was conducted with the general objective of identifying parental perceptions about the meaning of giftedness and the development of giftedness, which might have a positive effect on potentially gifted children. As reflected in the research questions below, it was anticipated that parental perceptions would have a major impact on the creation of a positive home environment for stimulating children's cognitive development.

That is, it is important to identify parental perceptions about giftedness even before the child is identified because:

1. The parents may already display certain *typical* perceptions of the cognitive development of their child

2. These *typical* parental perceptions may contribute to the creation of a home environment influencing positively the development of cognitive giftedness in a child

More specifically, this study has six objectives, the first two were investigated within a qualitative research design, and the latter four were tested within a quantitative research design.

Within a descriptive or qualitative model, this study has a twofold objective, to identify and describe the specific parental perceptions about:

1. The meaning (or definitions) of giftedness

2. The influence of internal (biological) and external (environmental) factors on the development of cognitive giftedness in preschool children.

These two descriptive objectives are addressed by the use of four screening instruments:

1. A parents' survey for their child's referral for giftedness evaluation, used for sample selection and for the identification of parental perceptions about the meaning and the development of giftedness

2. A teacher's survey for the referral of potentially gifted children, used for sample selection purposes

3. Parent interview questions, used for identifying parental perceptions about internal and external factors influencing children's cognitive development

4. Classroom participant observations

Then, within a statistical model using multiple regression and correlation tests, three more objectives were investigated, to study if:

1. The identified parental perceptions, uncovered in the qualitative data, were predictive of their own child's scores on cognitive skills measures (Kaufman Assessment Battery for Children—K-ABC, Kaufman & Kaufman, 1983, and Qualitative Use of English and Spanish Tasks—QUEST)

2. There is any relationship between four home environmental factors (i.e., amount of time parents spend with their child, parents' work hours, parents' educational attainment, and the number of siblings) and the child's scores on cognitive skills measures (K-ABC and QUEST)

3. There is any relationship between the parents' SES (based on the parents' combined income range) and their child's scores on cognitive skills measures (K-ABC and QUEST)

These latter three statistical research questions are addressed by the use of seven instruments (listed in order of administration, from referral and screening to diagnostic tools):

1. A parents' survey for their child's referral for giftedness evaluation, used for sample selection and for identifying parental perceptions about the meaning of giftedness and the development of giftedness

2. A teacher's survey for the referral of potentially gifted children, used for sample selection purposes

3. A demographic questionnaire, developed by the authors, for gathering data on the five home environmental factors

4. Parent interview questions, also developed by the authors, for identifying parental perceptions about the meaning and development of giftedness

5. The American Guidance Service Home/Health Survey (Harrison, 1990), used as a screening tool for identifying the overall home environment

6. The K-ABC

7. The QUEST (Gonzalez, 1994, 1995)

Developmental Conceptual Framework for the Study of Parents' Perceptions and Home Environmental Factors Affecting Giftedness

The conceptual theoretical framework provided below critically discusses important external variables affecting the development of children's giftedness, which need to be further studied. This study contributes to the extensive literature on the description of the characteristics of gifted children and their home environments by investigating two novel factors:

1. The influence of parental perceptions on the creation of a positive psychological home environment for the development of children's potential for giftedness

2. The pre-existing nature of these parental perceptions about cognitive development to the children's identification of giftedness

Much research has been conducted for the purpose of describing the characteristics of gifted children, and their families and home environments (e.g., Cornell & Grossberg, 1986; Karnes & D'Ilio, 1988; Kulieke & Olszewski-Kubilius, 1989). Researchers have touched on many issues centered around gifted children including problems of parents of gifted children, family adaptation, sibling relationships, social and adjustment issues, and educational concerns (e.g., Abelman, 1987; Ballering & Koch, 1984; Hackney, 1981; Keirouz, 1990; Passow, 1994). The literature is also saturated with several different definitions of giftedness (e.g., Banks & McGee-Banks, 1993; Bracken, 1991; Witt, Elliot, Kramer, &

Greshem, 1994). Statistical results are also readily available to outline the typical demographic characteristics of gifted children and their families (e.g., VanTassel, Olszewski-Kubilius, & Borland, 1989). It is not difficult to find applications of this research data in describing the *typical* portrait of a gifted child's family (e.g., Moss, 1990; Sebring, 1983).

Traditional and contemporary theories have been used in describing the effect that home environmental characteristics can have on children's cognitive development. Traditionally, it was suggested that only higher SES homes were able to produce a child with *gifted* cognitive abilities (Khatena, 1982). In spite of what the traditional research findings indicate, it may be that children from higher SES homes are commonly identified as gifted merely because they are referred by their teachers and parents more often than children from lower SES homes (Awanbor, 1991).

On the other hand, contemporary authors have suggested that some other home environmental factors, besides SES, may contribute to a child's cognitive development (Harrison, 1990), such as:

1. Time parents spend with their child

2. Parents' work hours

3. Parental level of education

4. The number of siblings living in the home.

The traditional SES factor, and the latter four home environmental factors identified by contemporary literature, are going to be used in this study as independent variables for investigating their predictive power and relation to:

1. Parental perceptions about children's cognitive development

2. Two measures of cognitive development (K-ABC and QUEST)

It is our argument that parental perceptions about external factors influencing giftedness create certain psychological home environments that positively influence the cognitive development of children. The influences in a very young child's life are centered in the home environment; such as parental perceptions influencing the quality of the communicative and emotional relationship the child has with his parents. That is, the manner in which a parent influences a child's cognitive development is not only dependent upon the parental SES related to the actual physical home environment, but also dependent upon the parental perceptions creating a psychological home environment. In fact, it is our argument that parents' perceptions are a major influence imposed on the developing child, and could be considered one of the most crucial factors in the child's intelligence development. As suggested by Baumrind (1978), parents can not avoid influencing very strongly the personality, character, and competence of their children.

In this study, the parents are referring their child for giftedness evaluation. Thus, the parents have already developed implicit perceptions about their child's abilities, and beliefs of what giftedness means. Then, these perceptions are implicit beliefs consisting of intellectual constructions that already reside in the mind's of the individuals (Sternberg, 1985; Sternberg & Lubart, 1993), which are expressed in the form of culturally defined values such as achievement expectations. Through their own perceptions, parents may create and uphold certain expectations of their child. Strom, Johnson, and Strom (1990) have suggested that the extent to which youngsters, particularly those from ethnic and low income families, have the opportunity at home to develop skills and behaviors that are indicative of a gifted child depends greatly on parents' expectations. People's perceptions of giftedness have many components; among them a development of individual, implicit explanations about the nature of giftedness (Gagne, Belanger, & Motard, 1993). Many studies reveal perceptions among professionals about the definition of giftedness, and the factors contributing to cognitive development (Sternberg, 1993; Sternberg & Lubart, 1993; Gagne, et al., 1993). This wide variety of perspectives among specialists in gifted education suggests similar diversity among others, including parents.

Contemporary research has taken a more holistic and dynamic approach to understanding the influence demographic factors have on the cognitive development of a child. Presently it is acceptable to consider evaluation for giftedness for children from all ethnic, SES, and cultural backgrounds (Bracken, 1991; Witt, Elliot, Kramer, & Gresham, 1994). The labeling of a child as gifted is no longer an exclusivity for children born into certain social class or ethnic group. Since new definitions of giftedness, such as Gardner's (1983) theory of multiple intelligences and Sternberg's (1995) theory of "implicit" giftedness, have been presented and accepted, the label of giftedness is possible for children from all SES and ethnic backgrounds.

A study by Awanbor (1991) suggested that the SES home background has no significant effect on whether a child is evaluated for possible giftedness. However, it is less likely for a child from a lower SES to be referred and ultimately assessed for intellectual giftedness. For instance, the Head Start Program has increased the emphasis on educational opportunities for children from low SES homes and culturally diverse backgrounds. However, even in this target program for low SES children, the focus is still on serving children experiencing some educational difficulty, rather than potential cognitive giftedness (Karnes & Johnson, 1991). Confirming the lack of programs for lower SES gifted children are the results of a study by Stile, Kitano, Kelley, and Lecrone (1993). They found that only 52% of the US states responding to their survey study reported having gifted children from disadvantaged families who were receiving some type of special consideration.

Even though statistics suggest urgent need for educational programs for lower SES gifted children, this study recognizes also need for considering children from all backgrounds for potential cognitive giftedness. In this study, it is proposed that children from low SES backgrounds are merely not referred for giftedness evaluation as often due to misconceptions still predominant among educators. Thus, it is expected that the SES of the child's family will have little or no bearing on the child's ability to perform cognitively, provided that assessment measures tap potential for giftedness, and not amount of information learned.

Thus, we have observed that traditional and contemporary literature is exhaustive in examining the parental perceptions and home environmental factors influencing gifted children's cognitive development, but only *after* the child's giftedness has been identified. Descriptive characteristics of gifted children and their parents dominate the body of contemporary research with the assumption that parental perceptions emerged only *after* the identification of their child's giftedness. That is, the unique personality features developed by parents once their children are identified as gifted has also been investigated by contemporary research. Studies typically indicate that parents have unique concerns and expectations regarding their gifted child (Keirouz, 1980). Information is also available about studies on the characteristics of families with children identified as gifted (Barbe, 1975).

In addition, we believe that the parents' behaviors, identified by contemporary literature as the four major home environmental factors mentioned above, have a powerful effect on gifted children's development. However, we also argue that these four contemporary home environmental factors represent a reflection of parental perceptions, which in turn create a specific psychological home environment that stimulates the children's cognitive potential. Furthermore, it is our argument that parental perceptions are pre-existing environmental influences to the child's giftedness. That is, it is our position that parental perceptions are not a result of labeling the child as gifted, but rather *pre-exist* the giftedness identification process. Thus, several questions are left unanswered by contemporary research. There is need to further investigate the effect of parental perceptions on the creation of a home environment that stimulates their child's potential for giftedness, *before* the identification process has been initiated. As discussed in the section below, parental perceptions affecting the development of potentially gifted children are the focus of this study.

Some of these open research questions lead us to design the present study, such as:

1. What do parents think giftedness means?

2. How do parents define the characteristics of a gifted child?

3. How do parents believe giftedness is developed in a child?

4. What do parents do to encourage the development of giftedness in their own child?

5. What are the major factors that parents believe stimulate cognitive development?

Developmental Position Taken in the Study

In this study, an interaction developmental position is taken by recognizing that the environment (including parental perceptions) to a greater extent, and genetics to a lesser extent, contribute to the development of giftedness in a child. This position endorsed supports that children are born with some individual degree of cognitive potential which can be further develop when exposed to a rich environment. This view proposes cognitive development as a dynamic process that changes with learning within the context of the home environment. In this sense, it is believed that the extrinsic influences, imposed by the parental perceptions within the context of the home environment, could be one of the most crucial in the formation of a child's intelligence development. In this study, a more contemporary view is proposed in light of the most recent definitions of giftedness. This contemporary perspective views intelligence as a dynamic process, one that is independent of ethnicity, gender, or SES. It is recognized that parental educational attainment (often reflected by the parents' professions) is not a direct indication of whether or not a child is cognitively gifted (Awanbor, 1991).

Furthermore, it is considered that external factors contributing to the development of a child's cognitive giftedness exist in the home environment even *before* the child is diagnosed as gifted. However, researchers have neglected to examine the influence of parental perceptions about cognitive development on the creation of a home environment before a child is identified as gifted.

This study contributes to the literature by exploring external influences in potentially gifted children, who were referred by their parents and teachers for further cognitive evaluation. This study contributes a multidimensional perspective to the literature on giftedness identification and external factors influencing giftedness. This study recognizes that the home environment is critical to the child's development in social, psychological, moral, emotional, cognitive, linguistic, and academic learning areas.

In addition, it is important to include parents and teachers in the referral or screening process of potentially gifted children. It is considered that parents and teachers are the most important social and moral agents affecting the development of children. Educational decisions should not be made on one test or assessment, this is particularly true when the child is a minority or from a lower SES background (Zeidner & Most, 1992). Therefore this study supports the use of multiple assessment instruments in the identification of giftedness in a child, which should be designed for specific population, and diagnosis and instructional planning purposes. Moreover, gifted young children warrant early identification due to: (1) need to interact with other peers of similar talents and abilities (Strom et al., 1990), (2) greater range of levels of academic competence (Hall, 1993) and (3) the potential development of negative attitudes toward school and learning (Shaklee, 1993).

Research Questions

Within a qualitative research design to descriptive research questions were examined:

1. What are the parental perceptions about the meaning of giftedness?

2. What are the parental perceptions of the influence of internal and/or external factors on the child's cognitive development?

Then, within a quantitative design, two more research questions were tested statistically with a multiple regression and a correlation model:

3. Is there a relationship between some home environmental factors and the child's performance in cognitive measures?

4. Do parents' perceptions predict their child's performance in cognitive measures (K-ABC, Kaufman & Kaufman, 1983; and QUEST, Gonzalez, 1994, 1995)?

Methodology

Participants

Two populations were used to select two different groups of participants for this study: (1) a high SES preschool, and (2) three low SES preschools. The children ranged in ages from 4.0 years to 6.11 years, and had not already been identified as gifted. Both populations consisted of mostly Caucasian children (N=6), with two minority children in the high SES group (one African-American child adopted by White parents, and one Asian-American child from a Thai background). The middle-high SES population was from an urban are in the Southwest region of the US. The low SES population was from a rural are located in the North central region of the US.

From both populations, the sample was selected based on several criteria:

1. The child was presently attending the preschool

2. A parent consented to their child's participation in the study

3. The child was referred for potential giftedness by a parent, a teacher, or both a parent and a teacher

4. The child was not already identified as gifted

Low SES Group

The pool of subjects was selected from children attending three private preschools serving a five square mile low income clientele in the North central region of the US, in which there were no identified gifted children. The pool of subjects was comprised of 137 children who came from low SES homes, all with a parental combined annual income of less than $20,000. The referrals were received from 18 parents. The final sample consisted of 13 subjects, 8 males and 5 females, ranging in ages from 4.3 to 6.3. All of the subjects in this low SES group were Caucasian.

High SES Group

The pool of subjects was selected from children attending a private preschool in a middle-size metropolitan area in the Southwest region of the US, in which there were no identified gifted children. The pool of subjects was comprised of 60 children who came from high SES homes. The referrals were received from 9 parents, 3 parents and teachers, and 1 teachers. The final sample consisted of 13 children, 8 girls and 5 boys, whose ages ranged from 4 years, 1 month to 6 years, 5 months. The children's ethnicity was primarily Caucasian (N=11, 84.6%), with one African-American child adopted by White parents, and one Chinese-Thai child. All children in the sample lived in a two-parent household.

Instruments

Six instruments were used to obtain qualitative and quantitative information for this study:

1. Parent's and teacher's surveys for referral of giftedness

2. A demographic questionnaire

3. The American Guidance (AGS) Home Survey (Harrison, 1990)

4. An interview for parents

5. The Kaufman Assessment Battery for Children (K-ABC, Kaufman & Kaufman, 1983)

6. The Qualitative Use of English and Spanish Tasks (QUEST, Gonzalez, 1991, 1994, 1995).

Parents and Teachers Surveys for Referral of Giftedness

The teachers' survey was developed by the authors and used *only* for sample selection purposes. The parents' survey was developed by the authors and used for sampling purposes as well as for investigating the parents' perceptions about the meaning of giftedness.

The teachers' and parents' surveys included six open-ended questions:

1. What does giftedness mean to you?

2. Why do you think this child is gifted?

3. What special language abilities does this child have?

4. What special problem-solving abilities does this child have?

5. In what ways does this child interact with other children?

6. Does this child have any other specific talents/abilities?

These questions were preceeded by a statement of intent of the authors. For constructing these surveys, ten students taking a course in preschool assessment at an Educational Psychology Department served as judges. Judges feedback, and suggestions provided by Nielsen and Buchanan (1991) were used for the specificity of changes. As a result, the clarity of the language and format of the surveys (face validity) was improved; and content and construct validity was increased, assuring that the variables intended to be measured by the survey questions were represented exhaustively. The surveys were also pilot-tested on a sample of five teachers and five parents, and their suggestions were followed in order to assure face validity for these surveys.

Demographic Questionnaire

It was developed by the authors for the purpose of identifying home environment characteristics: the parents' educational level, age, income range, SES, and work hours. Most questions used an affirmative-negative and multiple-choice format. Some questions were open-ended, requiring a brief description or explanation. This questionnaire was also reviewed by the same ten graduate students acting as judges for the parents' and teachers' surveys. The use of judges assured face, content, and construct validity of this instrument.

American Guidance Service Home Survey

This survey includes 12-items to be completed by the parents. The items sample variables of the home environment and parent-child interactions that have been shown by previous research to contribute to a child's overall development, including cognitive development (Harrison, 1990). This survey was standardized in a US large stratified sample representing geographical regions and cultural backgrounds. This survey was used for the parents to rate the overall home environment of the child.

The items represent four areas of the overall home environment:

1. Types of play materials

2. Number of books in the home

3. The frequency of parental reading, talking, and playing with the child

4. The amount of responsibility given to the child

Parents' Interview

The interview questions were designed to examine the parental perceptions about the influence of internal and external factors on their children's development of giftedness. The interview questions also help clarify perceptions expressed by the parents in their written responses to the surveys. This instrument's face, content, and construct validity was assured by using the same ten students acting as judges for the parents' and teachers' surveys, and demographic questionnaire.

Five open-ended questions were developed by the authors:

1. What do you think have been the major influences on your child's advanced development?

2. Do you think that some resources in your home have influenced your child's advanced development?

3. Do you think that any biological factors have influenced the advanced development of your child?

4. Who is the primary caretaker of this child? Why?

5. How do you think the quality of this relationship with the child has influenced his/her development?

Kaufman Assessment Battery for Children (K-ABC)

The K-ABC is a standardized battery appropriate for preschoolers that measures intellectual functioning and achievement (Kaufman & Kaufman, 1983). In this instrument, intelligence is defined as an individual's ability to solve problems in novel situations, and is measured by two Mental Processing Scales: Sequential and Simultaneous. These two scales are combined into a Mental Processing Scale. This test separates achievement into a different scale, which is defined as previously acquired factual knowledge and skills. In general, the K-ABC appears well normed; as it was standardized using a stratified sample considering age, race, gender, parental education, geographic region, SES, and community size variables. The reliability coefficients reported in the K-ABC Interpretative Manual (Kaufman & Kaufman, 1983) indicate that it is a useful instrument for psychoeducational assessment. Test-retest reliability coefficients determined for children age 4 years, 0 months to 8 years, 11 months ranged from .61 to .84 for the Mental Processing Scale and .87 to .98 for the Achievement Scale. Then, the K-ABC seems to be a valid measure of problem-solving abilities in novel situations, and factual knowledge in young children.

The Qualitative Use of English and Spanish Tasks (QUEST)

Gonzalez (1991, 1994, 1995) developed a model that explains the verbal and non-verbal concept formation process in children . This model identifies two knowledge representational systems dependent on the particular cognitive, linguistic, and cultural characteristics of the content learned. The model from which the classification tasks were derived was based partially on Piagetian theory (Piaget, 1967) and on the constraint model (Markman, 1984, Waxman, 1990), and it was found to have construct validity as shown by parametric and non-parametric tests (Gonzalez, 1991). Stimuli for the five classification tasks consist of plastic full-color objects (animals and food) representing 14 groupings reflecting the interaction of cognitive, cultural, and linguistic factors. Stimuli groupings were validated using judges and three pilot tests for assuring content validity; and a stepwise multiple factor analyses for assuring construct validity.

Three of these five classification tasks are verbal including labeling, defining, and verbal justification of sorting; and two tasks are non-verbal including sorting and category clue. Tasks are described following the pre-established order of administration (for a more complete description of tasks see Gonzalez, 1991, 1994). For the labeling task, the child is presented plastic objects and asked to name them (What *do you call this?*), while giving her one item at a time, followed by the defining task at the production level in which the child is asked four different probes to elicit a description of the object(s) (*What is a ___?* ; *What is a ___ like?* , *Tell me something about a ___* , and *What does a ___ look like?*). After, for tapping the comprehension level of the defining task, the child is given a definition that points to verbal and non-verbal clues for class inclusion categories of objects (taxonomic categories: superordinate, intermediate, and subcategories). This definition is repeated three times, and after the child is asked to define three different kinds of items. For the sorting task, the child is asked to group the objects by linguistic gender; followed by the verbal justification of sorting task in which the child is asked to explain the order imposed on the objects, and she is presented with metalinguistic counterexamples that change groupings and labels. Finally, for the category clue task, the child is provided with a model of how to group objects using two pictures of identical dolls; and then she is asked to sort the objects following the model provided, to explain her groupings, and to answer metalinguistic counterexamples that change groupings and labels.

Even though QUEST has two language versions, only the English version was used for this study since the children were monolingual. QUEST was an appropriate instrument for measuring the cognitive development of potentially gifted children because of the developmental adequacy of its model, tasks, and materials. QUEST is an alternative measure that can alleviate certain traditional methodological problems when assessing cognitive and language development in potentially gifted children who are young, such as the need to: (1) control for external factors influencing validity and reliability (e.g., appropriate clarity and complexity of the language used in the instructions, individualizing administration of the items, providing a strong model that has been empirically tested for assuring construct validity), (2) provide a non-verbal scale by which children's cognitive development can be assessed independently from language behaviors, (3) use tasks that measure potential in cognitive non-verbal and verbal processes since the amount of learned factual knowledge is still small in preschoolers, and (4) use problem-solving tasks that have open-ended and unlimited possible solutions that recognize creativity and unique individual responses in its developmental scoring categories. For further information of the administration, scoring, and technical characteristics of QUEST see Gonzalez (1991, 1994, 1995); and Gonzalez, Brusca-Vega, and Yawkey (1997).

Procedure

First, all the parents and teachers were invited to nominate children to participate in this study. If parents wanted to refer their children for giftedness evaluation, then they had to: (1) sign a consent form, (2) fill out a Parent Survey, and (3) agree to self-participate in the home interview. Secondly, all the referred children by their parents and/or teachers, whose parents had signed the consent form, were observed in their classroom on at least two occasions by graduate educational psychology students. The observers worked in pairs and were asked by the instructor for the course (second author) to interact with the children during the observations.

The purpose of these observations was for the graduate students to become familiar with the children before administering individually the K-ABC. Descriptive and event observations of the children's cognitive and linguistic development were conducted. Even though recording of the observations separating context from behaviors, and interpretations from descriptions of behaviors, were written; they were not used as data in the study. Thirdly, children were individually administered the K-ABC (Kaufman & Kaufman, 1983) by the graduate students. Forthly, QUEST (Gonzalez, 1991, 1994, 1995) was individually administered to the children by the second author of this paper. Both cognitive measures were administered in a quiet room at the preschool. Finally, the first author scheduled an appointment at the parents' convenience to conduct a home visit . During this visit, at least one parent for each child was required to complete the demographic questionnaire before the interview was conducted. The interview was tape-recorded for assuring validity in data analysis.

Results and Discussion

Data Analysis Design and Coding

Both qualitative research question are addressed with a representation of trends in the data (gathered by the parents' interview and survey) accompanied by quotes and examples from parents' responses from the low and high SES groups. The third and fourth quantitative research questions were analyzed by means of descriptive statistics and Pearson Product Moment correlation coefficients. Descriptive statistics are presented for all the demographic characteristics of the children and their parents, as well as for the children's performance in the two measures of cognitive skills. Only the significant correlations are presented for the home environmental factors and the children's performance in cognitive measures. The last quantitative research question was analyzed using a regression test, and only the significant results for the parents' SES and the children's performance in cognitive measures are presented.

Then three detailed case studies for each low and high SES are presented to exemplify the patterns found in the qualitative data, and the significant results obtained in the statistical analysis of data. The case studies provide a lively context for understanding the conclusions merging qualitative and statistical findings presented as a summary of the results and discussion section.

Research Question 1:
What are the Parental Perceptions of the Meaning of Giftedness?

A total of six patterns were found, from which five were found to be common for both the low and high SES groups, and one pattern was present only in the low SES group. These patterns were classified in relation to the parents' perceptions of the children's verbal and non-verbal abilities (the first five patterns correspond to verbal abilities, and the latter two patterns correspond to non-verbal abilities), for which some frequencies are given at the end of this section as a summary.

The first pattern found was that parents often defined giftedness in terms of language abilities, in relation to four trends:

1. Advanced verbal abilities or early language learning. For example one parent said, "Her conversations are at adult levels..., " another parent commented "He has always been able to form complex sentences and paragraphs beyond his age level." Other comments, each given by a different parent, include "She was an early talker. She has a large vocabulary", "her language abilities showed at an early age. By 18 months she was speaking in full sentences and singing clearly."

2. Advanced ability and interest in rhymes. For example, one parent said "He loves to find rhyming words. Sometimes he makes up his own words, but he understands the concept of rhyming."

3. Advanced ability to understand conceptual language. For instance, one parent shared, "He can correctly incorporate words into his speech after the word is defined by me only one or two times."

4. Advanced ability to produce conceptual language. For example, one parent noted, "She likes to make up stories and songs. Right now she is making up a song about her own life." Another parent commented, "She makes up quite good stories and situations with her stuffed animals."

The second pattern found relates to parents describing their children as having a strong desire to learn, based on two traits:

1. The child is described as being inquisitive or seekers of new knowledge. For instance, one parent said, "Right now she is extremely anxious to learn how to read." Other parent said, "He asks questions above his age level." Another parent noted, "He asks unusually insightful, theological questions and has a very good memory. He will ask questions ion logical progressions that lay the foundation for his ultimate inquiry."

2. The child enjoys to learn and engages on his own in problem solving situations. For instance, this trend is made very clear by one parent response, "He will hear a word on television and ask us how to spell it. Even before we are able to give him an answer, he figures out how to spell it correctly on his own!"

The third pattern found refers to children having good memory skills. Parents tend to describe their child's cognitive abilities by referring to an advanced ability to remember in two ways:

1. The child could remember directions, location, and places very well. For example, one parent commented, "She remembers where every bridge is between one town and another." Another comment illustrates the children's ability to remember directions, "She has a tremendous memory for directions to different places... if I go the wrong way home she will tell me it is the wrong way." One parent wrote a comment about her child describing how to get somewhere, "You need to go to the toy store at the mall, in the last aisle and get one of these so you can be like me."

2. The child had an advanced ability to remember information. For example, one parent noted, "She could remember songs after hearing them only a few times, and she could 'read' a certain book cover to cover by memory by 2 1/2 years." Similarly, another parent commented, "By age 2 he knew the lord's Prayers completely by memory." Another parent explained, "She can re-tell a story she has heard weeks later."

The fourth pattern found was that most parents described their child's advanced abilities as encompassing a good imagination. For instance, one parent responded, "He has a very vivid imagination. He comes up with really neat things to build or play." Another comment made by a parent illustrates her child's imagination, "She talks a lot about dreams and heaven."

The fifth pattern was parents' tendency to describe their child as having advanced puzzle-solving skills. For instance, one parent responded, "By the time she was 3 years old, she was able to piece together a 60 piece puzzle." Another parent noted, "Her puzzle building abilities at age 2 and 3 were exceptional. She could take a 125 piece puzzle and assemble it with no guessing or 'trying' pieces in under 3 minutes with the puzzle picture face down." Similarly another parent wrote, "She does puzzles very quickly, and recently put together and adult shaped puzzle without any help."

The sixth pattern represents the low SES parents' tendency to describe their child as having advanced gross motor or athletic ability. For example, one parent commented, "He has a lot of natural athletic ability. He is a natural at his tumbling and baseball throwing. It is all in his coordination." Another parent noted, "She has the ability to bathe herself, and do her own hair. She can braid her own hair." Similarly, another parent described her son, "He is taking ice skating lessons. He is also very interested in gymnastics. He plays on the trampoline and does flips on his swing set."

In summary, qualitative analysis of the Parents' Survey and the at-home interview resulted in three general categories of the parents' perceptions of their child's development: verbal abilities, non-verbal abilities, and overall abilities. Three parents (11.5%) described their child's verbal abilities as average, 16 parents (61.5%) described them as above average, and 7 (26.9%) parents described them as superior. Six parents (23.1%) described their child's non-verbal abilities as average, 13 parents (50%) described them as above average, and 7 parents (26.9%) described them as superior. More qualitative analysis suggested only two sub-categories for parents' perceptions of their child's overall abilities. Seventeen parents (65.4%) described their child's overall abilities as above average, and 9 parents (34.6%) described them as superior.

Research Question 2:
What are the Parental Perceptions of the Influence of Internal and/or External Factors on the Child's Cognitive Development?

Five patterns were found in relation to the second research objective: to identify what factors parents think influenced their child's cognitive development. The first pattern indicated that eleven of the parents (42%, from which six from the high SES group and five from the low SES group) believed in an *equal combination of both genetics and environment* on the development of their child. One parent responded, "I think they get genetic and outside environmental influences." Another parent said, "I think that nature is one part of it, and nurture is the other." One parent commented on the biological factors influenced by the environment, "We have allowed him to develop his potential."

The second pattern found revealed that seven parents (27%, from which three from the high SES group, and four from the low SES group), described their belief that *mostly environmental*, bust also some genetic factors, had contributed to their child's cognitive development. For example, one parent responded, "Some he has born with, but most of his abilities it is stuff he has learned."

The third pattern revealed that five parents (19%, from which two from the high SES group, and three from the low SES group) hold the belief that *mostly genetic*, but also environmental factors had influenced their child's cognitive development. One parent indicated that "Probably some factors in the home have influenced my son's development, but also both my husband and I have several members in our families of origin who are very intelligent and very successful in life. We also believe that both my husband and I are above average in our intelligence. Another parent responded, "I do not think that we have anything in our home that most people do not have. I think that my husband and I are both intelligent."

The fourth pattern revealed that very few parents, only two (8%) from the high SES group, described the factors contributing to the development of their child based *only on environmental* variables. One respondent was the parents of an adopted child. When interviewed and asked if she thought that any environmental factors had influenced the development of her child, this mother emphatically responded, "Yes. The fact that she is healthy and can focus a lot and pay attention. Neither of her parents are geniuses though, and there are not any geniuses in the family or anything like that. However, she does not have to worry about any biological or genetic problems."

The fifth pattern found indicated that there was only one parent (4%) from the low SES group, who described the factors contributing to her child's development based *only on genetics* . She answered, "I think she was born with what she can do. Yeah, she was born with it because some people are not. We do not have much and I do not spend much time with her. Her preschool is not very good at teaching, they just play."

Thus, in summary more parents believed that environmental factors made a stronger influence on their child's cognitive development, with lower number of parents perceiving that internal or genetic factors would make a major contribution. In addition, most parents perceived that an equal combination of both environmental and genetic factors would contribute to the child's cognitive development.

Descriptive Analyses of Data

In Table 6.1., the children's K-ABC Scores are summarized into seven categories, from low extreme to upper extreme. In Table 6.2. the QUEST performance is presented in relation to the five developmental categories used for coding their verbal, non-verbal, and overall performance. Children's scores in the K-ABC ranged from below average to the upper extreme for all the categories (i.e., simultaneous, sequential, MPC, non-verbal, and achievement). In general, children's performance in the QUEST ranged from pre-conceptual: perceptual to concrete, with a predominance of the pre-conceptual: perceptual range.

Table 6.3. presents descriptive statistics, in the form of frequencies and percentages, for some of he home environmental factors, including time parents spend with their child, parents' work hours, parents' educational attainment, number of siblings, and parents' SES.

Parametric Analysis of Data

Research Question 3:
Is There a Relationship Between Some Home
Environmental Factors and the Child's Performance
in Cognitive Measures?

Four home environmental factors turn out to show a significant correlation with the child's performance in cognitive measures:

1. Mother's work hours with the K-ABC achievement score ($r=.430$, $p<.05$). The positive correlation indicates that the fewer hours the mother works, the higher the score the child attains on the achievement portion of the K-ABC. This finding is consistent with research

indicating the positive role of the home environment in the child's cognitive development, which is partially based on the time the parent spend with their child. Much research indicates that more parent interaction with a child will enable him/her to develop further his/her cognitive skills (Harrison, 1990, Moorehouse, 1991). In addition, Scott, Perou, Urbano, Hogan, and Gold (1992) suggested that one of the characteristics found in a family with a gifted child is an ongoing communication and involvement with the child, which may be a reflection of a parents who works less hours outside the home.

2. Mother's educational attainment with the child's simultaneous K-ABC score ($r=.034$, $p<.05$). This finding suggests that the higher the educational level attained by the mother, the higher the score the child will attain on the K-ABC simultaneous scale.

3. Mother's educational attainment with the child's sequential K-ABC score ($r=.477$, $p<.05$). This finding suggests that the higher the mother's educational attainment, the higher the score the child will attain on the K-ABC sequential scale.

4. Mother's educational attainment with the child's K-ABC MPC score ($r=.508$, $p<.01$). This finding suggests that the higher the mother's educational attainment, the higher the score the child will attain on the K-ABC MPC scale.

5. Mother's educational attainment with the child's achievement K-ABC score ($r=.471$, $p<.05$). This finding suggests that the higher the mother's educational attainment, the higher the score the child will attain on the K-ABC achievement scale.

6. Mother's educational attainment with the child's non-verbal K-ABC score ($r=.471$, $p<.05$). This finding suggests that the higher the mother's educational attainment, the higher the score the child will attain on the K-ABC non-verbal scale.

7. Father's educational attainment with the child's sequential K-ABC score ($r=.493$, $p<.05$). This finding suggests that the higher the father's educational attainment, the higher the score the child will attain on the K-ABC sequential scale.

8. Father's educational attainment with the child's K-ABC MPC score (r=.430, p<.05). This finding suggests that the higher the father's educational attainment, the higher the score the child will attain on the K-ABC MPC scale.

9. Father's educational attainment with the child's non-verbal K-ABC score (r=.438, p<.05). This finding suggests that the higher the father's educational attainment, the higher the score the child will attain on the K-ABC non-verbal scale.

10. Father's educational attainment with the child's QUEST non-verbal performance (r=.400, p<.05). This finding suggests that the higher the father's educational attainment, the better the child's performance would be in the QUEST.

In summary, the correlation findings suggest that the higher level the educational attainment of both parents, the higher the child's performance would be in cognitive measures. This is consistent with the literature that suggests the effect of parents' level of education on their attitudes, behaviors, and perceptions about academic achievement on their own child's cognitive abilities (Braungart, Plomin, Fluker, & DeFries, 1992; Leon & Feldhusen, 1993). The perceptions the parents have developed about educational performance and achievement, which may be based on their own level of academic experiences, may have an effect on their child's performance level (Winner, 1996). Emphasizing the importance of cognitive development and academics can have an effect on the child's cognitive development (Bloom, 1985; Strom, Johnson, & Strom, 1990) and be demonstrated by their cognitive performances.

Research Question 4:
Do Parents' SES Predicts the Child's Performance
in Cognitive Skills Measures?

Using regression analysis, five significant predictors were found:

1. The parents' SES and the child's K-ABC sequential score (F=8.3, p<.01). This finding suggests that the higher the income range of the parents, the higher the score the child attained on the K-ABC sequential scale.

2. The parents' SES and the child's K-ABC simultaneous score (F=5.9, p<.05). This finding suggests that the higher the income range of the parents, the higher the score the child attained on the K-ABC simultaneous scale.

3. The parents' SES and the child's K-ABC MPC score (F=8.0, p<.01). This finding suggests that the higher the income range of the parents, the higher the score the child attained on the K-ABC MPC scale.

4. The parents' SES and the child's K-ABC achievement score (F=12.1, p<.01). This finding suggests that the higher the income range of the parents, the higher the score the child attained on the K-ABC achievement scale.

5. The parents' SES and the child's QUEST non-verbal performance (F=8.1, p<.01). This finding suggests that the higher the income range of the parents, the higher the score the child attained on the non-verbal area of the QUEST.

In summary, all of these significant regression analysis results are in support of the literature that suggests gifted children to have the tendency to come from higher SES backgrounds (Barbe, 1975; Belsky, 1988; Hackney, 1981; Khatena, 1982; Nevo, 1994; Schwartz, 1994; Terman, 1925). Harrison (1990) suggested that the home environment is influenced by several determining factors, including the SES of the parents. We are not suggesting that gifted children come only from a family with a higher SES. However, results suggest that the income range of the parents may be possibly related or associated (correlation tests), and become also predictive (regression tests) with certain home environmental factors, which may contribute to a child's ability to perform higher on cognitive skills measures. It is also interesting that in this study we used both a more traditional, standardized test of cognitive skills and achievement (K-ABC); as well as an alternative cognitive, verbal, and non-verbal assessment (QUEST). One feasible interpretation of these findings is that the parental SES level possibly *mediates* exposure to other important influential home environmental factors. For instance whether or not one parent works at home or does not work may be related to their educational level, the flexibility of their work hours, time spent with their child, and ultimately may be related to their SES level; which in turn may predict and be correlated with their child's performance in cognitive measures. For instance, in this study mothers' work hours are positively correlated with the child's performance in cognitive measures. Findings of the regression analysis tests take results even further, indicating that the parents' SES can actually predict the child's performance in measures of cognitive development.

Theoretical and Practical Implications of this Study

This study was focused on parental perceptions and environmental factors that might have an influence on the child's cognitive development. Through conducting qualitative analysis, this study found that parents do have certain perceptions about their child's cognitive abilities and what constitutes giftedness even *before* their children are identified as gifted. More importantly, parents also have certain beliefs about what internal an/or external factors influence the cognitive development of their child. Most parents' perceptions include the influence of external factors on giftedness development. In fact, parental perceptions and beliefs about cognitive development and giftedness also form part of the home environment to which children are exposed to. Thus, the perceptions that a parent has hat their child might be gifted, may have influenced the home environment even before the data was collected for this study. Thus, a *reciprocal causation* where each factor (parental perceptions and home environmental factors) affect one another may be the best interpretation for these findings.

As conceptualized in this study, even parents from different SES backgrounds have the same perceptions and beliefs about giftedness development. A possible explanation for the found similarities may be that most of all the parents studied shared the same mainstream cultural background. It would be interesting to include in the sample of future studies parents from minority backgrounds, coming from both high and low SES backgrounds; who would provide for their children monolingual and bilingual home language environments. The inclusion of those variables in the sample would provide some evidence for what role does cultural and language background play in the parental perceptions about giftedness, and the actual children's performance in cognitive measures. It would also be interesting to include in future studies a control group of children already labeled as gifted, in order to better understand the role of parental perceptions of what constitutes giftedness on how they shape the external home environment in which their child lives. This new data could be used to determine whether or not certain home environmental factors and parental perceptions exist before or after (i. e., precede or result from) giftedness identification in their child.

In addition, by means of correlation tests, this study found a relationship between the mother's and father's educational attainment, and the fewer hours a mother worked; and the child's performance in cognitive measures. These environmental variables may be influenced by many other factors that be indirectly (mediational variables) or directly contributing to the child's cognitive performance. It is also possible that there were other home environmental factors acting as confounding variables, which were not measured in this study. More studies need to be conducted to determine the extent that these home environmental factors (and many others) have on the cognitive development of a child. Gaining understanding of external home environmental factors may enable parents and educators to better stimulate the development of the full potential of children's cognitive development.

In addition, by means of regression tests, this study found that the parents' SES level predicted the child's performance in cognitive measures. Again the parents' SES level may be influenced by many other mediational variables influencing indirectly the child's cognitive performance. Thus in light of these results, when referring their children for possible giftedness, it would be valid to ask the parents to predict their child's performance on cognitive measures. Then, rather than just merely describing their child's ability level, parents can demonstrated better their perceptions and beliefs about what constitutes giftedness by predicting their child's assessment performance.

Limitations of this Study and Future Research Suggestions

This study has some limitations. Firstly, the sample of subjects was too small to draw generalizations; however, results are comparable to previous research findings, and different qualitative and statistical models applied to the data draw the same conclusions. Secondly, parents referred their children for giftedness before they were interviewed, which presents two extraneous factors, parents: (a) already perceived their child in a "gifted" way before the interview, and (b) may have "created" an environment that appears conducive to their child's cognitive development just for the purpose of this study. In other words, the parents responded to the interviewer knowing that this was a study on gifted children which might have had a "halo" effect influencing implicitly or explicitly the parents' responses to the survey and interview.

Thirdly, even though the study used several valid measures of the variables investigated, more direct measures of parents' and children's actual behaviors in the home environment should be collected. If more direct measures of the behaviors under study are taken in the home context, then they can be compared with the parental perceptions reported verbally. More research needs to be conducted on the influence of external factors (home environment and parental perceptions) on the cognitive development of a child. This study suggests that the home environment created by parents is also influenced by their perceptions about what external and/or internal factors are important contributors of advanced cognitive development or giftedness. Thus, studying potentially gifted children even before they are identified can help educators to understand what pre-existing home environmental factors were "created" by the parents and their child. Another variable that needs to be studied is the effect of the "gifted" child in the home. The gifted child can help "create" the overall home environment. This latter variable may be why this study found relatively little variation in the home environments of the children. Thus, the perceptions a parent has that their child might be gifted, may have influenced the environment even before the data was collected for this study. In sum, including more external variables for the study of potentially gifted children can help researchers, educators, and parents to better understand the intelligence development of a child. Through this type of research, environments can be better constructed, so that children are able to develop in a more healthy, productive, and advanced level.

Forthly, a graduated scale might have been more effective in data collection, and for data analysis purposes. Future studies might benefit from the use of a Likert scale for the measurement of parental perceptions. This Likert scale measure could have eliminated coding data using nominal categories only, which provides richer data for the qualitative analysis, but makes more difficult the statistical analysis of data. Thus, the addition of a Likert-type scale for collecting data on parents' perceptions, and for the actual prediction of their child's performance in cognitive measures would have increased the validity of the findings. Probably, the use of both open-ended instruments, such as an interview, and Likert scale survey items would be the ideal combination for measuring parental perceptions within a qualitative and statistical research design.

Fifthly, possibly the two groups chosen based on their annual income producing a low and a high SES level, and the parents' referral of their child for giftedness evaluation; may have created not matching groups in other variables not controlled. Possibly, these two groups are significantly different in certain other variables, which could have had a confounding effect on the overall statistical validity of this study. Probably it would be better to use a cross-section of a population, in order to eliminate the two distinct groups and to create a better flowing range of the confounding variable SES. In addition, other correlation coefficients could have been computed to determine any intercorrelation among variables. For instance, Are the hours a mother works significantly correlated with the parents' SES, or Are the parents' work hours significantly correlated with the time parents spend with their child? Such intercorrelations might help explain some of the results. The variables that were found to be significantly related to a child's performance in cognitive measures might be directly and significantly influenced by other home environmental factors.

Case Studies Representing the Patterns Found Across Research Questions

The following three case studies represent the general trends found across research. Pseudonyms have been used to protect the identity of subjects.

First Case Study: Laurel

Reason for Referral. Laurel was referred for evaluation by both her father and mother based on her perceived advanced language, social, and memory skills. Her mother stated: "we took her to see 'The Beauty and the Beast' when it first came out, after seeing it only twice, she had memorized the prologue in its entirety, with words she had never heard before." She was also referred due to her puzzle-solving skills. Her mother commented: "At age 2 and 3 she could take 25 piece puzzles and assemble them with no guessing or trying pieces, in under 3 minutes, even with the puzzle picture face down." On several occasions, the mother strongly emphasized her belief that Laurel was probably not really gifted with comments like: "I am not sure she is gifted, but she is advanced in her language skills."

Demographic Characteristics. Both of Laurel's parents had an education beyond a 4-year college degree, work outside the home as teachers, and provided a low-middle income for the family. Both parents spent a lot of time with Laurel and her younger sister.

Home Environment. The home environment was found to be family-centered, with a garden, and many books and hands-on children's activities readily available. There was no television in the home, but the children occasionally watched it elsewhere.

Parent's Interview. Laurel's mother believed that her child's development wasinfluenced by the quality time that both parents spent with her. The mother's responses were insightful, thought-out, and lengthy; and they were focused on her belief in the importance of environmental influences on the development of her child. She stated: "I do not think biologically or genetically she has been influenced at all, there aren't any geniuses in the family or anything like that. Basically her father and I were really concerned about developing the whole child."

K-ABC Results. The clinical observations of the examiner indicated that Laurel was very motivated and eager to do the sub-test activities. She was a very talkative child with an advanced ability to communicate in comparison to peers. In the Mental Processing Composite (MPC), Laurel's scores ranged between 123-137, within the superior category. Her Sequential Processing Scale score ranged between 123-139, placing her in the gifted category. Her Simultaneous Processing Scale score again was in the above average category, ranging from 113 to 129. Her Achievement Composite Scale score also indicated that Laurel had an advanced knowledge base, her score ranged from 106 to 118. Thus, Laurel's abilities felt in the superior range in comparison to peers for cognitive processes involving learning novel concepts.

QUEST Results. Laurel performed verbally at the functional level, which is within developmental expectations for her chronological age. She could explain her non-verbal groupings and could sort objects at the concrete level, which is above expectations for her age.

Recommendation. Thus, Laurel's performance in the QUEST indicated that she should be offered a gifted educational program in which she could further develop her verbal and non-verbal cognitive potential.

Second Case Study: Paul

Reason for Referral. Paul was referred for evaluation for giftedness by his parents because of his ability to understand abstract concepts, memory skills, creativity, extensive vocabulary and language skills, and problem-solving and social skills. Paul's mother gave extensive examples of each of his outstanding abilities in the parents' survey. For instance she wrote: "His memory seems incredible, he loves to learn; but mostly, he seems to truly understand some abstract concepts that I just have not seen other children his age even been interested in." She also referred to some anecdotal events as examples of Paul's outstanding abilities: "When he was 4 years old, he said he was going to spell his name backwards. Verbally he did it without the help of writing letters down. Now, he can switch letters to spell any words backwards."

Demographic Characteristics. Paul lived with both parents and a younger brother in a high SES home. The home was found to be child-centered with readily available games, activities, and visually stimulating materials in every room, including the kitchen. There was also a play room and a back yard designed for the use of the children's play. His parents prohibited the view of network television, but allowed Paul to watch selected videos. Both parents were well educated, the mother had a college degree; while the father had several university graduate level degrees, and worked as a medical doctor. The mother stayed at home full-time to care for the two children.

Parent's Interview. The mother responded to the in-home interview. When the mother was asked about the major influences she thought her child has had, she replied: "I try not to brush off any questions, I try to take the time to answer him. My husband spends a lot of time explaining things to him at a more advanced level than I would do." The mother also thought that some resources in the home probably had contributed to Paul's advanced development, such as books. She also suggested that some biological factors may had contributed to Paul's development: "....he is a lot like my husband, he has so many interests...Paul is good with three-dimensional things....and my husband is probably similar to him." Paul's mother discussed extensively her son's multiple interests which she considered were more advanced than peers his age. For instance, she stated: "I see that his interest go beyond what is right around him. He is really interested in the solar system. He also needs to know how everything works and is put together. His interests lead him farther out of his own little world. It is just a need in him, every-day life is just not interesting enough for him."

K-ABC Results. Paul's scores on the K-ABC indicated a very high aptitude in the areas of visual-motor perception, visual-motor organization, and reading. The clinical observation conducted by the examiner during the administration of the K-ABC indicated an exceptional spatio-temporal ability to solve three-dimensional puzzles (in the Triangles subtest). In the Mental Processing Composite (MPC), Paul's scores ranged between 128-139, placing him within the gifted category. Her Sequential Processing Scale score ranged between 125-140, placing him in the gifted category. His Simultaneous Processing Scale score was in the above average category, ranging from 115 to 127. His Achievement Scale score indicated that Paul had an advanced knowledge base, his score ranged from 109 to 120.

QUEST Results. Paul performed at the concrete level in the non-verbal tasks, which is well beyond developmental expectations for children of his chronological age. He showed potential verbal concept formation at a much higher level when prompted by the examiner. He also showed good short-and-long-term memory skills, and used prior experience in the form of stories.

Recommendation. Based on his performance in the QUEST, it was recommended that Paul be offered a gifted educational program in which he would be further stimulated to develop his conceptual abilities.

Third Case Study from the Low-SES Group: Scott

Reason for Referral. Scott was referred for his perceived advanced ability and determination to learn new information. In the Parents' survey, he was described as creative, motivated, personable, and one who has 'a lot of natural ability'."

Demographic Characteristics and Home Environment. Scott is a 4.10 year old boy, with two brothers (one older and one younger), living in a two bedroom home in a rural area in the North central region of the US. Scott lives with both his natural mother and father. His home is a family-centered environment, with books, toys, and miscellaneous items scattered everywhere, both inside and outside the house. However, the house was in need of some obvious repair work (e.g., the bedroom doors were merely sheets hanging from nails). Both of Scott's parents work more than 30 hours per week. So, Scott attends a full-day, five day a week child-care/preschool center. Scott's mother has 1-3 years of technical school training, while his father has only a high school diploma.

Interview. Scott's mother was eager to participate in the at-home interview, which took place at the kitchen's table. The mother did not offer a tour of the house and was distracted during the entire interview by the three boys at home. All of the mother's responses to the questions were very short and simple. For example, when she was asked what she thought were the major influences on her sons development, she responded, "Watching his older brother come home from school. He likes to try to do the same work and have him tell him what he did at school." When she was asked if she thought any resources in the home have influenced Scott's development, the mother responded, "He loves to read his books. He reads a lot, and listens to Disney music tapes." With the purpose of encouraging more comments from the mother, she was asked about any special interests Scott might have. The mother spoke extensively about his natural athletic ability. She replied, "He can play baseball very well. I coached the team and he was the best player on the team. He was older than most of the other players though. he has a natural swing with the bat and no one ever taught him. He started when he was real young and watched his older brother a lot. Almost every day he practices in the front yard."

In spite of the difficulties experienced during the interview (e.g., interruptions, noise, and tendency to deliver only short responses), the mother had already made comments on the Parents' Survey, which prove to be very valuable in the data analysis. In particular, she wrote, "He has a lot of natural athletic ability. He is a natural at his tumbling and baseball throwing. It is all in his coordination."

K-ABC Results. Scott's cognitive score profile indicated that he has an average/above average ability level. The scores dominated in the above average ability range for most important sub-tests comprising the Mental Processing Composite (MPC). He showed no obvious weaknesses or learning problems. His strongest score was in the Gestalt Closure sub-test, which relies on "mental images" to provide a correct answer. He also scored high in areas of achievement that require knowledge about common objects, mathematical computations and numbers, and common places and people. Scott's achievement profile was slightly lower than his cognitive profile. This suggests that Scott could be performing educational tasks and have a knowledge based that is at a higher level than the one he showed at the time of evaluation.

QUEST Performance. Scott was able to classify objects non-verbally at the concrete level, which was well beyond developmental expectations for his chronological age. In addition, he showed verbal conceptualization at a much higher level than expected. He expressed creativity in organizing and classifying the objects, and used familiar experiences to explain the object classifications.

Recommendation. Based on Scott's performance across instruments, it was recommended that he eventually be screened for entrance into an accelerated or gifted program.

References

Abelman, R. (1987). Child's giftedness and its role in the parental mediation of television viewing. *Roeper Review, 9*(4), 217-220.

Awanbor, D. (1991). Giftedness as an artifact.   *Gifted Education International, 7*(3), 153-156

Ballering, L. D., & Koch, A. (1984) Family relations when a child is gifted. *Gifted Child Quarterly, 28*(30), 140-143

Banks, J. A., & McGee-Banks, C. A. (1993).   *Multicultural education: Issues and perspectives* (2nd ed.). Massachusetts: Allyn & Bacon.

Barbe, W. B. (1975). A study of the family background of the gifted. In W. B. Barbe, & J. S. Renzulli (Eds.), *Psychology of the gifted.* New York: Irvington.

Baumrind, D. (1978). Parental disciplinary patterns and social competence in children. *Youth & Society, 9*(3), 239-272.

Belsky, J. (1988). The "effects" of infant day care reconsidered. *Early Childhood Research Quarterly, 3,* 235-272.

Bloom, B. S. (1985). Developing talent in young people. New York: Ballantine.

Bracken, B. A. (1991). *The psychoeducational assessment of preschool children.* Massachusetts: Allyn & Bacon.

Braungart, J. M., Plomin, R., Fluker, D. W., & DeFries, J. C. (1992). Genetic mediation of the home environment during infancy: A sibling adoption of the study HOME. *Developmental Psychology, 28,* 1048-1055. Bryant, D. M., Burchinal, M., Lau, L. B. & Sparling, J. J. (1994). Family and classroom correlates of head start children's developmental outcomes. *Early Childhood Research Quarterly, 9,* 289-309.

Burts, D. C., Hart, C. H., Charlesworth, R., Fleege, P. O., Mosely, J. & Thomasson, R. H. (1992). Observed activities and stress behaviors of children in developmentally appropriate and inappropriate kindergarten classrooms. *Early Childhood Research Quarterly, 7,* 297-318.

Cornell, D. G., & Grossberg, I. W. (1986). Siblings of children in gifted programs. *Journal for the Education of the Gifted, 9*   (4),   253-264.

Gagne, F., Belanger, J., & Motard, B. (1993). Popular estimates of the prevalence of giftedness and talent. *Roeper Review,16*(2), 96-102.

Gonzalez, V. (1991). *A model of cognitive, cultural, and linguistic variables affecting bilingual Spanish/English children's development of concepts and language.* Doctoral Dissertation. Austin, Texas: The University of Texas at Austin. (ERIC Document Reproduction Service No. ED 345 562).

Gonzalez, V. (1994). A model of cognitive, cultural, and linguistic variables affecting bilingual Spanish/English children's development of concepts and language. *Hispanic Journal of Behavioral Sciences, 16*(4), 396-421.

Gonzalez, V. (1995). *A model of cognitive, cultural and linguistic variables affecting bilingual Hispanic children's development of concepts and language.* Austin & Winfield: Bethesda, MR.

Gonzalez, V., Brusca-Vega, R., & Yawkey, T. D. (1997). *Assessment and instruction in culturally and linguistically diverse students: From research to practice.* Allyn & Bacon, Needham Heights, MA.

Hackney, H. (1981). The gifted child, the family and the school. *Gifted Child Quarterly, 31*(2), 51-54.

Hall, E. G. (1993). Educating preschool gifted children. Gifted Child Today, 16 (3), 24-27.

Harrison, P. L. (1990*). The manual for the American Guidance Service early screening profiles.* Minnesota: American Guidance Service.

Leon, K., & Feldhusen, J. (1993). Teachers' and parents' perceptions of social psychological factors of underachievement among the gifted in Korea and the United States. *Gifted Education International, 9*(2), 115-119.

Karnes, F. A., & D'Ilio, V. R. (1988). Comparison of gifted children and their parents' perceptions of the home environment.   *Gifted child Quarterly, 32(*2), 277-279.

Karnes, M. B., & Johnson, L. J. (1991). The preschool/primary gifted child. *Journal for the Education of the Gifted, 14*(3), 267-283.

Kaufman, A. S., & Kaufman, N. L. (1983). *Interpretive manual for the Kaufman Assessment Battery for Children.* Minnesota: American Guidance Service.

Kaufman, A. S., & Kaufman, N. L. (1983).   *Administration and scoring manual for the Kaufman Assessment Battery for Children.* Minnesota: American Guidance Service.

Keirouz, K. S. (1990). Concerns of parents of gifted children: A research review. *Gifted Child Quarterly, 3* (2), 56-62.

Khatena, J. (1982). *Educational psychology of the gifted.* New York: John Wiley.

Kulieke, M. J., & Olszewski-Kubilius, P. (1989). The influence of family values and climate on the development of talent. In J. H. Borland (Ed.), *Patterns of influence on gifted learners.* New York: Teachers College.

Markman, E. M. (1984). The acquisition of hierarchical organization of categories by children. In C. Sophian (Ed.). *Origin in cognitive skills.* The 18th Annual Carnegie Symposium on Cognition (pp. 376-406). Hillsdale, N. J.: Lawrence Erlbaum.

McCartney, K. (1984) The effect of quality of day care environment upon children's language development. *Developmental Psychology, 20,* 244-260.

Moorehouse, M. J. (1991). Linking maternal employment patterns to mother-child activities and children's school competencies. *Developmental Psychology, 27*(2), 295-303.

Moss, E. (1990). Social interaction and metacognitive development in gifted preschoolers. *Gifted Child Quarterly, 34(*1), 16-20.

Nevo, B. (1994). Definitions, ideologies, and hypotheses in gifted children. *Gifted Child Quarterly, 38*(4), 184-186.

Nielsen, M. E., & Buchanan, N. K. (1991). Evaluating gifted programs with locally constructed instruments. In N. K. Buchanan & J. F. Feldhusen (Eds.), *Conducting research and evaluation in gifted education: A handbook of methods and applications.* New York: Teachers College Press.

Passow, A. H. (1994). Growing up gifted and talented: Schools, families, and communities. *Gifted Education International, 10,* 4-9.

Peterson, D. C. (1977). The heterogeneously gifted family. Gifted Child Quarterly, 21(3), 396-411.

Piaget, J. (1967). Piaget's theory. In P. H. Mussen (Ed.), *Carmichael's manual of child psychology,* Vol. I , (pp. 703-732). New York: John Wiley.

Schwartz, L. L. (1994). *Why give gifts to the gifted?* Thousand Oaks, CA: Corwin Press.

Scott, M.S., Perou, R., Urbano, R., Hogan, A., & Gold, S. (1992). The identification of giftedness: A comparison of White, Hispanic, and Black families. *Gifted Child Quarterly, 36,* 121-139.

Sebring, A. D. (1983). Parental factors in the social and emotional adjustment of the gifted. *Roeper Review, 6,* 97-99.

Shaklee, B. D. (1992). Identification of young gifted students. *Journal for the Education of the Gifted, 15(*2), 134-144.

Sternberg, R. J. (1985). *Beyond IQ: A triarchic theory of human intelligence.* New York: Cambridge University Press.

Sternberg, R. J., & Lubart, T. (1993). Creative giftedness: A multivariate approach. *Gifted Child Quarterly, 39*(2), 88-94.

Stile, S. W., Kitano, M., Kelley, P., & Mecrone, J. (1993). Early intervention with gifted children: A national survey. *Journal of Early Intervention, 17*(1), 30-35.

Strom, R., Johnson, A., & Strom, S. (1990). Home and school support for gifted children. *International Journal of Disability, Development, and Education, 37*(3), 245-254.

Terman, L. (1925). *Genetic studies of genius* (Vol. 1). Stanford, CA: Stanford University Press.

VanTassel, J. L., Olszewski-Kubilius, P., & Borland, J. H. (Eds.). (1989). *Patterns of influence on gifted learners: The home, the self, and the school.* New York: Teachers College.

Waxman, S. R. (1990). Linking language and conceptual development: Linguistic cues and the construction of conceptual hierarchies . *The Genetic Epistemologist, 17,13*-20.

Winner, E. (1996). *Gifted children: Myths and realities.* New York: BAsic Books.

Witt, J. C., Elliot, S. N., Kramer, J. J., & Gresham, F. M. (1994). *Assessment of children: Fundamental methods and practices* . Dubuque, IA: Brown & Benchmark.

Zeidner, M., & Most. R. (1992). *Psychological testing: An inside view.* Palo Alto, CA: Consulting Psychologists Press.

Table 5.1.

K-ABC Scores and QUEST Performance by Minimum and Maximum, Mean, Mode, and Standard Deviation (s.d.)

K-ABC Scale	Minimum	Maximum	Mean	Mode	s.d.
Simultaneous	2.00	6.00	4.04	4.00	0.92
Sequential	3.00	6.00	3.92	3.00	0.84
Mental Processing Composite (MPC)	2.00	6.00	4.04	3.00	0.93
Non-Verbal	1.00	6.00	4.04	3.00	1.03
Achievement	2.00	6.00	3.50	3.00	0.66

Key:
0   lower extreme
1   well below average
2   below average
3   average
4   above average
5   well above average
6   upper extreme

Table 5.2.

QUEST Performance by Minimum and Maximum, Mean,
Mode, and Standard Deviation (s.d.)

QUEST Area	Minimum	Maximum	Mean	Mode	s.d.
Verbal	2.00	4.00	2.96	2.00	0.73
Non-verbal	2.00	4.00	3.58	2.00	0.44
Overall 2.00	2.50	4.00	3.27	1.50	0.46

Key:
1   No classification
2   Pre-conceptual: Perceptual
3   Pre-conceptual: Functional
4   Concrete
5   Metalinguistic

Table 5.3.
Frequencies and Percentages of Some Home
Environmental Factors

Home Environmental Factor	Frequency	Percentage
Time Parents Spend with their Child		
• Almost every day	20	76.9%
• At least 3/4 times/week	4	15.%
• 2 or 3 times/month	2	7.7%
Parents Work Hours Mothers		
• Mothers staying at home full time	11	42.3%
• Mothers working regular 9-5 M-F schedules	9	34.6%
• Mothers working at Part-time making her own hours	5	19.2%
• Mothers working more than 9-5, M-F schedules	1	3.8%
Fathers		
• Fathers staying at home full time	3	11.5%
• Fathers working regular 9-5 M-F schedules	13	50%
• Fathers working at Part-time/ making her own hours	3	11.5 %
• Fathers working more than 9-5, M-F schedules	7	26.9%

. . . continued

Table 5.3 continued . . .

Parents' Educational Attainment Mothers

• Mothers with a post-graduate degree	4	15.4%
• Mothers with a college degree	7	26.9%
• Mothers with a 4+yr. college completion, but no degree	1	3.8%
• Mothers with 1-3 yrs. of college or technical school	9	34.6%
• Mothers with a high school diploma	5	19.2%

Fathers

• Fathers with a post-graduate degree	5	19.2%
• Fathers with a college degree	6	23.1%
• Fathers with a 4+yr. college completion, but no degree	1	3.8%
• Fathers with 1-3 yrs. of college or technical school	4	15.4%
• Fathers with a high school diploma	7	26.9
• Fathers with less than high school	3	11.5%

. . . continued

Table 5.3 continued . . .

Number of Siblings

• One sibling living in the home	12	46.2%
• No siblings	8	30.8%
• Two siblings living in the home	5	19.2%
• Three siblings living in the home	1	3.8%%

Combined Annual Parents' Income

• $60,000 or more	8	3.8%
• Between 40,000-49,000	4	15.4%
• Between $20,000-29,000	1	3.8%
• Between $10,000-$19,900	9	34.6%
• Less than $10,000	4	15.4%

6

DEVELOPMENTALLY ADEQUATE ASSESSMENT PRACTICES WHEN SCREENING CLASSROOM PERFORMANCE IN KINDERGARTNERS

ಸಃಀ

Susan Leadem and Virginia Gonzalez

Summary

C hapter 6 provides an alternative conceptual and methodological research view to the study of development, assessment, and academic performance in monolingual young learners. Chapter 6 highlights the theme of the need for an alternative *developmental* view to assessment and academic performance when studying and serving young learners. That is, the study presented in Chapter 6 is used to illustrate the important role of teachers' evaluations of cognitive, linguistic, and social-emotional development when screening kindergartners for readiness and academic performance.

More specifically this study examined the predictive validity of one qualitative measure of social-emotional development (moral judgment tasks adapted by the authors from those created by Eisenberg-Berg & Hand, 1979), and of two standardized tests measuring cognitive-linguistic development and achievement (Kaufman Assessment Battery for

Children, K-ABC, Kaufman & Kaufman, 1983), and social-adaptive development (Vineland Adaptive Behavior Scales, Sparrow, Balla, & Cicchetti, 1985), on kindergartners' classroom performance. Twenty high-middle socioeconomic status (SES), 4 years-9 month to 5 years-9 month old children were individually administered the moral judgment tasks and the K-ABC, and their teachers rated their social-adaptive development. Multiple regression analyses indicated that: (1) the Vineland scores were the best predictors of classroom performance, followed by the K-ABC scores, and (2) social-emotional development was not predictive of children's classroom performance. Derived educational implications show that teachers' evaluations of social-adaptive development should be used for screening young children's readiness to begin school.

Purpose and Objectives

It is proposed in this study that classroom-teachers' evaluations of social-adaptive development need to be used as the most important method of screening for future school readiness in young children. It is hypothesized in this study that the mastering of social-emotional skills, not just cognitive-linguistic abilities, indicates readiness to participate in a structured group setting (such as the classroom) and may be predictive of subsequent success in the early school years. Some research studies have shown that teachers and parents often value the achievement of social competence and moral character over academic accomplishments (see e.g., Krumboltz, Ford, Nichols, & Wentzel, 1987). Even though this higher emphasis on social-emotional development is placed primarily by minority parents (e.g., African-Americans define a "gifted" individual as one who excels in interpersonal relationships—Patton, 1992), majority parents also nurture the child to grow emotionally. In addition, some other studies have shown that teaching children appropriate classroom social skills can lead to significant gains in academic achievement (Hopps & Cobb, 1974).

However, no known studies have directly examined the relationship between measures of young children's social-emotional development and their performance in the classroom. Assessment of social-emotional skills may be especially important when predicting a kindergartner's readiness to perform and succeed in the school, since in young children the assessment of pro-social and moral behaviors may be better measures of their genuine ability to perform required classroom skills than are standardized intelligence tests.

This study also proposes that teachers are an underutilized resource in the school system in the screening of the developmental strengths and weaknesses of young children. Past studies have indicated that kindergarten teachers are good resources for the identification of children at-risk for underachievement, even better than test batteries (e. g., Adelman, 1982). For instance, Stevenson, Parker, Wilkinson, Hegion, and Fish (1976) found that after only three months of observation and interaction, kindergarten teachers were able to accurately predict how well their students would be doing in school over 40 months later. However, the questionable validity of the standardized achievement tests and the lack of inclusion of social-emotional developmental measures in these past studies indicate that further research is warranted in this area.

Theoretical Conceptual Framework Proposed

First, the assessment of intelligence will be considered, with an emphasis on definitions of intelligence, current trends in assessment, and the relationship between intelligence test scores and classroom performance. Next, the assessment of social-emotional development to classroom performance will be discussed critically, with special emphasis on adaptive behavior and moral development.

Assessment of Intelligence

The accurate assessment of intelligence in young children is a challenging task, primarily because there is not a well-defined construct that can be represented validly in tests. Early researchers assumed that intelligence tests measure an inherited and fixed biological trait that would predictably unfold as an individual matured (Wodrich & Kush, 1990). Early intelligence tests, such as those developed by Binet and Simon, represented intellectual ability as a single score or intelligence quotient (Samuda, 1991). Back in 1927, Spearman stated that intelligence had become a mere vocal sound, a word with so many meanings that it had none (Samuda, 1991).

In contrast to early views many current theories propose that external sociocultural factors have a strong influence on internal genetic potentials inherited; however it is in the interaction with external stimulation and experiences that potentials develop into skills and abilities. In addition, contemporary research shows that intelligence develops dynamically and can change dramatically between the ages of 2 and 17 years

(Wodrich & Kush, 1990). In addition, research now shows that intelligence is multidimensional and encompass complex cognitive processes such as problem-solving, decision making, creativity, metacognition, learning strategies, critical thinking skills, etc. (Blythe & Gardner, 1990; Kaufman & Kaufman, 1983; Witt, Elliot, Dramer, & Gresham, 1994).

Despite these changing views, the definition of the construct of intelligence is still problematic. For instance, many of the contemporary models of intelligence are somewhat vague and do not acknowledge the cultural dimensions and the multiple interactions with external environmental settings (i.e., home, school, community, minority and mainstream contexts, etc.). Thus, most intelligence standardized tests are loaded with mainstream cultural content that reflects traditional intelligence theories endorsed, with the assumption that intelligence is innate when in fact these tests represent learned information. Moreover, when dealing with young children, the assessment of intelligence becomes even more difficult. Relatedly, Beiley (as cited in Wodrich & Kush, 1990) conducted a longitudinal study during the 1960s and 1970s with children from infancy through adolescence. Bailey concluded that scores on instruments of infant mental performance should be mainly used to assess current developmental status. Thus, intelligence tests should not be used to predict subsequent ability or cognitive performance levels. Likewise, Wechsler (as cited in Love, 1990) questioned whether items often included in scales for young children (age 2 years and under) were validly related to intelligence or any future performance.

As quoted by Love (1990), Wechsler stated,

> The main reason for the low correlation between IQs obtained on infant intelligence scales and those derived from the scales administered at later ages is that the tests used at the earlier ages do not measure the same "functions" as those employed later. This is no default of the tests, but it is due to the very nature of the maturation process. It is not possible to appraise the child's intellectual potential in the earlier years by the same means or in the same way that one can do it later on (p.45).

Based on this quote, it appears that Wechsler might defend that when using standardized tests with young children, there is need to use other measures for predicting accurately intelligence. This principle of using a complete assessment battery is proposed by many authors. The rationale for this principle is that one test is just a sample of behavior, and thus this information needs to be complemented by multiple informants across measures and contexts. For instance, in a study of potential "at-risk" kindergarten students, Roth and colleagues (1993) concluded that standardized assessment batteries have some limited predictive value, but they must be used in conjunction with other qualitative assessments of their strengths and weaknesses. Kochanek, Kabacoff, and Lipsett (1990), made an important point in stating that a child's development can not be predicted or diagnosed independently of caretakers feedback, and that models of assessment that are founded only on child-centered data are of suspect validity. Finally, Olson and Hoza (1993) proposed that classroom observations of actual performance on academic tasks needs to be included in assessments of cognitive ability.

Then, while researchers have made great strides since the development of early tests, it is apparent that many flaws still exist in the assessment of intelligence, such as:

1. Many tests continue to use measures of language ability or logico-mathematical skills as the only indicators of cognitive ability (Blythe & Gardner, 1990; Olson & Hoza, 1993)

2. Many tests include items, resources, and procedures that are more familiar to mainstream cultures than to minority cultures (Gonzalez, Brusca-Vega, & Yawkey, 1997; Moss, 1992)

3. Scores obtained from some tests by young children are used for predicting school achievement when in fact they do not show evidence of predictive validity (Anastasi, 1988; Wodrich & Kush, 1990). In fact, Adler (1995) concluded that intelligence tests are only predictive of the person's ability to take tests.

In this study we assume that different qualitative and quantitative measures are needed for measuring validly intelligence in young children, including teachers' evaluations and classroom observations of the actual performance of kindergartner students. Numerous studies confirm the accuracy of teachers when rating their own students' achievement levels (see e.g., Itskowitz, Navon, & Strauss, 1988; Mercer, Algozzine, & Trifiletti, 1979; Stevenson, et. al., 1976; Vitaro, Tremblay, Gagnon, & Pelletier, 1994). Qualitative assessments will be used for expanding the definition of intelligence to social-emotional developmental areas that can influence school performance in young children. In particular, two areas of social-emotional development, adaptive behavior and pro-social moral development, will be examined as not traditional areas of intelligence. Some research studies have started to demonstrate during the 1990s that classroom achievement is a reflection of many skills such as a student's cognitive abilities, interest in school work, motivation to learn, and social skills (see e.g., Blythe & Gardner, 1990; Wentzel, 1991, 1993). The constructs of adaptive behavior and pro-social moral development are similar to the interpersonal and intra-personal intelligence proposed by Gardner (1983). His theory of multiple intelligences defined this construct as the capacity to solve problems or fashion products which are valued in one or more cultural settings. However, Gardner's theory is not predictive of school achievement, but of determining an individual's niche once he or she graduate from high school. In addition, Gardner proposed that culturally valued intelligences should be measured using qualitative tools that represent games, and storytelling and creative activities that allow students to be assessed in natural and non-threatening contexts (Blythe & Gardner, 1990).

Thus, this study will examine if social—emotional intelligence, measured through alternative assessments using teachers as informants, can create and predict a more accurate picture of classroom performance in kindergartners. Then, this study can further the understanding of the value of screening instruments designed for teachers to rate their young students' adaptive behaviors and social-emotional development, which can be predictive of their school academic performance.

Assessment of Social-Emotional Development and Adaptive Behavior

Unlike the assessment of intelligence, developing measures of social-emotional development has a relatively short history. Until the 1970s, the lives of preschool children were primarily family centered. Young children were considered to have fairly simple social and emotional lives, and most parents believed that they were capable of understanding this aspect of their children's development without professional assessment or consultation (Martin, 1991). Thus, few studies examined the social-emotional development of preschool children.

Evidence showing the importance of social-emotional development when determining a child's readiness for school started to be developed during the middle 1960s. Ilg and Ames (1965, cited in Vander Zanden, 1993) started to incorporate what were back then some rather questionable predictors in the physical and behavioral developmental maturity of children in relation to school performance. They aimed to diagnose at what developmental age the child was behaving as a total organism, to find developmental clues for school placement of young children. Since then, during the decade of the 1990s, numerous studies have linked social-emotional development to academic achievement, but mostly in older children. For instance, Wentzel (1993) found that some aspects of social competence are powerful predictors of academic performance in middle school students. Wentzel's study results suggested that appropriate social behavior may facilitate learning in cooperative groups or situations where adherence to specific rules is necessary to complete a project. In addition, socially appropriate behavior may result in more positive, academically relevant interactions with teachers and peers, which in turn may facilitate the completion of academic tasks. In both instances, therefore social behavior may act as an indirect mediator in classroom achievement.

According to the American Association on Mental Deficiency (AAMD), adaptive behavior is defined as the effectiveness of degree with which individuals meet the standards of personal independence and social responsibility expected for age and cultural group (Grossman, 1983). Adaptive behavior is also considered to be developmental in nature, defined by the expectations or standards of other people, and is limited to typical performance, not capacity to perform (Harrison, 1985). In addition, adaptive behavior is often incorporated into the broader construct of social competence, which also includes social skills (Harrison, 1991).

Traditionally the construct of adaptive behavior has been linked to the diagnosis of mental retardation (Harrison, 1985, 1991). For many years, after the introduction of intelligence tests in the early 1900s, mental retardation was diagnosed solely on IQ scores (Anastasi, 1988; Harrison, 1985). Increasing concerns over the use of a single instrument for diagnostic purposes led the AAMD to add deficits in adaptive behavior to the definition of mental retardation in 1959 (Platt, Kamphaus, Cole, & Smith, 1991; Sparrow et al., 1985). However, it was not until the passage of the Education for All Handicapped Children Act of 1975 (Public Law 94-142) that the study of adaptive behavior began in earnest (Harrison, 1985). Since that time, many researchers have tried to characterize adaptive behavior as a construct and examine the relationship between adaptive behavior and intelligence. Some researchers have proposed that the construct of adaptive behavior, and its measures, contributes information different from that of an intelligence test (Rozkowski & Bean, 1980; Platt et al., 1991). The first point of difference is that intelligence measures generally focus on maximum performance in cognitive functioning, while measures of adaptive behavior focus on every day behavior and typical performance. Secondly, intelligence scores in standardized tests tend to be more stable, while adaptive behavior scores may change dramatically with training. Platt and colleagues (1991) conducted a review of the literature, and found that most studies indicate a moderate correlation ($r=.40$ to $.60$) between adaptive behavior and intelligence; concluding that the two are independent but related constructs. However, the specific relationship between classroom performance and adaptive behavior has not been researched extensively yet in young children. Thus, using the classroom teacher as an informant for rating their young students' social adaptive behaviors may be an effective tool for predicting school achievement, and for making readiness and placement decisions with preschoolers.

Assessment of Moral Development

The study of moral development in children originated with Piaget who proposed in the 1930s that moral development was linked to sequential stages of intellectual growth in which they interact and transform their environment (Vander Zander, 1993). During the 1950s, Kohlberg applied Piaget's theory to the study of moral development, and particularly to the study of moral judgments in children; which would show a universal sequence of development, with only variation in the specific age at which stages were reached. In his original study of moral judgment completed in 1958, Kohlberg presented his subjects (a sample of 10 and 16 year old boys and girls) with a series of moral dilemmas based on hypothetical situations (Colby & Kohlberg, 1987). Kolhberg (1987) was not interested in whether his subjects believed the main characters' actions in each story were right or wrong, but instead he focused on the *reasoning processes* of the subject confronted with the dilemma. Kohlberg believed that in the study of moral behavior, "it is essential to determine the actor's interpretation of the situation and the behavior since the moral quality of the behavior is itself determined by the interpretation" (cited in Colby & Kohlberg, 1987, p. 2). As explained by several authors (Gardner, 1978; Kohlberg, Levine, & Hewer, 1983; Vander Zanden, 1993), Kolhberg identified 6 stages in the development of moral judgment , resulting from the children's and adults' responses to the moral dilemmas.

The six stages identified by Kolhberg (1987) are grouped into three general levels:

1. The *pre-conventional level*, typical of most children under 9 years of age, characterized by egocentric reasoning that uses self-serving reciprocity

2. The *conventional level*, characteristic of most adolescents and adults, at which individuals are mostly concerning with meeting and conforming to the expectations of others in order to avoid their disapproval

3. The *post-conventional level*, attained by less than 25% of the subjects, at which individual attempt to determine and define personal values apart from the rules and expectations of socially defined groups. At this level the bases of one's actions becomes one's own conscience, rather than group expectations. Individuals reaching this third level of moral reasoning also showed higher intellectual levels

Other views of moral development have also been proposed more recently. For instance, while Gilligan (1982) supported the general framework developed by Kohlberg, she also argued that men and women generally view morality differently. Gilligan (1982) hypothesized that men view morality as a system of rules for taming aggression and maintaining individual's rights; while women depict morality as a means of protecting the integrity of relationships and maintaining human bonding. Thus, in Gilligan's view, men's reasoning skills are coincident with Kohlberg's stages, and thus they generally score higher than women in his moral reasoning stages.

Another view of moral development is proposed by Rest (1986), who hypothesized that moral development does not occur as an individual passes through successive stages, as a result of people's traits. Instead, in rest's view, moral development results from an *interaction* of four components or *processes* involved in the production of a *moral act*. According to Rest (1986), in order to "behave morally" an individual must:

1. Realize that he or she can do something that would affect the interests, welfare, or expectations of other people

2. Make a judgment of which course of action is morally right, resulting in labeling what a person must do in a particular situation
3. Decide whether to give priority to moral values above other personal interests that may compromise the moral ideal

4. Execute and implement a plan of action so that he or she can follow through on his or her intention to behave morally

Thus, while Kohlberg (1958) defined moral development in terms of the path of reasoning an individual takes when confronted by a moral dilemma, Rest (1986) viewed moral development in terms of actual choices and behaviors an individual exhibits when forced to make a decision in real-life situations. While authors such as Kohlberg, Gilligan, and Rest have expanded our understanding of moral development in adolescents and adults, only a few researchers have investigated the development of moral judgment in young children. For instance, Piaget (cited in Vander Zanden, 1993) hypothesized that moral development is still fairly undeveloped in preschoolers, so there may be little variation in the types of moral reasoning exhibited in young children. However, research conducted after the original Kolhber's studies, has revealed that young children have been found to exhibit moral reasoning skills, following Kohlberg's levels. For instance, Eisenberg-Berg and Hand (1979) found that preschoolers exhibited pro-social moral behavior that was related to: (1) their tendency to be sociable; (2) a desire to avoid personal conflict; and (3) an ability to interpret others' emotional states; rather than a reflection of true moral concerns or desire to gain approval of others. Thus, these latter authors suggested that there may be a relationship between empathic moral reasoning and the development of social skills, such as pro-social behaviors. This study will expand on examining this possible connection between pro-social behavior, pro-social moral judgments, and classroom performance (as measured by responses given to adaptations of Eisenberg-Berg and Hand's moral judgment stories).

This study proposes that the development of moral judgment may influence classroom performance in two possible ways:

1. Children may exhibit higher levels of pro-social moral judgment, because they may be advanced in their overall development, ability

that indirectly would influence the presence of higher readiness levels, resulting in successful performance in a kindergarten classroom

2. Children with higher levels of moral judgment may tend to be more sociable, ability that would indirectly influence their higher functional level within a structured group (such as the classroom environment)

Position Taken in this Study

The importance of identifying children at-risk of later developmental disabilities has been well documented during the 1980s and 1990s (Adelman, 1982; Kochanek, Kabacoff, & Lipsitt, 1990; Olson & Hoza, 1993; Roth, McCaul, & Barnes, 1993; Satz & Fletcher, 1988; Vitaro et al., 1994). However, the best method for assessing young children for educational placement still remains in question.

During the 1990s researchers have demonstrated that in children under 5 years of age the best predictors of later academic and social achievement, intellectual ability, psychological well-being, and conduct problems are factors in the home environment, including:

1. Maternal occupation and educational level (Kochanek et al., 1990)

2. Perceived attachment to parents (Brinich, Drotar, & Brinich, 1989; Raja, McGee, & Stanton, 1992)

3. Level of stress in the home (Gelfand, Teti, & Fox, 1992; Webster-Satton, 1990).

Yet by the time a child enters elementary school, scores obtained from standardized tests of cognitive-linguistic skills are often assumed to be the best predictors of a student's academic performance (Cole, Usher, & Cargo, 1993; Olson & Hoza, 1993; Roth et al., 1993). However, the exclusive use of standardized intelligence tests for the educational placement of young children may be problematic because these tests measure a very small sample of a child's overall capacities (Gardner, cited in Scherer, 1985). In particular, intelligence tests have limited value when used as predictors of young children's readiness to begin school, since many of the skills needed for succeeding in kindergarten (e.g., the ability to listen attentively to a story, to care for toileting needs, to participate in games or activities with others, etc.) are not represented in the construct and items of intelligence tests. In addition, according to Wentzel (1991), discrepancies frequently occur between students' standardized test scores and their actual classroom achievement. One hypothesis stated by Wentzel (1991) as to why these differences occur is that standardized intelligence tests measure only specific cognitive skills, while classroom teachers evaluate both students' intellectual and social skills. Therefore, the use of standardized test scores of cognitive-linguistic skills as an exclusive screening method for school readiness in young children may not be a developmentally adequate practice.

In sum, measures used in this study have the potential to become accurate screening tools of kindergartners' school readiness, since these measures represent the three factors discussed in the conceptual theoretical framework presented above:

1. The limited range of skills measured by intelligence tests

2. The possible association between the acquisition of social-emotional skills and school readiness

3. The importance of using teachers' ratings of their students' adaptive behaviors and social-emotional development for predicting their classroom performance

Four research questions are addressed in this study:

1. Are kindergarten teachers' evaluation of students' adaptive behavior predictive of classroom performance?

2. Is pro-social moral development related to classroom performance in kindergarten students?

3. Is cognitive development, as measured by standardized intelligence tests, predictive of classroom performance in kindergarten students?

4. Of the instruments used in this study, which is the best predictor of classroom performance in kindergarten students?

Methods

Research Design

A quasi-experimental design was used in which the four research questions were represented in qualitative and quantitative measures, and the data was analyzed using regression tests.

Participants: Children

Twenty children (9 girls—45%-, and 11 boys—55%) ranging in age from 4 years-9 months to 5 years-9 months at the time of assessment participated in this study. The mean and the median age was 5 years, 2 months, with a SD of 2.95. Eighteen of the children were White (90%), one was Hispanic (5%), and one was of a Middle Eastern/Hispanic descent (5%). The children were enrolled in either a regular or a developmental kindergarten class in which children with more advanced skills were placed. All the children attended a private preschool, which was located in an upper-middle class neighborhood of a middle sized metropolitan community in the Southwest region of the US. All the children from the selected classes whose parents gave consent participated in the study.

Participants: Teachers

Three teachers also participated in this study as informants. They rated the children's:

1. Social-adaptive development using the Vineland Adaptive Behavior Scales, Classroom edition (Sparrow et al., 1985)

2. Cognitive skills and academic achievement using a Likert Scale developed by the first author

All of the participating teachers were female, had either a bachelors or masters degree in education, and had at least 8 years of teaching experience at the kindergarten level. Two teachers were White, and one was a bilingual Hispanic teacher.

Instruments

Five instruments were used to obtain qualitative and quantitative data for this study. Two standardized instruments were used to obtain quantitative data:

1. The Vineland Adaptive Behavior Scales, Classroom Edition (Sparrow et al., 1985) are intended for use with students ranging in age from 3 years to 12 years, 11 months. The items on the Vineland scales are grouped into four domains (i. e., communication, daily living skills, socialization, and motor skills), which are then further divided into sub-domains. This instrument was used to measure the variable of social adaptive behavior, and the scores obtained from this instrument was used to test the first research question. This instrument was filled out by a teacher familiar with the daily activities of the child being assessed.

2. The Kaufman Assessment Battery for Children (K-ABC, Kaufman & Kaufman, 1983) was used for measuring the children's cognitive-linguistic abilities and achievement. This instrument is designed for children ranging in age from 2 years, 6 months to 12 years, 6 months. Cognitive-linguistic processes are measured by two mental processing scales, which provide estimates of an individual's learning potential and preferred style of learning. The achievement scales assess factual knowledge and skills, which are usually acquired in a school setting or through alertness to the environment. According to the K-ABC manual (Kaufman & Kaufman, 1983), scores from both mental processing and achievement scales are related to school performance. However, scores from the achievement scale are the most useful in predicting future success or failure in school. Scores obtained from the mental processing and achievement scales of the K-ABC were used to address the third research question.

In addition, qualitative information was collected using three instruments:

1. Three pro-social judgment stories adapted from those created by Eisenberg-Berg and Hand (1979), which purpose was to examine the children's moral development in the area of *pro-social moral reasoning*. Thus, their actual   *actions* or behaviors were not observed, but

their reactions to the main protagonist' vicarious experiences were recorded. The adaptations of the stories had the purpose of reflecting contemporary children's cultural and social experiences. In these tasks, the children were asked how the protagonists in each story should respond when confronted with three different moral dilemmas, and to explain why the protagonists should act in the child's proposed manner. Children's responses were then recorded on videotape for increasing the validity of the data coding. See Table 6.1. for the actual story texts.

2. *Teachers' rating scale.* Teachers' ratings of each child's cognitive ability, academic achievement, and classroom performance using a 5 point Likert scale (from well above average to well below average) of both past observed typical classroom performance (rated by classroom teachers), and actual portfolio products (rated by independent expert teachers); resulting in two separate ratings. The Likert scale includes 25 cognitive and academic achievement skills as they are performed in an actual classroom setting. Each of these 25 skills were derived from one or more sub-test of the K-ABC, so that the children's performances in these two instruments could be compared. These rating scales were developed by the first author following strict pilot test procedures. Before the rating scales were used in the study, they were first evaluated by three kindergarten teachers serving as independent judges to improve the construct validity of the instrument. Teachers were to assure the representation of K-ABC sub-tests constructs in the areas included in the teachers' rating scale, and also how well the survey represented actual classroom behaviors relevant to predict the children's readiness. In addition, teachers participating as judges also improved the face validity of the rating scale by clarifying the language used, any phrases or words that were ambiguous or difficult to understand were replaced with words that more clearly defined the skills to be measured. The resulting revised survey was then showed to the judges in addition to three other preschool teachers to assure that the original problems were corrected. The teachers' rating scale provided useful information for evaluating the children's classroom performance, and also for the relationship between scores on all K-ABC scales and actual classroom performance as measured by alternative assessments. Table 6.2. presents the actual Teacher's Rating Scale, and Table 6.3. presents the rela-

tionship between skills measured by the K-ABC sub-tests and skills represented in the Teachers' Rating Scale constructed.

The portfolio ratings were obtained using the samples of actual children's classroom work including:

1. A *handwriting sample* obtaining approximately after 4 months of the beginning of the school year. Prior to the collection of this sample, the teachers had spent time teaching the skills required to make the letters of the alphabet, and the children had numerous opportunities to practice this skill. For collecting this sample, the children were asked to copy a phrase that the teacher had written on the board. The children were encouraged to do "their best work" since this assignment was part of a holiday gift card to be sent home to their parents. If a child had difficulty copying the phrase, the child received additional help and was allowed a second attempt to complete the assignment. The best handwriting sample produced by each child was collected and photocopied for later scoring.

2. A *self-portrait* task for which the child was encouraged to draw the "best picture" of himself or herself. The drawings were to be saved for inclusion in a memory book to be sent home at the end of the school year. In some instances a family portrait drawn during the same week of school was used for analysis if the judges rating the drawings decided that it was a better example of the child's "best effort." Photocopies of the drawings were collected for later scoring.

3. A *listening activity* in which the subjects were given verbal instructions for completing a written assignment. The purpose of this activity was to measure the child's attention span, ability to understand and follow verbal directions, fine motor coordination, and ability to complete tasks despite distraction

4. An op*en-ended questionnaire of teachers' observations of children's classroom performance*. The three classroom teachers were asked to respond to six open-ended questions concerning the subject's performance in daily classroom activities. These 6 questions were developed by the first author as a general measure of how well the children performed in a real classroom setting the actual K-ABC skills measured. These 6 questions included: How do this child' language

skills help/hurt classroom performance of tasks?, How do this child's social skills help/hurt classroom performance of tasks?, What types of pro-social (helping) behaviors does this child exhibit?, To the best of your knowledge, how does this child's home environment influence classroom performance of tasks?, What are the child's strengths?, and What are the child's weaknesses? These 6 questions were also pilot tested with the same three kindergarten teachers acting as judges that participated in the construction of the Teachers' Rating instrument. The purpose of these 6 questions was to provide a qualitative description of the children's classroom performance in several areas; and to determine the extent to which factors such as language, social skills, pro-social behaviors, and the home environment influence classroom achievement. In addition, the teachers were encouraged to provide any additional comments they felt were necessary to describe the child's classroom performance.

Procedures

A participant-observer model was used for collecting data for this study. Beginning on the second day of school, the first author participated in regular classroom activities in the three selected kindergarten classes. The first author divided her time equally among the three classes, and she was involved in all aspects of the school day, including academic activities, snack time, recess, art, and music.

There were two primary advantages to the first author becoming a participant observer in the Kindergarten classes:

1. The children started the school year with the assumption that the researcher was one of the teachers or aides (resulting in an expected presence in the classroom allowing observations of the everyday children's classroom performance under natural conditions)

2. During formal assessment periods, the children were already familiar with the researchers, and might probably felt more comfortable interacting with her

Procedures: Assessment of Cognitive Skills

During the fourth week of school, the first author began to administer the K-ABC to the children. The test was administered in the school library, a room which was both familiar to the subjects and quiet enough to allow them to complete the K-ABC with minimal distractions. The children were given as much time as needed for the not timed sub-tests. Immediately after each child finished the test, the researcher recorded her observations of each child's behaviors during assessment.

Procedures: Assessment of Moral Development

Approximately three months after the beginning of the school year, the subjects were assessed for pro-social moral development using stories adapted from Eisenberg-Berg and Hand (1979). The subjects worked individually with the researcher to complete the stories, and were assessed in the school library also. The children's responses were videotaped for assuring validity of data analysis.

Procedures: Assessment of Adaptive Behavior

Each teacher participating in the study as an informant was asked to complete the Vineland Adaptive Behavior Scales, Classroom Edition (Sparrow et al., 1985) for each subject in her class. Before the teachers completed the Vineland Scales, the researcher provided them with a complete explanation of the administration procedure. The Vineland Scales were given to the teachers approximately three months after the beginning of the school year, and all surveys were completed within two months.

Procedures: Teachers' Survey of Cognitive Skills and Classroom Achievement

Approximately three months after the beginning of the school year, the teachers were asked to rate each child's *typical* classroom performance. All surveys were completed within two months.

Procedures: Portfolio Rating

Throughout the fall semester, copies of the children's school work were collected for analysis. The self-portraits were drawn during the first week of the school year, while the handwriting and listening activity samples were obtained approximately four months after the beginning of the school year.

Results and Discussion

First data analysis design and coding procedures information is presented. Second descriptive statistics are used to characterize the subjects and their scores on the various assessment instruments used. Third the results of regression tests is presented in relation to the four research questions tested. Fourth case studies are presented to illustrate descriptive and statistical findings, which will lead to a fifth section of discussion of major findings and the resulting revised model.

Data Analysis Design and Coding

In this quasi-experimental study, a multiple regression model was used to determine the extent to which each independent variable (adaptive behavior, pro-social moral development, cognitive-linguistic development, and achievement) predicted the dependent variable (classroom performance). For the two standardized measures used (the Vineland Adaptive Behavior Scales, and the K-ABC), standard scores were used as predictors of the classroom performance variable.

Data Analysis Design and Coding: Coding of the Children's Classroom Performance

Scores obtained from four sources (i. e., Teachers' Ratings Scale, and portfolio samples—handwriting sample, self-portrait, and listening activity) were combined to produce a composite score representing total classroom performance. This composite score averaging the scores obtained on the four qualitative measures obtained were treated as a continuous variable when entered into the regression model. The teachers' observations of classroom performance were not scored numerically, but used as qualitative input for comparing it with other measures of classroom performance.

Each child's classroom performance was rated by independent judges as: (1) well-above average, (2) above average, (3) average, (4) below average, and (5) well below average. In the case of the Teachers' Rating Scale, a mean score was obtained for the mental processing skills, achievement skills, and a combination of the skills assessed (as they related to the classification of the skills measured by the K-ABC).

All of the portfolio samples were independently rated by three public school teachers, who were not familiar with the subjects. This eliminated any bias on the part of the first author and the classroom teacher, who were already familiar with both the subjects' scores on other instruments and their typical school behavior. Keeping in mind the age of the subjects and the month of the school year in which the samples were collected, the raters were asked to score the writing and listening activity samples using the same 5 point Likert scale. Scores obtained from the three raters were averaged to obtain a mean score for the writing and the listening activity tasks.

The self-portrait drawings were scored by the first author using an empirically devised system derived from Koppitz (1968) and Mortensen (1991). Scores obtained by the first author were independently confirmed by two other raters who were familiar with the subjects. One point was awarded for the inclusion of each item from a specific set of characteristics (see Table 6.4.). According to Koppitz (1968), human figures drawn by a typical 5 year-old child are expected to contain 7 or 8 items from the list of characteristics. Therefore, a drawing including 6 to 9 items (81-120% of the expected number of items, $\pm$ 1 SD from the mean) was rated as average. A drawing containing 3 items or less (less than 70% of the expected items; more than 1 SD below the mean) was rated as below average. A drawing containing 10 to 12 items or less (121-160% of expected items; more than 1 SD above the mean) was rated as above average. Finally, a drawing containing 13 or more items (161% of expected items; more than 2 SD above the mean) was rated as well above average.

Data Analysis Design and Coding: Coding of the Moral Judgment Tasks

Each of the subjects' responses was placed into one of six empirically derived categories, based partially on those created by Eisenberg-Berg and Hand (1979), and Kohlberg (as cited in Vander Zanden, 1993). These six developmental categories are listed sequentially, from less to more advanced levels: (1) no reasoning, (2) hedonism/revenge, (3) needs oriented or stereotyped reasoning, (4) mutual benefit orientation, (5) adherence to social conventions, and (6) internalized laws or value systems. Previous research by Eisenberg-Berg and Hand (1979) and Kolhberg (cited in Vander Zanden, 1993) indicate types of reasoning, definitions, and categorizations of level of moral reasoning shown in Table 6.5.; scoring system that was used in this study.

The children's responses were videotaped at the time of assessment and transcribed into written form at a later date. All responses were scored by the first author, and independently rated also by two judges who were unfamiliar with the subjects. The responses were scored based on the reasoning underlying the children's moral judgments.

Results: Descriptive Level

The range of scores, median, Z scores, and standard deviations for all K-ABC scores are presented in Table 6.6. While the mean and median scores for all K-ABC scales were above 100 (the national average), the scores obtained on the Sequential Processing, Simultaneous Processing, Mental Processing Composite, and Non-Verbal Scales were significantly higher than the national mean. These results indicate that the sample of children participating in this study is not representative of the national norm group in these areas. However, scores obtained in the Achievement scale by participating children were not statistically different from the national mean. Thus, while these children tend to have above average cognitive potential and problem-solving abilities, their learned knowledge and skills were within the average range.

The range of scores, median, Z scores, and standard deviations for all Vineland Adaptive Behavior scores are presented in Table 6.7. The mean scores for the Daily Living Skills, Motor Skills, and Adaptive Behavior Composite domains were significantly higher than the national mean scores. The Communication and Socialization scores were not significantly different from the national mean scores. It is interesting to note that the range of mean scores was much smaller for adaptive behavior than for the mental processing composite components of the K-ABC. However, the range of scores for adaptive behavior and achievement, which both measure learning in a specific culture, were much smaller.

Developmental levels attained by the children on the moral judgment tasks ranged form the first level of no reasoning (score of 1) to the highest level of internalized laws or valued systems (score of 6). The mean composite score was 3.5 (Standard Deviation=1.12) and the median score was 3.47. It is interesting to note that while children appeared to respond at the same level for stories 1 (Mean=3.4, Standard Deviation=1.43, Median=3) and 2 (Mean=3.2, Standard Deviation=1.12, Median=3), many of them responded at a somewhat higher level for story 3 (Mean=3.95, Standard Deviation=1.51, Median=5). Thus, some factors present in the story content or linguistic structure (e. g., length of story, difficulty level of language used, level of complexity of content, reading level of story, etc.) may have influenced the children's performance.

A composite score for classroom performance was obtained by averaging scores from two sources: (1) the teachers' ratings of cognitive skills and academic achievement, and (2) the portfolio composite score. Scores from each source represented 50% of the total classroom performance score. For all instruments, a Likert scale was used, were 1corresponded to average performance, 2 corresponded to above average performance, 3 indicated average performance, 4 corresponded to below average performance, and 5 indicated well below average performance. The range of the mean and median scores, and the standard deviation for the classroom performance components are summarized in Table 6.8. The Portfolio Components reported include the raw scores for the self-portrait drawing and the listening activity which were also converted to scores on a Likert-type scale, the handwriting sample scores using only a Likert-type scale. The Portfolio Composite was calculated by averaging the scale scores obtained for the three portfolio components (self-portrait, listening activity, and writing sample). As can be observed in Table 6.8., the children's composite scores were broken down into Mental Processing Skills and an Achievement Component, resulting into very similar scores attained by children when evaluating their actual classroom performance. This is an interesting finding, since K-ABC scores indicated a significant difference between the subjects' mental processing scores and their achievement scores. Therefore, the results from this survey may indicate that standardized test scores may not be reflective of the students' actual performance in the classroom. In addition, a Composite Classroom Performance score was obtained averaging scores from two qualitative instruments, the Teacher's Rating Scale and the Portfolio Composite scores. Both scores represented 50% of the total Classroom Performance Composite score. These results are also shown in Table 6.8.

In conclusion, the children participating in this study performed generally very well in both standardized and alternative measures. On the K-ABC Mental Composite Scales, all scaled scores were within the average to well above average range. However, all children scored within a narrower and lower mean in the K-ABC Achievement Scale and also in all four Vineland adaptive behavior domains, staying only within the average range. Scores for the qualitative instruments were somewhat more varied, although the children generally performed very well on these measures as well. The mean score for the moral judgment stories indicated that the participating children typically performed at Kolhberg's stage 3, with a varied performance depending on the content and language structure of the story (resulting in more advanced responses for story 3 than for stories 1 and 2). Thus, for the age of the participating children, they were showing an advanced moral development.

The scores resulting from the Teachers' Rating Scale of Cognitive Skills and Academic Achievement showed slightly above average ratings for both the Mental Processing Component and the Achievement Component. Then, teachers' ratings were not coincident with the K-ABC scores, because the latter indicated a significant difference between their Mental Processing Scale scores and their Achievement Scale scores. In addition, other alternative measures were also supportive of the teachers' ratings, including the mean Portfolio Composite scores and the total Classroom Performance Composite scores (which were also slightly above average).

Thus, contradictory findings based on standardized and alternative assessments were obtained, which can be explained by many possible factors:

1. The presence of two different *informants* (evaluators for the K-ABC testing, and classroom teachers for the rating scale)

2. The provision of evidence for supporting a difference in children's performance across *contexts* (the K-ABC testing situation and the actual classroom performance for the teachers' ratings)

3. The collection of only a *small sample of behavior* in the K-ABC testing situation in comparison to the teacher using *real-life daily experiences* with the child's academic performance in the   *classroom* as a basis for ratings.

Major Statistical Findings

Multiple regression analyses were conducted in relation to the research questions presented in Table 6.9. While this particular major results did not directly answer a research question, there was a significant relationship when each of the independent predictors in research questions 1, 2, 3, and 4 were considered together, but not when tested independently. The most important results indicated that when the Mental Processing Composite and the Adaptive Behavior Composite were considered simultaneously, they were fairly accurate predictors of the children's classroom performance (R squared=0.512, p=< .01). Thus, the variability in the two predictor variables considered simultaneously accounted for 51.2% of the variance in classroom performance.

Most significant results showed than when scores from the four adaptive behavior domains of the Vineland Scales were considered simultaneously, they were highly predictive of the children's classroom performance (R squared=0.721, p=< 0.001). Then, the variability in the four adaptive behavior domains of the Vineland Scales considered simultaneously accounted for 72.1% of the variance in classroom performance. Thus, the Vineland Scales measuring social adaptive behavior showed even better predictive values than the Mental Processing Composite and Moral Development Composite scores considered together.

When scores from the three moral judgment stories were considered simultaneously in the Moral development Composite score, they were not predictive of the children's classroom performance (R squared=0.000, p=n. s.). Not even the children's responses at a higher developmental level for the third moral story were predictive of the composite score for the children's classroom performance (R squared=0.038, p=n. s.). Even though no moral judgment story predicted the children's classroom performance, the measurement of this variable using other tools warrants further research because some limitations and biases may have been present in the instrument used.

In addition, as shown in Table 6.9., the scores from four K-ABC scales (Sequential Processing, Simultaneous Processing, Non-Verbal, and Achievement) were significantly predictive of the children's classroom performance (R squared=0.421, p < 0.05). However, when scores from the Mental Processing Scales were considered alone (including only the Sequential Processing Scales and the Simultaneous Processing Scales), they were slightly more predictive of the children's classroom performance (R squared=0.469, p < 0.01) than when the four K-ABC Scales were considered simultaneously. Interestingly, scores from the K-ABC Achievement Scale were much less predictive of classroom performance (R squared=0.199, p < 0.05) than were adaptive behaviors scores of the Vineland Scales or Mental Processing Scales scores of the K-ABC. As mentioned above, the variability in the four adaptive behavior domains of the Vineland Scales considered simultaneously accounted for 72.1% of the variance in classroom performance; while the K-ABC four K-ABC scales accounted for 42.1% of the variance, and the two Mental processing Scales accounted for 46.9% of the variance, and the Achievement Scale accounted for 19.9% of the variance only. This latter finding is in contrast to statements made in the K-ABC Interpretative manual

(Kaufman & Kaufman, 1983), claiming that out of all of the K-ABC scores, the Achievement scores should be most predictive of children's actual academic performance.

In conclusion, multiple regression analyses indicated that teacher scales of adaptive behavior (Vineland Scales) are most predictive of classroom performance, followed by standardized measures of cognitive abilities (K-ABC Mental Processing Scales). Results showed that developmentally based, alternative measures of moral reasoning skills were not predictive of children's classroom performance.

Discussion of Findings and the Revised Model

In this section, the relationship between each of the three independent variables measured through standardized and alternative assessments (adaptive behavior, moral development, and cognitive development) and their predictive power for classroom performance in kindergartners will be discussed. In this discussion, final remarks will be reached for the four research questions proposed in this study.

Discussion of Findings and the Revised Model: Research Questions 1 and 3

For over 50 years, standardized intelligence tests have been used for the educational placement of children (Samuda, 1991). Even though results from this study confirm that K-ABC scores are significant predictors of academic achievement, findings also show that measures of social adaptive behaviors are the *best* independent predictors of young children's readiness for Kindergarten and classroom performance (see Table 7.9.). This finding coincides with other studies (Feiring & Lewis, 1991; Feldman & Wentzel, 1990; Wentzel, 1991, 1993) showing that some aspects of social competence were highly predictive of academic performance in elementary and middle school students. These findings also confirms Platt's hypothesis (1991), showing that adaptive behaviors and intelligence are separate but related constructs, as confirmed in this study in the moderate Pearson correlation found between cognitive skills measured by the K-ABC and adaptive behavior measured by the Vineland Scales (r=0.592).

Results of this study providing evidence that that adaptive behavior scores are highly predictive of classroom performance in kindergartners provides two important contributions to the field of educational assessment. Firstly, this is one of the few studies that compare the usefulness of measures of cognitive-linguistic and social-emotional development when predicting school readiness and classroom achievement in young children. The results obtained in this study indicated that while advanced problem-solving abilities and prior learning of factual knowledge certainly enhance school performance, measures of child's overall level of functioning (observed on a daily basis by a teacher) are better predictors of a child's readiness to learn and participate in a classroom setting. Therefore, it appears that the ability to perform certain adaptive behavior skills on a regular basis (e.g., understanding language and communicating adequately, caring for personal needs, interacting with other individuals and showing responsibility and sensitivity to others, and having the motor skills necessary to manipulate objects and play games with others) is more important to kindergarten success than mastering the skills measured by standardized intelligence tests.

Secondly, this study illustrates the potential role that teachers may have in the assessment of children. Classroom teachers have often been undervalued as evaluators for two main reasons:

1. Teachers are intimidated by "psychology experts" who tend to underestimate the importance of their daily interactions with their students for their accurate assessment (Gardner as cited by Scherer, 1985)

2. Past studies have indicated that teachers may be biased in how they view their students' performance (Itskowitz et al., 1988; Jussim, 1989; Kenealy, Frude, & Shaw, 1990) resulting in inaccurate assessments

In actuality the accuracy of teachers' judgments of their students is supported by researchers who found that given adequate time to observe and interact with their students, teachers are:

1. Quite accurate in their students' perceptions (Stevenson et al., 1976)

2. Often more accurate at predicting students' performance than are scores on a battery of tests (Mercer, Algozzine, & Trifiletti, 1979)

In addition, findings of this study suggest that teachers may be the best informants for screening young children's school readiness because they are familiar with their natural behaviors in daily classroom activities. In the assessment of adaptive behaviors, teachers provide information that can not be obtained by an outside unfamiliar evaluator, who ob- servers the child's behavior for only a short period of time. Teachers also have been exposed to a large cohort of children and have internalized developmental "norms" or expectations that can increase the accuracy and validity of their evaluations. In addition, the accuracy of teachers' perceptions of their students' skills was also confirmed in this study in the high correlation found between cognitive skills rated by standardized tests and by teachers ($\underline{r}$=0.705).

While it appears that extensive formal training in assessment is not required for teachers to have a useful role in the screening of children for kindergarten readiness, awareness of other factors *is* required. Specifi- cally, Gonzalez and co-authors (1997) emphasized that any evaluator must become aware of the influence of his/her personality, cultural and linguistic background, and personal belief system when assessing chil- dren. In particular, since teachers typically do not receive training in as- sessment, it is essential that they become aware of the influence of their attitudes on the evaluation process.

In sum, the results obtained from this study indicated that the ability to perform adaptive behavior skills on a daily basis is highly related to classroom performance in kindergarten students. In fact, of the three in- dependent variables examined in this study, adaptive behavior was most predictive of future achievement in the classroom. Thus teachers' ratings of adaptive behavior may play an important role in the early screening of young children and in the prediction of future school performance.

Discussion of Findings and the Revised Model: Research Question 2

Moral development, as measured in this study, appears to be unre- lated to classroom performance, and thus is not useful in predicting aca- demic achievement in young children. Results showed that pro-social moral reasoning was unrelated to classroom performance (R squared=0.000, $\underline{p}$ < 0.626), Mental Processing (R squared ' 0.000, p < 0.521), factual knowledge (R squared=0.050, $\underline{p}$ < 0.175), adaptive behav- ior (R squared=0.007, $\underline{p}$ < 0.403), and age (R squared=0.035, $\underline{p}$ < 0.209).

These findings are in contrast to the theories of moral development proposed by Kohlberg (as cited by Colby & Kohlberg, 1987) and Eisenberg-Berg and Hand (1979), which linked moral, cognitive, and social development. We propose two possible explanations for the lack of association between moral development and classroom performance observed in this study. Firstly, this study examined only the subjects' pro-social moral *reasoning* rather than their pro-social actual actions or *behaviors*. Another possible explanation of findings is that this particular sample of children had already received extensive instructions in moral behavior at home and at school, since they attended a preschool that was associated with a community church. Then, it can be that these children's reasoning skills were more advanced than their emotional development. Thus, while these children may have understood logically what the correct moral response should be, their emotional immaturity may prevent them from practicing these moral behaviors on a daily basis. If actual pro-social moral behaviors exhibited in the classroom had been examined instead of pro-social moral reasoning in hypothetical situations, the statistical relationship between moral development and classroom performance may had been stronger.

Secondly, moral development may be a totally separate aspect of intelligence that was not measured by standardized tests of other alternative measures of classroom performance used in this study. This explanation would support Gardner's (1983) theory of multiple intelligences, which he proposed are often independent of one another and develop at different rates. Thus, competence in one aspect of development (i.e., cognitive-linguistic skills or adaptive behavior) may not be related to competence in another area (e.g., moral development). In addition, advanced moral reasoning may not be a skill required for success in a kindergarten classroom. Therefore, while moral reasoning skills may be related to other areas of life functioning, they appear to be unrelated to school performance in young children.

The level of moral reasoning observed in the children participating in this study varied from story to story. Thus, there was an effect of the content of the stories on the level of moral reasoning attained by the children. Most children performed at a higher level in story 3 than in story 1 and 2. Perhaps this result was influenced by the level of familiarity of the children with the content of the stories. The moral dilemma presented in story 3 was more familiar to young children as they had more actual experience dealing with similar situations. However, the three stories are examining moral *reasoning* only when hypothetical situations are presented to children in an assessment process rather than moral actions. Observing actual behaviors within the context of real-life experiences may result in higher moral reasoning levels attained by young children.

In summary, findings in this study across the four research questions tested showed that moral development was unrelated to classroom performance, adaptive behavior, and cognitive development. These findings suggest that the construct of moral development is independent from the constructs of adaptive behavior and cognitive development, as measured by the assessment tools used din this study. Moreover, it appears that advanced moral *reasoning* skills are not required to perform at a successful level in a kindergarten classroom. But, results also suggest that moral reasoning skills were related to the particular characteristics of the story used as discussed above (e.g., linguistic difficulty, reading level, sociocultural content). In addition, these results may also be influenced by the fact that the children's verbal responses to hypothetical situations were used as samples or moral *reasoning*, rather than actual *behaviors* in reaction to real-life experiences.

Discussion of Findings and the Revised Model:
Research Question 4

Results of multiple regression analyses obtained in this study indicated that standardized intelligence test scores were significant predictors of classroom performance (R squared=0.421, $p < .05$). However, considered alone, the intelligence test scores were not the best predictors of classroom performance. Instead, adaptive behavior scores appeared to be more predictive of classroom performance in kindergartners (R squared=0.721, p ' 0.001). Alternative measures of moral reasoning did not predict classroom performance in young children. These findings confirm the conclusions drawn by Blythe and Gardner (1990), and Roth and colleagues (1993), who argue that factors besides standardized test scores should be considered when making educational placement decisions.

These findings may be due to several factors. Firstly, the standardized intelligence test used, K-ABC, was administered under conditions that were not reflective of the actual classroom conditions in which children must perform. That is, following best assessment practices recommended by experts (e.g., Witt et al., 1994), standardized testing occurred in an ideal situation: in a quiet room with no distractions, and with the child receiving individualized attention from the evaluator. Then, even though the administration of the K-ABC was done taking into account several external factors that could have a confounding effect on the children's tests scores (e. g., level of familiarity of the evaluator to the children), still several other factors may have decreased the validity of the K-ABC in this study. In addition, the children were not tested if they were ill, tired, or "out of sorts."

Thus, intelligence test scores attained by the children in this study were more likely to reflect the *ideal* performance, rather than the *typical* performance of these children. Instead their typical performance was assessed by teachers' ratings and portfolio products. Thus, test scores may represent the child's potential to perform in an ideal setting, because real-life factors affecting the typical children' s performance in the classroom. (e. g., emotional, social, and physical development; daily home influences; and disruptions in the classroom) are recommended to be controlled for in test administrations. These real-life factors affecting the classroom performance of children are considered to be confounding factors in a testing situation.

In fact, the differences between skills measured in an ideal setting (during testing) with control of most external variables affecting the performance of young children versus a *natural* classroom setting, are highlighted when the K-ABC Mental Processing Scale scores are compared to the teachers' ratings of similar skills in a classroom setting. While the mean Mental Processing Scale score in the K-ABC test was 126.5 (categorized as a superior performance), the mean score from the teachers' ratings of these same cognitive and linguistic skills was only slightly above average. Several factors may explain the observed differences between the K-ABC Mental Processing Scale scores and the teachers' ratings of similar skills. We propose two possible explanations for these results. Firstly, teachers may be biased in their students' assessments because individual traits in both the teacher and the children (e.g., personality, physical appearance, and cultural background) may have caused them to underestimate their students' cognitive-linguistic abilities.

However, the use of two procedures for controlling confounding factors suggested that this possible bias in teachers' evaluations actually may have not happened in this study. The first control procedure indicated that the mean portfolio scores given by classroom teachers (2.32) and by independent raters (2.69), who were unfamiliar to the children, were very similar. In addition, since the portfolio products reflected the actual performance of many of the same skills assessed by the teachers' ratings, the similarity in scoring indicated that the teachers were fairly accurate in the assessment of their students. The second control procedure indicated that due to the contextual and non-verbal clues present in the classroom setting, teachers have been found by previous researchers to *overestimate*, rather than *underestimate*, their students' skills in areas such as language development (Witt, et al., 1994). Therefore, the possibility that the teachers in this study significantly underestimated their students' cognitive skills is unlikely.

Another major factor influencing the more predictive power of adaptive behavior in comparison to the K-ABC scores may be that the latter measures only the child's conceptual understanding of certain skills, rather than the child's ability to express this understanding in a typical classroom environment. For instance, the child' test scores may have indicated an advanced understanding of many academic concepts or problem-solving skills as expressed by verbal or non-verbal (e.g., pointing) behaviors. However, typical and normal developmental limitations of young children (e.g., lack of fine motor skills, distractibility, or emotional immaturity) may have inhibited the expression of these skills in the classroom through more complex and "natural" verbal and non-verbal behaviors. In addition, the K-ABC measures only cognitive-linguistic development and may not measure many of the perceptual, social, emotional, and self-control skills taught in kindergarten. Thus, the K-ABC may have inadequate curriculum validity for kindergartners.

Discussion of Findings and the Revised Model: Case Studies Illustrating Findings

Three case studies are included to illustrate how the patterns of performance in individual children matched the overall performance trends observed in the statistical analysis. In all case studies, pseudonyms are used instead of the children's real names.

Conclusions

Multiple regression analyses indicated that scores from the Vineland Adaptive Behavior Scales were the best predictors of classroom performance. When considered simultaneously, scores from the Vineland Scale, K-ABC Scales, and moral judgment tasks significantly predicted classroom performance, but to a lesser extent than when the Vineland was used alone. Likewise, scores from the K-ABC Scales were significantly predictive of classroom performance, but were not as predictive as the Vineland Scales. Moral development was observed to be unrelated to classroom performance in kindergarten children.

Considering the developmental limitations of young children, the finding that adaptive behavior scores are more predictive of classroom performance than are intelligence test scores is not unexpected. Before an individual can physically or verbally express a concept or skill, he or she must first acquire a cognitive understanding of the concept. However, because young children are still limited in their physical, emotional, verbal, and social skills, they may have difficulty expressing their understanding of academic concepts or problem-solving skills in a classroom setting. Thus, standardized intelligence tests may indicate a level of cognitive development above that expressed on a daily basis.

This developmental trend was observed in the children participating in this study. For all 20 children, K-ABC Mental Processing scores were higher than their Adaptive Behavior Composite scores. For 12 out of the 20 children, the K-ABC Mental Processing scores indicated a cognitive ability above that expressed in the classroom on a daily bases (e.g., K-ABC scores indicated above average cognitive ability, while classroom performance was only average). Only 7 children had K-ABC Mental Processing scores in the same developmental range as their classroom performance. Thus, K-ABC Mental Processing scores generally tended to measure *potential* cognitive developmental level, which were above the performance level observed by teachers in the children's classroom performance.

On the other hand, for 13 out of the 20 children, performance on the Vineland Adaptive Behavior Scales was in the same developmental range as their classroom performance.

In sum, while advanced problem-solving abilities and prior learning of factual knowledge enhanced a child's school performance, it appears that the ability to perform certain adaptive behavior skills on a regular basis (as evaluated by the child's classroom teacher) are better indicators of a child's readiness to learn and participate in a classroom setting.

Limitations of the Study

This study was limited by three major factors, including:

1. The small and homogeneous sample, limiting the generalization of findings to other populations. All the children participating in this study were from a two-parent, middle-to-upper-middle class home, where both parents tended to be well educated. In addition, 90% of the children were Anglo, and all of the children felt within a narrow

age range. Therefore, one should use caution when making general-izations to children with different ages, home environments, ethnic and cultural backgrounds, or socioeconomic levels. In addition, a larger sample would decrease the chance of error in all statistical tests performed.

2. The examination of only school-related predictors of classroom per-formance. However, many other factors in the home environment have been shown by the literature to be closely connected to the school performance, especially in young children. See Chapter 4 for an example of a study focused on home environmental factors affect-ing advantaged and disadvantaged children's cognitive development. For example, maternal occupational and educational level (Kochanek et al., 1990), perceived attachment to parents (Brinich et al., 1989; Raja et al., 1992), level of stress in the home (Gelfand et al., 1992; Webster-Statton, 1990), and parents' commitment to the productive use of time spent with the child (Bloom, 1985) have all been shown to be related to a child's later intellectual ability, psychological well-being, and conduct problems. Therefore, this study examines only a small number of the many factors that are related to future school success.

3. The use of only one standardized and alternative instrument for each skill measured. The results could have been different if other more traditional standardized intelligence tests would have been used, such as the Wechler or Stanford-Binet Scales that tap more learned knowl-edge rather than the K-ABC 's cognitive potential tapped. For the case of pro-social skills, only an alternative measure of moral *rea-soning* rather than the observations of actual *actions* was used as the only measure of social-emotional development. Finally, only one sample of each class work considered (e.g., drawing, listening, and writing samples) was scored to obtain the portfolio ratings. While these authors feel that scores obtained from these single samples were fairly representative of the overall level of class work per-formed by the children, accuracy in ratings would increase if more samples were used as a measure of classroom performance.

Theoretical and Practical Implications of the Study:
Future Research Questions

Even though this study has some limitations, several important contributions to the field of educational assessment are still derived from its findings. Firstly, observations of kindergarten students' adaptive behavior skills on a daily basis are highly related to their ability to perform in school. It appears that the observation of adaptive behavior skills provides important information about the developmental readiness of children that is not obtained from standardized intelligence tests. Thus, adaptive behavior scales (such as the Vineland) may be inexpensive screening tools for classroom teachers to rate kindergartners' school readiness. Teachers have the potential to play a meaningful role in assessment because they are "experts" in children's daily academic behaviors, which are most predictive of their future classroom performance. Finally, the results of this study indicate that the administration of standardized intelligence tests to determine kindergarten readiness may not be necessary for all children. While standardized intelligence tests provide diagnostic information that may be essential in some cases, the use of observation-based instruments by classroom teachers may be adequate screening devices for many young children.

The results of this study indicated that some aspects of social-emotional development (i.e., adaptive behavior) are highly related to classroom performance, while others areas such as pro-social moral reasoning appear unrelated to classroom performance in young children. It would be interesting to examine other areas of social-emotional development (i.e., self-concept, coping abilities, and interactions with peers) to determine their relationship to classroom performance in young children. In addition, results obtained from this study indicated that standardized achievement tests may not measure many of the skills required for success in the classroom, and thus are not truly representative of a child's actual classroom performance. It appears that alternative forms of assessment (i. e., teachers' observations and ratings of cognitive skills) may be more accurate measures of performance in the classroom than are standardized achievement tests. Therefore, further research on alternative, qualitative forms of assessment could benefit the field of educational assessment for young children.

Finally, future studies should investigate if the same relationships between the independent variables and classroom performance occur in a different sample group. It is possible that the regression coefficients would tend to increase given a larger and more heterogeneous sample, indicating an even stronger relationship between certain predictors (e. g., adaptive behavior) and classroom performance.

Case Studies Representing the Patterns Found Across Research Questions

First Case Study: Joseph

Joseph was a 5 year, 9 month old Kindergarten student by the time of assessment, and was the oldest child participating in this study. Joseph's scores from all forms of assessment are shown in Table 6.10.

K-ABC Results. Joseph K-ABC scores tended to be quite high. On four of the K-ABC Scales (Sequential processing, Simultaneous processing, Mental Processing Composite, and Nonverbal) his scores were higher than the mean scores for children participating in this study (which in turn were significantly higher than the national mean scores). However, Joseph's K-ABC Achievement scores were only average, even though his teacher rated his classroom performance as above average.

Vineland Adaptive Behavior Scale. Joseph also received high scores on the Vineland Scales, although his scores on this adaptive behavior scale were somewhat lower than his K-ABC Mental Processing scores. For a child of his age, Joseph scored quite high on the Communication Scale of the Vineland.

Moral Judgment Stories. Joseph's responses to the pro-social moral judgment stories indicated that in the first two stories he was reasoning at Kohlberg's stage 3, which is needs oriented and shows stereotypic reasoning with mutual benefit orientation. For the third story, Joseph showed a higher level of moral reasoning, performing at the level of adherence to social conventions. While the statistical analysis indicated that moral reasoning is unrelated to classroom performance, Joseph's pattern of performance on these stories was very similar to the other children participating in the study, who generally performed at a higher level on the third moral story.

Teachers' Rating Scale. Joseph's teacher also considered his cognitive skills to be advanced, rating him well above average in six of the skills measured and above average in 19 of the skills measured on the teachers' rating scale of cognitive skills and academic achievement. Joseph's advanced cognitive skills are expected, given his home environment. For example, his teacher noted that Joseph's parents are very supportive of him. They spend a lot of time reading to him, working on reading (phonics) and on his math skills. They are involved in church activities and Joseph is involved in sports.

Joseph's teacher also confirmed the high communication skills resulting from the Vineland Scales. Joseph's teacher stated, "He is always willing to share ideas and participate in discussion. He expresses himself well with words, has began to read, and has shown great improvement in reading comprehension." Joseph's teacher also noted other socialization skills, as she stated, "He is able to follow directions and able to work independently. He accepts responsibility well. He has a great attitude and spirit of cooperation which is reflected not only ion school work, but also in his relationship with peers." Thus, Joseph's teacher considered him to have good social and language skills, which enhance his classroom performance.

Joseph's performance in the moral judgment stories was also confirmed by his teachers' feedback. Joseph's teacher observed that while he showed many pro-social behaviors (such as helping others to clean up, showing patience with others, and taking care of school property), these behaviors are somewhat different from those mentioned in the stories. Thus, it is difficult to make a comparison between reasoning about hypothetical situations (the children's responses to the moral stories) and actual moral behaviors exhibited in the classroom (the natural experiences that served teachers to provide feedback in their ratings).

In general, Joseph's teacher gave his overall classroom achievement a high rating (1.69, above average level). Independent evaluators also confirmed Joseph's high level of performance in his class work, giving samples of products similar ratings (1.67, above average level). Thus, Joseph's performance in the classroom was consistent with his adaptive behavior scores attained in the Vineland Scales, but it was also somewhat higher than his K-ABC Achievement Scale score, and somewhat lower than predicted by his K-ABC Mental Processing Composite score (indicating a cognitive level somewhat above his performance level exhibited in the classroom as rated by his teacher).

Since, Joseph's adaptive behavior scores appeared highly related to his teachers' ratings using alternative instruments, it appears that the Vineland Scales may be a better instrument for assessing the skills required in an actual kindergarten classroom than are standardized intelligence tests such as the K-ABC.

Second Case Study: Linda

Linda was 5 years and 1 month old by the time of the assessment, and she was enrolled in a regular kindergarten class. Linda's scores obtained for all the instruments are presented in Table 6.11.

K-ABC Results. Linda's K-ABC mental Processing scores were quite high. All were above average, and her scores on three scales (Simultaneous, Mental Processing Composite, and Nonverbal) indicated possible giftedness. Linda's score on the K-ABC Achievement Scale, however was in the low average range.

Vineland Scales. Linda's Vineland Scale scores were much lower than her K-ABC Mental Processing scores, and indicated an average performance in all areas of adaptive behavior.

Moral Judgment Stories. Linda's responses indicated that she is reasoning at an advanced level for her age. However, Linda's responses were somewhat different from those given by many other children, since she reasoned at the same level across the three stories. Her moral reasoning level did not seem to be dependent on the situation or context on which moral decisions were made.

Teachers' Ratings. Linda's teacher noted that her language and social skills were a mixed blessing for her. For example, the teacher stated that, "Linda asks questions, which help her to complete tasks. However, sometimes her lack of concentration or distractibility keeps her from doing her best work." In addition, Linda's teacher observed that "she is concerned about what others are doing, and this causes her to loose track of her responsibilities." Her teacher indicated that Linda also exhibits pro-social behaviors in the classroom, as she stated that "Linda loves to assist students and the teacher with tasks. She is very caring. She is a nurturer of others. She is very affectionate."

Linda's teacher rated her overall classroom achievement as average (score=3.04). Independent evaluators rated her portfolio products also confirmed an average rating for her age and grade level (score=3.22). Linda's home environment may provide some explanation for her school performance. Her teacher noted that Linda's mother home schools the older sister and has a new baby. Thus, the teacher inferred that due to responsibilities with the other two children, Linda's mother does not have much one-to-one time with her. As reported by Linda's teacher, there is no evidence of TV watching, some reading is done at home by parents. Thus, while education appears to be highly valued by Linda's parents (as evidenced by the time spent home schooling an older sister), it seems that Linda's parents may also be distracted by other activities and obligations. Therefore, they may not have the time and energy to reinforce the skills and concepts Linda learns at school.

In sum, Linda's scores on the standardized instruments were very close to the mean scores obtained by the other children participating in the study. While Linda's scores on the K-ABC Mental Processing Scales indicated her cognitive developmental *potential* to be at the near-gifted level, her level of *actual achievement* in the classroom was rated as average, as well as her adaptive behavior scores were within the average range. Even though there was disagreement between standardized and alternative measures of cognitive development and adaptive behavior, there was consistency in the achievement measures, showing similar average performances.

Third Case Study: Billy

Billy had just turned 5 years old by the time of the assessment. Billy's scores on all instruments are shown in Table 6.12.

K-ABC Results. While Billy received high scores on all K-ABC Scales, his performance in some areas was quite noteworthy. For example, Billy's core for the Simultaneous processing Scale was 160, indicating that his score was four standard deviations above the mean, and his performance in this area was better than 99.9% of same-age children. Billy's nonverbal score of 144 was also well into the gifted range, and was almost three standard deviations above the mean. Thus, Billy's problem-solving and cognitive abilities appear to be quite advanced.

Vineland Scales. Billy's adaptive behavior scores also tended to be above average. although they were significantly lower than his K-ABC Mental Processing Scale scores.

Moral Judgment Stories. Billy's pattern of moral reasoning was very similar to that shown by Joseph and many of the other children participating in this study. Billy's responses to the pro-social moral judgment stories indicated that he was reasoning at Kohlberg's stage 3 (needs oriented or stereotypic reasoning, or mutual benefit orientation) for the first two stories. However, for the third story, Billy showed a higher level of moral reasoning (adherence to social conventions), as also shown by most children participating in this study. Thus, while Billy's moral reasoning was advanced for his age, he was also influenced by the context in which the hypothetical decision was made.

Teachers' Ratings. Billy's teacher observed that many of his social and language skills enhanced his classroom performance. For example, in relation to Billy's language skills, his teacher noted, "He has a good grasp of language and as a result has done very well in learning his sounds and numbers." In addition, Billy's teacher also noted that he had good social skills, as she stated, "Billy cares for each person and encourages everyone to do their best work, which has helped him to do his best work as well." His teacher also observed that he had an incredible ability to stay focused on tasks despite numerous distractions, a skill that is unusual in a child his age. In other observations, Billy's teachers also stressed the many pro-social behaviors that he exhibited in class, as she stated, "Billy is a child who focuses on helping his peers in need of assistance. He takes time to explain and encourage good performance. He includes peers in his plays. He is very patient." Billy's teacher recognized as his strengths being compassionate and helpful, and being gentle and caring with his peers. "Billy's teacher rate his overall classroom achievement as above average (score'2.31). She considered his performance as average in 8 of the assessed skills, and above average in 18 other skills.

Likewise, outside evaluators rated his class work as above average (score=2.11).

In summary, Billy's adaptive behavior scores appeared to be more consistent with his teachers' ratings, while his K-ABC scores appeared to be tapping his potential rather than his actual classroom performance. In addition, while moral reasoning appeared to be unrelated to classroom performance, Billy's level of social abilities seemed to help him in his classroom performance as discussed and rated by his teacher. Thus, his pattern of performance appeared to be quite congruent in comparison to his peers. His cognitive *potential*, as measured by the K-ABC mental Processing Scales, was much higher than his *actual* classroom achievement, as measured by alternative instruments for which teachers were the informants.

References

Adelman, H. S. (1982). Identifying learning problems at an early age: A critical appraisal. *Journal of Clinical Child Psychology, 11*, 255-261.

Adler, E. (1995). Relax: SAT's not an intelligence test. *The Arizona Daily Star, October 14*, p. A3.

Anastasi, H. S. (1982). *Psychological testing.* New York: Collier Mcmillan Publishing Co.

Blythe, T., & Gardner, H. (1990). A school of all intelligences. *Educational Leadership, 47*, 33-37.

Brinich, E., Drotar, D., & Brinich, P. (1989). Security of attachment and outcome of preschoolers with histories of non-organic failure to thrive. *Journal of Clinical Child Psychology, 18, 142*-152.

Colby, A., & Kohlberg, L. (1987). *The measurement of moral judgment.* New York: Cambridge University Press.

Cole, P. M., Usher, B. A., & Cargo, A. P. (1993). Cognitive risk and its association with risk for disruptive behavior disorder in preschoolers . *Journal of Clinical Child Psychology, 22*, 154-164.

Eisenberg-Berg, P., & Hand, L. (1979). The relationship of preschoolers' reasoning about moral conflicts to pro-social behavior. *Child Development, 50*, 356-363.

Gardner, H. (1978). Developmental psychology. Boston: Little, Brown, and Co.

Gardner, H. (1983). *Frames of mind.* New York: basic Books.

Gelfand, D. M., Teti, G., & Fox, C. E. R. (1992). Sources of parenting stress for depressed and non-depressed mother so of infants. *Journal of Clinical Child psychology, 24*, 262-272.

Gillingan, C. (1982). *In a different voice.* Cambridge: Harvard University Press.

Gonzalez, V., Brusca-Vega, R., & Yawkey, T. D. (1997). *Assessment and instruction of culturally and linguistically diverse children at-risk of learning problems.* Needham Heights, MA: Allyn & Bacon.

Grossmna, H. J. (Ed.) (1983). *Classification in mental retardation* . Washington DC: American Association on Mental Deficiency.

Harrison, P. L. (1985). *Vineland Adaptive Behavior Scales, Classroom Edition Manual.* Circle Pines, MN: American Guidance Service.

Harrison, P. L. (1991). Assessment of adaptive behavior. In B. A. Bracken (Ed.), *The Psychological Assessment of Preschool Children* . Boston: Allyn & Bacon.

Hopps, H., & Cobb, J. A. (1974). Initial investigations into academic survival-skill training, direct construction, and first-grade achievement. *Journal of Educational Psychology, 66,* 548-553.

Itskowitz, R., Navon, R., & Strauss, H. (1988). Teachers' accuracy in evaluating students' self-image: Effect of perceived closeness. *Journal of Educational Psychology, 80,* 337-341.

Jussim, L. (1989). Teacher expectations: Self-fulfilling prophecies, perceptual biases, and accuracy. *Journal of Personality and Social Psychology, 57,* 469-480.

Kaufman, A., S., & Kaufman, N. L. (1983). *Administration and scoring manual for the Kaufman Assessment Battery for Children.* Minneapolis, MN: American Guidance Service.

Kaufman, A., S., & Kaufman, N. L. (1983). *Interpretative manual for the Kaufman Assessment Battery for Children* . Circle Pines, MN: American Guidance Service.

Kenealy, P., Frude, N., & Shaw, W. (1990). Teacher expectations as predictors of academic success. *Journal of Social Psychology, 131,* 305-106.

Kochanek, T. T., Kabacoff, R. I., & Lipsett, L. P. (1990). Early identification of developmentally disabled and at-risk preschool children. *Exceptional Children, 56,* 528-538.

Kohlberg, L. (1987). *Child psychology and childhood education: A cognitive developmental view.* New York: Longman.

Kohlberg, L., Levine, C., & Hewer, A. (1987). *Moral stages; A current formulation and a response to critics.* Basel, Switzerland: Karger.

Koppitz, E. M. (1968). *Psychological evaluation of children's human drawings.* New York: Grune & Stratton.

Krumboltz, J., Ford, M., Nichols, C., & Wentzel, K. (1987). The goals of education. In R. C. Calfee (Ed.), *The study of Stanford and the schools: Views from the inside: Part II,* (pp. 134-167). Stanford, University Press.

Love, H. D. (1990). *Assessment of intelligence and development of infants and young children.* Springfield, IL: Charles C. Thomas.

Mercer, C. D., Algozzine, B., & Trifiletti, J. J. (1979). Early identification: Issues and considerations. *Exceptional Children, 46,* 52-54.

Mortensen, K. V. (1991). *Form and content in children's human figure drawings.* New York: New York University Press.

Moss, P. A. (1992). Shifting conceptions of validity in educational measurement: Implications for performance assessment. *Review of Educational Research, 62,* 229-258.

Olson. S. L., & Hoza, B. (1993). Preschool developmental antecedents of conduct problems in children beginning school. *Journal of Clinical Child Psychology, 22,* 60-67.

Patton, J. M. (1992). Assessment and identification of African-American learners with gifts and talents. *Exceptional Children, 59,* 150-159.

Platt, L. O., Kamphaus, R. W., Cole, R. W., & Smith, C. L. (1991). Relationship between adaptive behavior and intelligence: Additional evidence. *Psychological Reports, 68,* 139-145.

Raja, S. N., McGee, R., & Stanton, W. R. (1992). Perceived attachments to parents and peers and psychological well-being in adolescence. *Journal of Youth and Adolescence, 21,* 471-485.

Rest, J. R. (1986). *Moral development: Advances in research and theory.* New York: Praeger Publishers.

Roszkowski, M. J., & Bean, A., G. (1980). The Adaptive Behavior Scale (ABS) and IQ: How much unshared variance is there? *Psychology in the Schools, 17,* 452-459.

Roth, M., McCaul, E., & Barnes, K. (1993). Who becomes an "at-risk" student? The predictive value of a kindergarten screening battery. *Exceptional Children, 59,* 348-358.

Samuda, R. J. (1991). Multiculturalism: Perspectives and challenges. In R. J. Samuda, S. L.Kong, J. Cummins, J. Pascual-Leone, & J. Lewis (Eds.), *Assessment and placement of minority students* (pp. 5-13). Toronto, Canada: C. J. Hogrefe.

Satz, P., & Fletcher, J. M. (1988). Early identification of learning disabled children: An old problem revisited. *Journal of Consulting and Clinical Psychology, 56,* 824-829.

Scherer, M. (1985). How many ways is a child intelligent? *Instructor, 94,* 32-25.

Sparrow, S. S., Balla, D. A., & Cicchetti, D. V. (1985). *Vineland Adaptive Behavior Scales, Classroom Edition.* Circle Pines, MN: American Guidance Service.

Stevenson, H. W., Parker, T., Wilkinson, A., Hegion, A., & Fish, E. (1976). Predictive value of teachers' ratings of young children. *Journal of Educational Psychology, 68,* 507-517.

Vander Zanden, J. W. (1993). *Human development.* New York: McGraw-Hill.

Vitaro, F., Tremblay, R. E., Gagnon, C., & Pelletier, D. (1994). Predictive accuracy of behavioral and sociometric assessments of high-risk kindergarten children. Journal of *Clinical Child Psychology, 19,* 302-312.

Webster-Statton, C. (1990). Stress: A potential disruptor of parents' perceptions and family interactions. *Journal of Clinical Child Psychology, 19,* 302-312.

Wentzel, K. R. (1991). Classroom competence may require more than intellectual ability: Reply to Jussim. *Journal of Educational Psychology, 83,* 156-158.

Wentzel, K. R. (1993). Does being good make the grade? Social behavior and academic competence in middle school. *Journal of Educational Psychology, 85,* 357-364.

Witt, J. C., Elliott, S. N., Kramer, J., & Gresham, F. M. (1994). *Assessment of children: Fundamental methods and practices* Iowa City, IA: Brown & Benchmark.

Wodrich, D. L., & Kush, S. A. (1990). *Children's psychological testing: A guide for non-psychologists*. Baltimore, MA: Paul H. Brooks Publishing.

Table 6.1.
Pro-Social Moral Judgment Stories
(adapted from Eisenberg-Berg & Hand, 1979)

Story Title	Story Text
Story 1 *The Accident*	One day a girl named Mary was walking with her father to a friend's birthday party. On her way to the party, Mary saw a boy who had fallen down and hurt his leg. The boy asked Mary to go to his house and get his mother so that his mother could take him to a doctor. But if Mary **did** run sand get the boy's mother, she would be late to the party and she would miss the ice cream, cake, and all the games. What should Mary do? Why?
Story 2 *The Harvest*	Some farmers in a town called Wilcox had worked very hard for a whole year to grow some crops. They ended up harvesting just enough food to feed the people in the town, with no extra food left over. At the same time, farmers in a nearby town called Benson had also been working very hard to grow food. But a big flood came along and ruined all the food that the farmers in Benson had grown. The people in Benson were left with nothing to eat. The people in the flooded town of Benson asked the poor farmers in Willcox to share their food with them. But, if the farmers in Willcox shared their food, their families would go hungry, even though they had worked so hard to grow the crops. The people in Benson could not bring in food from other towns farther away because their roads were all washed out due to the floods. There was no place for an airplane to land, so they could fly in food either. What should the poor farmers in Willcox do? Why?
Story 3 *The Bully*	One day a boy named John was playing with his toys in his front yard. He looked up and saw that an older girl from another neighborhood was hitting the 3-year-old boy who lived next door. The smaller boy was crying and asking for help. John wanted to help the younger boy, but he knew that if he went over in the next yard, the mean girl might hurt him too. What should John do? Why?

Table 6.2.
Teachers' Rating Scale of Cognitive Skills and
Academic Achievement

How do you rate this child's classroom performance in the following areas?

Skill	1	2	3	4	5
Reading ability					
Word knowledge					
Verbal expression					
Letter identification					
Word pronunciation					
Knowledge of shapes					
Number identification					
Mathematical concepts					
Ability to repeat a series of numbers					
Logical classification skills					
Reasoning ability					
Problem-solving ability					
Long-term memory					
Short-term memory					
Ability to shift tasks quickly					
Ability to understand & follow directions					
Attention span					
Ability to complete tasks despite distractions					
Alertness to environment					
Auditory vocal memory					
Ability to work under time pressure					
Alertness to visual detail					
Whole-part relationships					
Acquired facts					
Fine motor coordination					
Interpersonal relationship skills					

1   Well above average
2   Above average
3   Average
4   Below average
5   Well below average

Table 6.3.

Relationship Between Skills Measured by K-ABC Sub-Tests and Skills Measured by the Teachers' Rating Scale

K-ABC Sub-Tests	Skills Measured by Both the K-ABC Sub-Tests and the Teachers' Rating Scale
Hand Movements	• Attention span • Short-term memory • Ability to complete tasks despite distractions
Gestalt Closure	• Alertness to the environment • Alertness to visual detail • Whole-part relationships • Long-term memory
Number Recall	• Attention span • Short-term memory • Auditory vocal memory • Ability to repeat a series of numbers • Ability to complete tasks despite distractions
Triangles	• Ability to work under time pressure • Problem-solving strategies • Whole-part relationships • Reasoning ability
Word Order	• Ability to shift tasks quickly • Ability to understand and follow directions • Ability to complete tasks despite distractions • Short-term memory • Verbal expression
Matrix Analogies	• Fine motor coordination • Problem-solving strategies • Attention to visual detail • Reasoning ability • Logical classification skills

Spatial Memory	• Short-term memory • Attention span • Ability to complete tasks despite distractions
Faces and Places	• Verbal expression • Long-term memory • Acquired facts • Alertness to the environment
Arithmetic	• Mathematical concepts • Attention span • Knowledge of shapes • Number identification • Alertness to the environment • Long-term memory • Reasoning ability • Acquired facts
Riddles	• Acquired facts • Logical classification skills • Long-term memory • Whole-part relationships • Verbal expression • Word Knowledge • Alertness to the environment • Reasoning ability
Reading/Decoding	• Letter identification • Reading ability • Word pronunciation • Verbal expression • Long-term memory • Word knowledge • Alertness to the environment

Table 6.4.

List of Items and Their Definitions Used for Scoring Self-Portraits
(from Koppitz, 1968) and Mortensen (1991)

Item	Definition
Head	Any representation with clear outline of head
Eyes	Any representation
Pupils	Distinct circles or dots within outlines of eyes required. A dot with a line over is scored as eyes and eyebrows
Eyebrows or eyelashes	Either brows or lashes or both
Nose	Any representation
Nostrils	Dots or nostrils shown in addition to nose
Mouth	Any representation
Two lips	Two lips outlined and separated by line from each other; two rows of teeth only are not scored
Ear	Any representation
Hair	Any representation or hat or cap covering hair or hiding hair
Neck	Definite separation of head and body
Body	Any presentation, clean outline necessary
Arms	Both arms presented by more than a single line
Arms in two dimensions	Both arms presented in more than a single line
Arms pointing downward	One or both arms pointing down at an angle of 30 degrees or more from horizontal position, or arms raised appropriately for activity figure is engaged in

Arms correctly attached at shoulder	Indication of shoulder necessary for this item, arms must be firmly connected to body
Elbow	Distinct angle in arm required, rounded curve in arm is not scored
Hands	Differentiation from arms and fingers necessary such as widening of arm or demarcation from arm by sleeve
Fingers	Any representation
Correct number of fingers	Five fingers on each hand or arm
Legs	Any representation in female item is scored if distance between waist and feet is long enough to allow legs to be present under a skirt
Legs in two dimensions	Both legs presented by more than a single line
Knee	Distinct angle in one or both legs, or kneecap; a round curve in leg is not scored
Feet	Any representation
Feet two dimensional	Feet extended in one direction from heel, and showing greater length than height
Profile	Head drawn in profile even if rest of figure is not entirely in profile
Clothing, one item or more	No clothing indicated or only hat, buttons, or belt, or outline of garments without detail
Clothing, two or three items	Includes items such as pants, skirt, shirt, hat, hair ribbon, barrette, necklace, shoes, purse
Clothing, four items or more	Four or more items listed above present
Good proportions	Figure looks right even if not entirely correct from an anatomical point of view

Table 6.5.

Moral Judgment Categories for the Type of Reasoning Scoring System

Code	Type of Reasoning	Definition	Examples
1	No Reasoning	• Child does not know how protagonist should respond in a given situation. • Child cannot explain why protagonist should perform	• I don't know what they should do • John should go over to help. I don't know why
2	Hedonism/ Revenge	• Child's actions are motivated by a selfish desire to gain rewards for self or others • Protagonist's mean or hurtful actions are justified because other characters were mean or hurtful first	• Willcox should keep the food because their town would get fed • It's OK for John to hurt the girl to keep the little boy from getting hurt more
3	Needs Oriented or Stereotyped Reasoning	• Child labels the physical or psychological needs of others and considers needs in his/her reasoning • Child justifies a given course of action with stereotyped conceptions of good and bad behavior	• Mary should help the boy because he's hurt • The Willcox farmers should help them because they are hungry • The should share because it's nicer • Mary should go to his mom because that's obeying God
4	Mutual Benefit Orientation	• Child justifies a given course of action with references to resultant gain for all interested parties	• The Willcox farmers should share because then they would both have food

| 5 | Adherence to Social Conventions | • Child shows acceptance of social conventions and rules
• Child shows respect for authority
• Child understands that some situations are beyond a child's capabilities and therefore should be handled by an adult | • John's older than the little boy so he should help
• john should go to the other house and tell the mom
• John can help by telling his mom |
| 6 | Internalized Laws or Value Systems | • Child's actions are based on an internalized value system
• Child gives priority to most important needs
• Child shows desire to solve problem by helping or improving another person | • They want her at the party, but the boy needs her
• Maybe he would teach her about God so she would be nicer to the boy |

Table 6.6.

Statistical Range, Mean, Standard Deviation, Median Score, Observed z, and P Value for the K-ABC Scores

K-ABC Scale	Range of Scores	Mean Score	Standard Deviation	Median Score	Observe z	p Value
Sequential Processing	78-141 range=63	115.85	15.42	113.5	4.73	p<.001
Simulta- neous Processing	92-160 range=68	126.10	17.33	125.0	7.78	p<.001
Mental Processing Composite	104-160 range=56	126.10	12.93	126.5	7.78	p<.001
Achieve- ment	84-128 range=44	105.00	10.35	105.5	1.49	n.s.
Nonverbal	88-160 range=72	124.25	16.35	122.0	7.29	p<.001

Table 6.7.

Statistical Range, Mean, Standard Deviation, Median Score, Observed z, and P Value for the Vineland Adaptive Behavior Scores

Vineland Scale Domain	Range of Scores	Mean Score	Standard Deviation	Median Score	Observe z	p Value
Communication	79-116 range=37	100.8	9.95	113.5	0.24	n. s.
Daily Living Skills	83-119 range=36	107.15	9.70	109.0	2.13	p<.05
Socialization	86-120 range=34	105.25	7.69	105.5	1.57	n. s.
Motor Skills	82-126 range=44	110.35	9.22	109.5	3.09	p<.01
Adaptive Behavior Composite	83-119 range=36	105.85	8.37	106.0	1.74	p<.05

Table 6.8.
Statistical Range, Mean, Standard Deviation,
and Median Score for the Qualitative Evaluation of the
Children's Classroom Performance

Portfolio Component	Range of Scores	Mean Score	Standard Deviation	Median Score
Self-Portrait (Raw Score)	6-20 range=14	10.6	3.53	10.0
Self-Portrait (Scaled Score)	1-3 range=2	2.15	.875	2.0
Handwriting	2.0-4.67 range=2.67	3.10	0.74	3.0
Listening Activity (Raw Score)	2-6 range=4	5.25	1.12	6.0
Listening Activity (Scaled Score)	1-4 range=3	1.70	0.98	1.0
Portfolio Composite	1.33-3.89 range=2.56	2.32	0.707	2.11
Mental Processing Skills		2.70	0.49	
Achievement Component		2.65	0.62	
Composite Classroom Performance Score	1.68-3.55 range=1.87	2.503	0.484	2.325

Table 6.9.

Summary of Multiple Regression Analyses of Predictor Variables
with Classroom Performance (Dependent Variable)

Predictor Variable	R squared	p value
• Mental Processing Composite • Adaptive Behavior Composite	0.512	p<.01

• Vineland Domain Scores
    Communication
    Daily Living Skills
    Socialization
    Motor Skills
	0.721	p<.001

• Moral Development Composite	0.000	n.s.
• Moral Development (story 3)	0.038	n.s.

• K-ABC Scales:
    Sequential Processing
    Simultaneous Processing
    Nonverbal
    Achievement
	0.421	p<.05

• K-ABC Scales
    Sequential Processing
    Simultaneous Processing
	0.469	p<.01

• K-ABC Achievement Scale	0.199	p<.05

Table 6.10.

First Case Study: Joseph's Scores in All Instruments

Instrument	Score	Performance Range	Percentile Rank
K-ABC Sequential Processing	131+- 7	Well-Above Average (Gifted)	98
K-ABC Simultaneous Processing	141+- 7	Well-Above Average (Gifted)	99.7
K-ABC Mental Processing Composite	144+- 6	Well-Above Average (Gifted)	99
K-ABC Nonverbal	138+- 7	Well-Above Average (Gifted)	70
AK-ABC Achievement	108+- 5	Average	86
Vineland Communication	116+- 7	Above Average	88
Vineland Daily Living Skills	118+- 7	Above Average	75
Vineland Socialization	110+- 7	Average	87
Vineland Motor Skills	126+- 2 (est.)	Above Average	87
Vineland Adaptive Behavior Composite	117+- 5	Above Average	87
Moral Judgment Story #1	3	Above Average	NA
Moral Judgment Story #2	4	Above Average	NA
Moral Judgment Story #3	5	Well Above Average	NA
Moral Judgment Composite	4	Above Average	NA

Teachers' Survey (Mental Processing Composite)	1.94	Above Average	NA
Teachers' Survey (Achievement Composite)	1.57	Well Above Average	NA
Self-Portrait (Raw)	12	Above Average	NA
Self-Portarit (Scaled)	2	Above Average	NA
Handwriting Score	2	Above Average	NA
Listening Activity (Raw)	6	Well Above Average	NA
Listening Activity (Scaled)	1	Well Above Average	NA
Portfolio Composite	1.67	Above Average	NA
Classroom Performance Composite	1.68	Above Average	

Table 6.11.

Second Case Study: Linda's Scores in All Instruments

Instrument	Score	Performance Range	Percentile Rank
K-ABC Sequential Processing	115+- 7	Above Average	84
K-ABC Simultaneous Processing	125+- 7	Above Average	95
K-ABC Mental Processing Composite	124+- 6	Above Average	95
K-ABC Nonverbal	129 +- 7	Above Average	97
AK-ABC Achievement	93+- 5	Average	32
Vineland Communication	100+- 5	Average	50
Vineland Daily Living Skills	109+- 6	Average	73
Vineland Socialization	102+- 7	Average	55
Vineland Motor Skills	102+- 12	Average	55
Vineland Adaptive Behavior Composite	103+- 4	Average	58
Moral Judgment Story #1	3	Above Average	NA
Moral Judgment Story #2	3	Above Average	NA

Moral Judgment Story #3	3	Above Average	NA
Moral Judgment Composite	3	Above Average	NA
Teachers' Survey (Mental Processing Composite)	3.00	Average	NA
Teachers' Survey (Achievement Composite)	3.07	Average	NA
Self-Portrait (Raw)	6	Average	NA
Self-Portarit (Scaled)	3	Average	NA
Handwriting Score	3.67	Below Average	NA
Listening Activity (Raw)	4	Average	NA
Listening Activity (Scaled)	3	Average	NA
Portfolio Composite	3.22	Average	NA
Classroom Performance Composite	3.02	Average	

Table 6.12.

Third Case Study: Billy's Scores in All Instruments

Instrument	Score	Performance Range	Percentile Rank
K-ABC Sequential Processing	115+- 7	Above Average	84
K-ABC Simultaneous Processing	160+- 7	Well Above Average (Gifted)	Above 99.9
K-ABC Mental Processing Composite	140+- 6	Well Above Average (Gifted)	99.6
K-ABC Nonverbal	144 +- 7	Well Above Average (Gifted)	99.8
AK-ABC Achievement	115+- 5	Above Average	84
Vineland Communication	109+- 5	Average	73
Vineland Daily Living Skills	119+- 6	Above Average	90
Vineland Socialization	120+- 7	Above Average	91
Vineland Motor Skills	116+- 12	Above Average	86
Vineland Adaptive Behavior Composite	119+- 4	Above Average	90
Moral Judgment Story #1	3	Above Average	NA
Moral Judgment Story #2	3	Above Average	NA
Moral Judgment Story #3	5	Well Above Average	NA
Moral Judgment Composite	3.67	Above Average	NA
Teachers' Survey (Mental Processing Composite)	2.24	Above Average	NA
Teachers' Survey (Achievement Composite)	2.40	Above Average	NA
Self-Portrait (Raw)	10	Above Average	NA
Self-Portarit (Scaled)	2	Above Average	NA

Handwriting Score	3.33	Well Above Average	NA
Listening Activity (Raw)	6	Well Above Average	NA
Listening Activity (Scaled)	1	Well Above Average	NA
Portfolio Composite	2.11	Above Average	NA
Classroom Performance Composite	2.21	Above Average	

7

ACADEMIC RESILIENCE IN YOUNG CHILDREN: UNDERSTANDING THE RELATIONSHIP BETWEEN TEMPERAMENT AND QUALITY OF THE PARWENT-CHILD RELATIONSHIP

ഉറ

Ellen Demas and Virginia Gonzalez

Introduction

The objective of study represents one of the themes present across chapters in this book: using an alternative view to study the effect of internal (i.e., early childhood temperament) and external (i.e., quality of the parent-child relationship, and family background—advantages or disadvantaged) factors on cognitive resilience in young children. Four preschool children (i.e., four to five-year-olds) and their families participated in this multiple case study design that used qualitative and standardized measures: (1) a demographic questionnaire, (2) the Kaufman Assessment Battery for Children (Kaufman & Kaufman, 1983a, 1983b), (3) the Temperament Assessment Battery for Children (Martin, 1988), (4) a projective technique for assessing temperament (adapted from research of Thomas & Chess, 1982), (5) the Parent Sense of Competence Scale (McDevitt & Carey, 1978), (6) parents' interviews, and (7) home and school observations. Results suggested that the classification of early childhood temperament varied according to context, informant, and the instrument format. An interaction between early childhood temperament and the quality of the parent-child relationship was evident in specific situations influencing academic performance in young children from advantaged and disadvantaged backgrounds.

Theoretical Perspective

Although research has uncovered evidence demonstrating that detrimental factors increase the risk of a child's maladjustment and poor academic achievement (Emery, 1982; Garmezy, 1993; Honing, 1984; Rak & Patterson, 1996), less was known about the children who are resilient to such conditions. This study attempted to clarify some still open research questions: Why are some children resilient to their disadvantaged circumstances, while others are not? In contrast, Why do some children from advantaged backgrounds have difficulty succeeding academically? Determining which factors contribute most to resilience can aide in fostering these conditions in at-risk children. This study has a twofold objective: (1) to identify the developmental internal and/or external factors that influence academic success in young children from disadvantaged and advantaged family environments, and (2) to examine the interaction between these internal and external factors.

Currently, numerous children are at-risk for developmental problems based on internal and external factors (Honig, 1984). The term "at-risk" suggests a potential for negative outcomes when faced with negative life circumstances (Rak & Patterson, 1996). Among the potential internal factors found to negatively influence development are low birth weight, congenital defects, and some dispositional attributes of the individual (i.e., temperamental characteristics, Garmezy, 1993). External factors placing children at-risk include aspects of the physical, social, and cultural environment. Examples of such external factors presented in the home environment include: low socioeconomic status (SES), poor nutrition, negative parental perceptions of a parent-child relationship, punitive disciplinary practices, lack of financial and emotional support, low parental expectations, low standards for education and achievement, familial dysfunction, violence, abuse, parental mental illness, and parents with minimal education. These factors may place the child at-risk if they disrupt the critical care-giving process by causing children to be less receptive to stimulation (Rak & Patterson, 1996; Wyman, Cowan, & Work, 1991; Van Tassel-Baska, 1989).

Although potentially damaging, these at-risk factors may be avoided (Rak & Patterson, 1996). The ability to cope and adapt well under high-risk environments is identified as resilience (Wyman, et al., 1991). In children, resilience is the capacity to overcome risk factors and avoid negative outcomes such as delinquency, behavioral problems, psychological maladjustments, academic difficulties, and physical complications (Hauser, Vieyra, Jacobson, & Wertreib, 1985). Research suggests the resilience in young children is influenced by both internal and external developmental factors (Wyman et al., 1991). For example, Neighbors, Forehand, and McVicars' study (1993), investigated resilient adolescents and inter-parental conflict, and found that internal (i.e., individual differences) and external factors (i.e., family environments) differentiated between resilient and non-resilient adolescents. Internal factors included biological and psychological processes, such as temperament, personality traits, motor skill abilities (e.g., primitive and postural reflexes of infants), neurological factors (i.e., plasticity and brain lateralizations in young children), phenotypic expressions of behaviors (i. e., energy levels, sleep patterns, perceptual preferences such as tolerance for noise and light, attention levels, etc.), and inherited characteristics represented by the individual's genotype (i.e., genetic patterns).

Much research has been conducted to uncover which internal factors place children at-risk for developmental difficulties (Adams, Hillman, & Gaydos, 1994; Emery, 1982; Garmezy, 1993; Honig, 1984; Rak & Patterson, 1996). However, an increasing number of studies have included an examination of possible internal factors functioning as protective mechanisms as well as risk factors. One internal factors repeatedly recognized as a critical influence on resilience was early childhood temperament (Garfmezy, 1993; Grizenko & Pawliuk, 1994; Kyrios & Prior, 1990; Werner, 1989; Wyman et al., 1991). Researchers have demonstrated the predictive power of early childhood temperament on later emotional disorders (Wolfson, Fields, & Rose, 1987).

In addition, research conducted on at-risk children has demonstrated that the quality of the parent-child relationship plays a critical role in the development of resilience. The findings reported from several research studies have suggested that negative characteristics present in the parent-child relationship (i.e., inadequate knowledge base regarding child development, negative attitudes toward parenting, and punitive parenting practices) may impede the child's cognitive and emotional development (Miller, Miceli, Whitman, & Borkowski, 1996).

Moreover, research findings have shown an interaction relationship between internal and external factors influencing resilience in at-risk children. These factors were said to interact continuously and dynamically to generate either success or failure. Several studies have demonstrated that the interaction between a family factors and an individual factor was required to differentiate between resilience and non-resilience in young children (Brooks, 1994; Garmezy, 1993; Neighbors et al., 1993; Werner, 1993).

Therefore, this study proposes that determining which developmental factors contribute strongest to the academic resilience of young at-risk children and better understanding the relationship and interaction between these factors will aide in the promotion of academic success. This study will contribute to the identification of these developmental factors which will guide and assist educators and psychologists in their efforts to design and implement screening and intervention programs as well as early diagnosis and educational programs to alleviate a child in academic "crisis" and identify children "at-risk" of developing learning problems.

Methodology

Research Questions

The following research questions were addressed in an attempt to evaluate the influence of early childhood temperament and the quality of the parent-child relationship on the academic resilience of children from advantaged and disadvantaged backgrounds:

1. What characteristics of early childhood temperament promote academic resilience in young children?

2. What qualities of the parent-child relationship (i.e., parental perceptions of satisfaction and competence) promote academic resilience in young children?

3. Do early childhood temperament and the quality of the parent-child relationship interact to influence academic resilience in young children?

4. Do early childhood temperament and quality of the parent-child relationship influence academic performance in children from advantaged family backgrounds, as well as those from disadvantaged backgrounds?

Research Design

This qualitative study examined four research questions investigating the influence of developmental internal (i.e., early childhood temperament) and external (i.e., family background—advantaged or disadvantaged, and quality of the parent-child relationship) factors on the academic resilience of young children. This study used a descriptive model for studying three variables: (1) early childhood temperament, (2) family background (advantaged or disadvantaged), (3) quality of the parent-child relationship, and (4) academic resilience. See Table 7.1. for the relationship among research questions, research model, variables, and research design.

The 2x2 research design utilized in this study represented children from advantaged and disadvantaged family environments, who showed either resilience or non-resilience. Four case studies representing these four factors were examined: (1) an advantaged family with a resilient child, (2) an advantaged family with a non-resilient child, (3) a disadvantaged family with a resilient child, and (4) a disadvantaged family with a non-resilient child. The construct of "resilience" traditionally reflects an outcome specific to populations from disadvantaged backgrounds. However, with respect to the 2x2 design the term "resilience" was applied to describe academic performance of individuals from advantaged as well as disadvantaged backgrounds. For purposes of this study, an advantaged family background was identified as a family unit with moderate to high income, high maternal educational attainment (i.e., Bachelor's degree minimum), and at least two adult care-givers (Entwisle & Astone, 1994). A disadvantaged family background was defined as a family unit with low income, low maternal educational attainment (i.e., no college degree), and a disruptive household structure (i.e., single-parent home, Entwisle & Astone, 1994). In addition, resilience and non-resilience were associated with academic performance. Children were placed at either the upper or lower end of the academic achievement spectrum. Therefore, children demonstrating potential learning problems were identified as non-resilient, while children showing possible giftedness were identified as resilient.

Participants

Four preschool children and their families participated in this study. The pool of participants was selected from two preschools in a middle-size metropolitan area in the Southwest region of the US. One preschool was located in a high to middle SES neighborhood, while the other was located in a middle to low SES neighborhood. The participants were four-to-five-year-old preschoolers from either advantaged or disadvantaged family backgrounds. Differentiation between the two environmental categories was based on available family resources and conditions (more information is provided in the Results and Discussion section, i.e., SES, parental level of education, family structure; Van Tassel-Baska, 1989).

Instruments

The seven instruments described below were used to collect qualitative data for this study. Some of these instruments were standardized and others were alternative measures.

Demographic Questionnaire. This measure was adapted from an instrument developed by Williams and Gonzalez (see Chapter 5 in this book). The questionnaire was used to describe characteristics of: the families including the age of the mother and the father, ethnicity or race of the mother and the father, combine annual household income range, and parents' educational attainment. The information collected was used to categorize the family as advantage or disadvantage.

Kaufman Assessment Battery for Children (K-ABC). For purposes of this study, the K-ABC was used to measure academic resilience. The K-ABC is a standardized battery of tests (containing three Scales), individually administered requires approximately 45-60 minutes for preschoolers) measuring intelligence and achievement for ages 2.5 to 12.5 years (Kaufman & Kaufman, 1983a, 1983b). The K-ABC has demonstrated to have validity and reliability for the population examined in this study. The Achievement Scale was designed to measure past knowledge and skills attained in school (i.e., vocabulary, language concepts, reading, arithmetic, and general information). In contrast, the Mental Processing Scales measure children's present level of intelligence (i.e., problem-solving skills, verbal and organizational abilities). According to Kaufman and Kaufman (1983a, 1983b) both the Achievement and Mental Processing Scales are necessary for understanding children's academic abilities. In this study, the children's cognitive and achievement abilities were evaluated with the K-ABC in order to identify them as either resilient or non-resilient. Children performing at high cognitive levels (i.e., giftedness) were considered resilient, while those performing at lower cognitive levels (i.e., learning problems) were considered non-resilient.

The Temperament Assessment Battery for Children (TABC). This measure was developed by Martin (1988), and it was adapted to measure the temperamental domains influencing academic resilience (see Tables 7.2 and 7.3). This assessment consists of three rating scales developed for teachers, parents, and clinicians, each using a Likert Scale response format. For purposes of this study, only the teacher and parent forms were used. According to Martin (1988), the parent form measures six areas of temperament: (1) activity level (i.e., gross motor vigor), (2) adaptability (i.e., ease and speed of adjustment to changed social environments), (3) approach/withdrawal (i.e., the initial tendency to approach or withdraw from novel social situations), (4) emotional intensity (i.e., magnitude of negative emotional expression), (5) distractibility (i.e., attention span), and (6) persistence (i.e., ability to continue with difficult tasks).

However, factor analysis performed by Presley and Martin (1994) on the TABC teacher form indicated that temperament domains assessed by this instrument can be reduced to three factors: (1) persistence (i.e., contains items from the distractibility, persistence, and activity scales), (2) approachability (i.e., contains items from the approach/withdrawal, activity, persistence, and adaptability scales), and (3) negative emotionality (i.e., contains items measuring intense negative emotional reactions and loud vocal reactions). Both validity and reliability were established for the TABC by Martin (1988).

Projective Technique for Assessment Temperament. This instrument was designed by the first author for the purpose of collecting direct, qualitative information on the children's temperaments (see Table 7.4.). This technique consists of a series of stories that are acted out by the evaluator and the child through the use of toys (i.e., stuffed animals). First, the scenario (i.e., story) was explained to the child. Then, the child was asked to retell the story to assure comprehension. Next, the child and research "played" out the story allowing the child to control the actions and verbalizations of the character. Finally, the child's actions and responses were recorded verbatim via notes taken by the researcher.

This instrument was constructed to reflect the following five dimensions of early childhood temperament: (1) approachability, (2) negative emotionality, (3) adaptability, (4) activity level, and (5) task orientation. The instrument was created by, first defining each temperament factor by referring to definitions utilized in temperament literature (Presley & Martin, 1994). Then, descriptive adjectives were provided to classify and operationalize behaviors that pertained to a specific domain. Next, stories were created by the researchers for presenting opportunities for the child to express the specific factor under consideration. Finally, construct validity of the projective technique was assessed via the responses of three graduate students, acting as judges, to a Likert-scale style questionnaire. The purpose of the questionnaire was to rate how closely the stories reflected the corresponding temperamental factors as defined by Presley and Martin (1994).

Parenting Sense of Competence Scale (PSOC). The PSOC is a 17-item scale developed by McDevitt and Carey (1978) assessing parenting self-esteem. The PSOC is comprised of: (1) sense of satisfaction, and (2) sense of competence as a parent. When constructed, this measure revealed two factors: (1) satisfaction, reflecting parenting frustration, anxiety, and motivation; and (2) efficacy, reflecting competence, problem-solving ability, and capability in the parenting role. For this study, parenting self-esteem represents the variable of the quality of the parent-child relationship. Specifically, the PSOC analyzed the two factors of satisfaction and efficacy using a 6-point scale ranging from strongly disagree (6) to strongly agree (1). The validity and reliability of this instrument were established by authors.

Parents' Interview. Six open-ended questions were created by the first author to examine early childhood temperament and the quality of the parent-child relationship. These questions expanded upon the items used in the TABC and PSOC assessment scales in order to allow parents to expand on close-ended questions. The first three questions were used to examined early childhood temperament, and included: (1) How would you describe your child's temperament?, (2) How do you react to your child's temperament?, and (3) Do you feel your child's temperament has influenced (i.e., benefited or hindered) his/her academic performance? If so, how? In addition, the last three questions were designed to examine the parent-child relationship, and included: (4) Do you fell satisfied as a parent?, (5) What skills do you believe are necessary to be competent as a parent?, and (6) Do you believe your relationship with your child has influenced his/her academic performance? If so, how?

Home and School Observations. Naturalistic observations of the children's temperaments and aspects of the parent-child relationship were performed by the researcher and recorded in writing, in both the home and the school contexts. Home observations were performed in parallel to the parent interview an spanned the entire course of the visitation (i.e., approximately 60 minutes per observation session). The school observations (i.e., 30 minutes per observation session) were executed prior to and during administration of the K-ABC and the projective technique for assessing temperament.

Procedures

Preschool directors were approached and solicited permission for children and their families to participate in the study. Participating preschool teachers, whose classrooms included four and five year-old children, were asked to distribute information packets to families they understood to best meet the participation criteria established for the study. Families interested in participating in this study were asked to complete either one or none of the referrals (i.e., for possible giftedness or the presence of learning problems), as well as the demographic questionnaire and subjects' consent form. After reviewing the demographic questionnaire, the participating families' backgrounds were identified as either advantaged or disadvantaged. Then, the academic resilience (i.e., defined as academic achievement for this study) of the participating children were assessed with the K-ABC (Kaufman & Kaufman, 1983a, 1983b). At this point in the study, the families were categorized as one of the following: (1) an advantaged family with a resilient child, (2) an advantaged family with a non-resilient child, (3) a disadvantaged family with a resilient child, and (4) a disadvantage family with a non-resilient child.

After the four cases were identified, the children's temperament were assessed using five measures: (1) three indirect measures utilizing parent and teacher forms of the TABC and the parent interview, and (2) two direct measures using the projective technique assessment and classroom observations. First, parents were asked to complete the parent form of the TABC (Martin, 1988), while teachers were asked to complete the teacher form of the TABC for their student participating in the study. Then, home visitations were conducted by the first author for administering the parental interviews and perform home observations. In addition, each child was observed for 60 minutes by the first author at school in order to assess the temperamental characteristics including activity level, task persistence, approachability, adaptability, and negative emotionality. Finally, the first author administered the projective technique in order to evaluate early childhood temperament. This measurement of social inhibition, negative emotionality, adaptability, activity level, and task orientation was conducted in a quiet classroom.

Finally, three measures were used to evaluate the quality of the parent-child relationship, including: (1) the PSOC (McDevitt & Carey, 1978), (2) a parent interview, and (3) home observations. Parents completed the PSOC, and then they were interviewed by the first author. Home observations were also conducted by the first author to collect information about two aspects: (1) the apparent level of closeness between child and parent, and (2) the emotional states of the parents and children.

Results and Discussion

Data Analysis Design

A qualitative analysis design was utilized for data coding with multiple instruments measuring each variable under study: academic resilience, family background, early childhood temperament, and the quality of the parent-child relationship. The definitions, descriptions, and operational definitions for each of the early childhood temperament variable with categories and subcategories are presented in Tables 7.1 and 7.2. Nominal categories were created and used for coding the variables under investigation, with resulting triangulation across several instruments measuring the same variables. The results of the qualitative analysis are presented as four case studies at the end of this chapter. Each case study presents an analysis of the results with respect to each of the research questions proposed in the study. Following the discussion of each individual case study, a summary representing the patterns discovered across all four case studies is presented.

Qualitative Analysis of the First Research Question

The first research question addresses the characteristics of early childhood temperament that promote academic resilience in young children. Parents' and teachers' perceptions about the participating children's temperaments were obtained from observations, interviews, an alternative projective technique, and surveys (TABC). The influence of temperamental characteristics on academic performance was found to be dependent on three factors: (1) context, (2) informant, and (3) instrument format (see Tables 7.5, 7.6., 7.7., and 7.8.).

Context. For each case study, we conducted an analysis of the temperamental characteristics that was dependent on context (see Tables 7.4., 7.5., 7.6., and 7.7.). That is, variability among the temperamental characteristics depended on whether the children were at home (i.e., informal context) or at school (i.e., formal context). In order to demonstrate the influence of context on the categorization of temperament domains, a comparison across case studies was performed using the results obtained from the projective assessment technique and classroom observations and K-ABC results. This comparison held the information and format factors constant (i.e., both instruments relied on the researcher's responses to open-ended questions), while it allowed the context factor to vary. For instance, the projective technique assessment indicated that Michael was less active in an informal setting (i.e., moderately active) than he was actually observed to be in a formal setting (i.e., mostly active). The projective technique assessment also showed that Lisa was more emotional (i.e., moderate negative emotionality) in an informal setting than she was observed to be at school (i.e., negative emotionality). In addition, Jill was slightly less persistent at home (i.e., mostly persistent) than she was at school (i.e., strongly persistent). Furthermore, Kevin was slightly less active at home than at school.

These results indicated that temperamental domains vary with context. Therefore, certain external factors may exist in the home and/or school, which alter the expression of various young children's temperamental domains. However, each temperamental domain did not necessarily change with context for each child in the same manner, allowing for individual differences. The influence of context on temperament was different for each child. For example, although Michael's activity level was different at home and at school, Lisa's activity remained constant. However, Lisa's negative emotionality depended on whether she was at home or at school, while Michael's emotionality was not affected by context. Therefore, the contextual factors responsible for altering the expression of the temperamental domains may also vary with each child. In summary, the results suggested that different children tended to have different temperamental characteristics in different situations, indicating individual differences. In addition, this study revealed that external factors may be present in the home or school settings that have contributed to the variability among the temperamental domains.

Informant. Variability among the categorizations of the temperamental domains may also have depended on the informant (see Tables 7.5., 7.6., 7.7., and 7.8.). For each case study, the temperamental domains may have been described differently by parents, teachers, and researchers because each informant has different perceptions. In order to examine the influence of informant variability on temperamental categorizations, a comparison between the parents' (i.e., parent interview) and researchers' perceptions (i.e., projective assessment technique) was performed. This comparison held the context and format factors constant, while allowing the informant factor to vary (i.e., both instruments used an open format to report behaviors exhibited in an informal setting).

For example, while Michael's parents described their son as moderately approachable, the projective assessment technique indicated that he was mostly approachable. In addition, the projective assessment technique revealed that Lisa expressed more negative emotionality (i.e., moderate negative emotionality) than indicated by her mother (i.e., slight negative emotionality). This comparison also found that Jill's mother perceived a slightly higher level of persistence than the projective assessment technique had indicated. Moreover, Kevin's mother perceived him to be more adaptable (i.e., strongly adaptable) than the projective assessment technique indicated (i.e., mostly adaptable).

These variations suggested that the categorization of temperamental domains may not be based solely on the behaviors exhibited by the children, but also on the perceptions of those reporting their observations of these behaviors. Therefore, following results suggested by this study, in the analysis of results, it is critical to consider who was evaluating the temperamental domains and how their perceptions may have altered the actual temperamental levels exhibited by the children.

Instrument format. The influence of instrument format on the categorization of temperamental domains was revealed in this study (see Tables

7.5., 7.6., 7.7., and 7.8.). Temperamental classifications appeared to vary with the instrument design (i.e., closed or open format). A comparison between the TABC parent form and the parent interview was performed to examine this potential influence, such that the context and informant variables were held constant. For instance, while the TABC parent form, completed by Michael's mother, rated his negative emotionality as slightly emotional, the parent interview revealed that he was strongly emotional. In addition, the TABC parent form revealed that Lisa was mostly active, yet her mother stated that she perceived her daughter as moderately active. While the TABC parent form, completed by her mother, rated Jill as mostly approachable, her mother reported that she was moderately approachable. Similarly, the TABC, completed by Kevin's mother, rated him slightly less persistent (i.e., mostly persistent) than his mother described him to be during the parent interview (i.e., strongly persistent).

Results of this comparison suggest that variability among temperamental categorizations may be simply a result of the instrument used to measure the factor. Since the open-ended format allowed more opportunity for informants to express their beliefs and perceptions, it appeared that the open-ended questionnaire provided a more accurate representation of the children's temperaments than the closed Likert Scale survey format.

Qualitative Analysis of the Second Research Question

The second research questions addressed what qualities of the parent-child relationship promoted academic resilience in young children. A descriptive analysis of the second research question regarding the relationship between the quality of the parent-child relationship and academic resilience was based on the results of the observations, interviews, and surveys (PSOC). This analysis indicated that a positive parent-child relationship, consisting of self-perceptions as competent and satisfied parents, contributed to young children's academic resilience. Specifically, a sense of satisfaction and competence as a parent appeared to influence children's academic performance. However, since each parent (i.e., both resilient and non-resilient children) participating in this study exhibited the positive parent-child relationships, it did not appear that a positive parent-child relationship ultimately promotes academic success. Therefore, a positive parent-child relationship was a necessary, but not sufficient, factor influencing children's academic performance. These results supported previous research findings. For instance, Wyman and colleagues (1991) reported that a nurturing caregiver-child relationship and parent self-perceptions as competent, effective caregivers were critical factors contributing to children's resilience to at-risk conditions.

In addition, this research study suggests that the teacher-child relationship may be critical to understanding the influence of children's social environments on their academic performance. Since the results of this study showed that academic performance may be influenced by factors that were context and informant specific (i.e., early childhood temperament), serious attention should be given to the influence of the teacher-child relationship on academic performance. For instance, in this study, teachers repeatedly had different temperamental ratings of the children than their parents. Either the children behave differently across contexts, school and home settings, or the teachers had different perceptions of the same behaviors children exhibited at home and school. In either instance, the teachers' observations of the children's behaviors would vary from those of he parents. Therefore, children's differences in academic performance may be influenced by the teacher-child relationship, as well as the parent-child relationship. The results of this study suggest that further knowledge regarding the dynamics of the teacher-child relationship was critical to understanding the influence of the environment on a child's academic performance.

Although most research has focused on the influence of the parent-child relationship on academic performance (i.e., Adams, et al., 1990; Brooks, 1994; Emery, 1982; Fauber, Foreland, McCombs Thomas, & Wierson, 1990; Garmezy, 1993; Grizenko et al., 1994; Miller, et al., 1996; Werner, 1989), these results were supported by the literature. For instance, in summarizing a series of studies investigating the influence of children's temperament on teachers' decisions, Keogh (1982) reported that teacher's responses to students were influenced by their perceptions of the children's temperaments. More specifically, these perceptions influenced teacher's views of students' ability to learn from instruction, estimates of students' cognitive and language abilities, and expectations for academic performance. That is, the educational opportunities and experiences available to the students depended on the teachers' perceptions of their temperament. Therefore, the teacher-child relationship appeared to have a critical influence ion a child's academic performance.

In sum, based on the results of this study, it appeared that the evaluation of both the teacher-child relationship and the parent-child relationship were critical to understanding the social influences on children's academic performance. Moreover, based on this study's results and evidence present in the literature, both factors (i.e., parent-child and teacher-child relationships) interact to influence academic resilience in young children.

Qualitative Analysis of the Third Research Question

The third research question focused on the interaction of the early childhood temperament and the quality of the parent-child relationship and its effect on the children's academic resilience. The results of this study suggest that an interaction exists between early childhood temperament and the quality of the parent/child relationship. However, it appeared that specific temperamental domains were interacting with qualities of the parent-child relationship. These factors interacted in such a way that favorable temperamental domain and positive qualities of the parent-child relationship resulted in resilient academic performance. In addition, negative temperamental domain interacted with a positive parent-child relationship and resulted in non-resilience.

For instance, the first case study demonstrated a child from a disadvantaged background exhibiting non-resilient academic performance. In this case, Michael's parents reported that they perceived themselves to be satisfied and competent in their roles as parents. Although Michael and his parents had a positive relationship, his academic performance indicated possible learning problems. Therefore, the presence of another mediating factor, negative temperament in both home and school contexts, may have reduced Michael's academic success and contributed to his non-resilience at school.

Another example is portrayed by the second case study, a disadvantaged child exhibiting resilient academic performance. Although Lisa demonstrated negative temperamental characteristics a t home (i.e., negative emotionality, adaptability, and activity levels), the interaction between her positive temperamental characteristics (i.e., approachability, adaptability, and persistence) at school and positive parent-child relationship may account for her resilient academic performance.

The third case study, Jill, demonstrated an advantaged child with non-resilient academic performance. Although each instrument measuring early childhood temperament reported a positive overall temperament for Jill (i.e., intermediate positive), the results suggested that the child exhibited some temperamental difficult areas (i.e., approachability and activity at home and school settings) that may have counteracted the positive parent-child relationship, and resulted in difficulties in academic performance. Specifically, Jill's teacher reported that she was moderately emotional at school. Even in the presence of a positive parent-child relationship, these negative attributed may have contributed to Jill's low performance on the K-ABC Achievement Scale.

The fourth case study, Kevin reported on an advantaged child exhibiting superior academic performance. Each instrument revealed that Kevin ha positive temperamental characteristics whether at home or in school. Based on this study's hypothesis, Kevin's positive temperamental qualities were interacting with a positive parent-child relationship to promote his academic success.

Thus, results from this study support previous research studies suggesting that the children's temperament and the quality of the parent-child relationship interact dynamically to influence academic resilience. It appeared that the child's temperament was a primary influence on academic performance; and more specifically, the child's temperament at school as perceived by the teacher, while the parent-child relationship was a mediational factor. A study performed by Wyman and collaborators (1991) demonstrated that an early positive temperament was critical in infancy and early childhood, and that a nurturing and supportive parent-child relationship was more likely to influence resiliency in older children. In addition, previous research has reported that teachers' perceptions of students' temperaments may influence their teaching practices (Keogh, 1982). However, further research examining the dynamics of the teacher-child relationship with respect to temperament and academic performance is needed. Finally, after a thorough literature search, no studies were found that explicitly compared parents' and teachers' perceptions of children's temperaments with respect to their influence in academic resilience.

Qualitative Analysis of the Fourth Research Question

The fourth research question investigated the interaction of early childhood temperament, the quality of the parent-child relationship, and the disadvantaged or advantaged family background. The results of this study suggested that temperamental factors may influence the academic performance of children from advantaged, as well as disadvantaged, backgrounds. For instance, the study suggested that Kevin's positive levels of each of the temperamental domains interacted with his positive parent-child relationship to promote his superior academic performance.

In contrast, the positive relationship between Jill and her parents inter-acted with her negative temperamental qualities to result in non-resilient academic performance. Therefore, even in the midst of resources, oppor-tunities, and a caring and nurturing parent-child relationship, negative temperamental characteristics may have contributed to Jill's low perfor-mance on the K-ABC Achievement Scale.

These results did not support the existing research literature on tem-perament which stated that internal and external factors (i.e., early child-hood temperament and the quality of the parent-child relationship) func-tion in a direct relationship within an at-risk environment. For instance, the study performed by Grizenko and Pawliuk (1994) found these factors to act as protective mechanisms against adversity. However, this study found that both, positive temperamental characteristics and a positive parent-child relationship were necessary for the academic success of chil-dren from advantaged and disadvantaged backgrounds. Thus, regardless of their socioeconomic status background, there are some children who have at-risk temperamental characteristics for developing problems at school, especially because they tend to elicit in teachers a negative per-ception of their behaviors.

Conclusions and Future Research Recommendations

This study found that both, early childhood temperament and the quality of the parent-child relationship, appeared to have contributed to the academic performance of the young children participating in this case study. Several patterns were found in how context (i.e., school versus home), informant (i.e., parent versus teacher), and format of the assess-ment (i.e., open-ended versus closed-ended) of early childhood tempera-ment influence whether or not it would affect academic resilience within and between children. Furthermore, this study revealed that temperament appears to have a primary influence on young children's resilience, while the quality of the parent-child relationship has a mediational role. How-ever, further research with larger samples is necessary to further validate these results, especially with the use of mixed research designs using both qualitative and statistical analysis of data.

Studies should also further investigate the effect of the format (i.e., open-ended versus closed-ended) of measurements used on results ob-tained. It is also recommended that future studies use other additional measures of cognitive abilities (other than the K-ABC used in this study), for its potential important effects on academic resilience of young children. Especially alternative and developmental measures (i.e., problem-solving tasks) of cognitive potential should be used for the case of young children.

This study supports previous research findings, but also opens up further research questions. For instance, What other characteristics of early childhood temperament and the parent-child relationship, not examined in this study, may have contributed to the academic performance of these children? That is, other temperamental domains mapped out in research, such as mood, rhythmicity, threshold, intensity, and distractibility (Thomas & Chess, 1982) have play a role in whether children would become resilient or non-resilient in academic performance. Future studies need to analyze more deeply the complexity of the various aspects of childhood temperament, in order to avoid oversimplification of the variable and expose individual differences and the multidimensionality of this variable. Other aspects of the characteristics of the parent-child relationship can also be studied such as resourcefulness, parents' mental health, time spent interacting with children, disciplinary style and strategies used, etc. Finally, the teacher-child relationship also needs to be studied in an attempt to better understand the social influences on children's academic resilience.

Limitations of the Study

The sample size utilized is this study was its most salient limiting factor. This study involved four case studies, with one child and his/her family for each case study. Due to its small sample size, this study was restricted to qualitative analysis of data. In addition, the case studies were not selected randomly, but rather the children and their families were purposely chosen based on family resources, as advantaged and disadvantaged family background was one of the variables investigated. The instruments could have been also a limiting factor in this study, because some of the instruments such as the questionnaire, the interview, and the survey were developed or adapted for this study. Even though a pilot test was conducted for assuring construct validity and reliability of the measures for the participants' characteristics, the pilot testing only used two families (i.e., one advantaged and one disadvantaged). Furthermore, the Achievement Scale of the K-ABC was reported to be less reliable than the other scales (Kaufman & Kaufman, 1983a, 1983b). Therefore, the classification of participants (as resilient and non-resilient) may been less accurate in comparison to other instruments of this construct.

Finally, authors recognize that parents and teachers may have been biased in their perceptions of temperament and the quality of the parent-child relationship. Therefore, some of the results may have been altered due to potential biases among informants. Furthermore, another potential limitation of the study may have been introduced by evaluating the parent-child relationship based only on verbal reports of parents; instead of collecting primary data based on direct observations.

Case Studies Illustrating Patterns Found in Research Questions

First Case Study: Michael
A Disadvantaged Family with a Non-Resilient Child

Family Background. Michael is a 5.3. years-old, Caucasian male child. He is from an intact home where both parents assume responsibility for his car. Both of his parents are Caucasian and in the age range of 40-49. His mother has attended 1-3 years of college, but does not have a college degree. His father is a high school graduate. Both of his parents work and earn a combined income in the low to middle range (i.e., 30,000-39,000) for a household size of four (Michael has an older brother. Michael's family background was categorized as a disadvantaged family background.

Academic Resilience. Scores on the K-ABC indicated that Michael had average ability in all areas. The Sequential Processing Scale of the K-ABC standard score was 100 (50th percentile). The Simultaneous Processing Scale of the K-ABC standard score was 106 (66th percentile). The Mental Processing Composite of the K-ABC standard score was 107 (68th percentile). The Achievement Scale of the K-ABC standard score was 100 (50th percentile). Although Michael demonstrated average cognitive abilities, there was evidence of some specific cognitive processes that were depressed. So, Michael demonstrated non-resilient academic performance.

Early Childhood Temperament. TABC (parent form) with participation of both parents indicated the following temperamental characteristics for Michael: mostly approachable, slightly emotional, mostly adaptable, moderately active, mostly persistent, and his overall temperament was intermediate positive. The *TABC* (teacher form) indicated the following temperamental characteristics for Michael: mostly persistent, moderately emotional, moderately approachable, and his overall temperament was slow to war-up.

Projective Assessment Technique. Results of this measure indicated that Michael's temperament was: mostly approachable, moderately emotional, mostly adaptable, and moderately active, moderately persistent. Michael's overall temperament was intermediate positive.

Classroom Observation. Based on this alternative measure, Michael's temperament was observed to be mostly active , moderately approachable, moderately adaptable, moderately persistent, and overall his temperament was slow to warm-up.

Parent Interview. Michael's father began the interview by describing him as moody ("he wants constant attention and interaction with us and if he can not have it, then he gets really moody and difficult. His parents also stated that "he is very active, he keeps going all day." His mother stated, "Michael is initially shy when meeting new people, but he gets over it quickly." His parents reported that Michael is persistent, as they stated "Michael may get angry at first if he is doing something hard, but he will keep on trying and trying." When parents were asked about how Michael responds to new situations (e.g., starting school), his parents said, "he seems to need some time to adjust, but he gets over it."   Michael's temperament often makes his parents feel frustrated. Michael's parents stated that his temperament "can be both good and bad. They considered that his persistence and activity levels could be beneficial, but his mood swings could be hindering his academic performance. Michael's parents perceived his disposition to reflect a slow to warm-up temperament, strong negative emotionality, strong levels of activity, moderate levels of approachability and adaptability, and mostly persistent.

Quality of the Parent-Child Relationship. The PSOC revealed that Michael's parents were effective, mostly competent, and strongly satisfied.

Home Observations. Michael has a very close relationship with his family. He repeatedly interrupted his play to join his parents and "cuddle" with parents during t he observation process. Michael was complaint to any requests that his parents made of him.

Parental Interview (both parents). Michael's mother expressed that "I feel satisfied, but some days I feel more satisfied than others. It (parenting) can be frustrating. You want to do the best you can for your children but you do not always know what is best. I do not feel I always know how to handle him." Both parents expressed frustration to the difficulty to adjust to "the way Michael is" and not always knowing how to handle his moody and difficult behaviors. The mother's expressed feelings of frustration and anxiety regarding parenting practices appeared to respond to Michael's difficult to warm-up and moody temperament. Both parents stated, "patience was crucial for raising their child ad they need to be flexible with him." Both parents also suggested that parenting classes should be mandatory for all new parents, so that they can better understand what children need during different stages. They stated that they "had tried to learn as much as they could about how to raise children and development. There are so many different opinions and possible choices that I hope we chose what is right for Michael." They stated, " they hoped that their relationship with Michael would benefit him, we try to provide with him with the best we can and do the best we can as parents."

Second Case Study: Lisa
A Disadvantaged Family with a Resilient Child

Family Background. Lisa is a 5.2. years-old, Caucasian female child . Lisa's parents are divorce (for two years at the time of the study) so Lisa lives with her mother and visits with her father on alternating weekends . Her mother is Caucasian between 30-39 years of age and has a Bachelors degree. Her father is African-American between 40-49 years of age and is a high school graduate. The annual income is in the low range (i.e., 20,000-29,000) for a household size of three (Lisa has an older brother) . Lisa's family background was categorized as a disadvantaged family background.

Academic Resilience. Scores on the K-ABC indicated that Lisa had above average ability in all areas . The Sequential Processing Scale of the K-ABC standard score was 124 (95th percentile). The Simultaneous Processing Scale of the K-ABC standard score was 123 (94th percentile). The Mental Processing Composite of the K-ABC standard score was 127, (96th percentile). The Achievement Scale of the K-ABC standard score was 111 (77th percentile). Lisa's performance indicated possible giftedness and she demonstrated resilient academic performance.

Early Childhood Temperament. TABC (parent form), was completed by Lisa's mother and revealed that the child was mostly approachable, strongly emotional, slightly negative emotionality, mostly persistent, and with an easy overall temperament. The TABC (teacher form) revealed that Lisa was mostly persistent, strongly approachable. moderately emotional, and she had an overall intermediate temperament.

Projective Assessment Technique. This instrument revealed that Lisa's temperament was strongly approachable, moderately emotional, strongly adaptable, slightly active, and mostly persistent. Lisa's overall temperament was intermediate positive.

Classroom Observation. Lisa's temperament was observed in the classroom to be strongly approachable, strongly adaptable, slightly active, strongly persistent, and her overall temperament was intermediate positive.

Parent Interview. Lisa' s mother described her as social and friendly, and persistent, as she stated "Lisa will stay with something difficult, but will fuss the whole time." Lisa's mother also stated that her temperament had a tendency to change, "if she has kept in her routine, her mood is more flat." Her mother described Lisa as moderately active, "but it also depends on her mood." Lisa's mother stated that the child's temperament "has and will benefit her academically because it provides her with leadership qualities...she is very organized, ordering, and controlling...I could see her in a supervising position some day..."

Quality of the Parent-Child Relationship. The PSOC revealed that Lisa's mother was mostly satisfied, and mostly competent.

Parental Interview (Lisa's mother). Lisa's mother stated that she felt mostly satisfied in her parenting role, but also frustrated at times , as she stated that "self-confidence, consistency, and communication" are important to be a competent parent." Lisa's mother hoped that her relationship with Lisa had influenced her in a positive way. She stated, "I try to do the best I can. I do not have all the answers, I just hope I do the best I can for my kids."

Third Case Study: Jill
An Advantaged Family with a Non-Resilient Child

Family Background. Jill is a 4.11. years-old, Caucasian female child. Jill's family is intact, and she has three older brothers . Both of her parents are Caucasian between 30-39 years of age and have Bachelors degrees. The annual income is in the high range (i.e., over $60,000) for a household size of six. Jill's family background was categorized as an advantaged family background

Academic Resilience. Scores on the K-ABC indicated that Jill had above average ability in some areas, and below average in other areas. The Sequential Processing Scale of the K-ABC standard score was 100 (50th percentile). The Simultaneous Processing Scale of the K-ABC standard score was 123 (94th percentile). The Achievement Scale of the K-ABC standard score was 100 (50th percentile). Jill's performance indicated possible problems in some areas related with sequential processes, and demonstrated a non-resilient academic performance

Early Childhood Temperament . The TABC (parent form), was completed by Jill's mother, and revealed that her temperament was mostly approachable, strongly adaptable, moderately active, slightly negative emotionality, and that her overall temperament as intermediate positive. The TABC (teacher form) revealed that Jill's temperament was mostly persistent, strongly approachable, moderately emotional, and that her temperament was overall intermediate positive.

Projective Assessment Technique. This measure revealed that Jill's temperament was moderately approachable, slightly emotional, strongly adaptable, slightly active, mostly persistent, and that she has an overall intermediate positive temperament.

Classroom Observation. This measure revealed that Jill's temperament was moderately approachable, slightly negative, strongly adaptable, slightly active, strongly persistent, and that her overall temperament was intermediate positive.

Parent Interview. Jill' s mother described her daughter's temperament as "very happy, easy going, flexible. The only time I see assertive or impatient behaviors is with her older brother." Jill's mother also stated, "she tends to shy away when she meets new people, but it does not take her long to get over it. She rather prefers quiet times." In reference to persistence, Lisa's mother reported, "Jill sticks with it if a task is challenging."Jill's mother believed that she reacts positively to Lisa's temperament because she is "very easy and content." Jill's mother stated that the child's temperament "will benefit her because she is very persistent."

Quality of the Parent-Child Relationship. The PSOC revealed that Jill's mother was strongly satisfied, and strongly competent.

Home Observations. Jill appeared to be close to her mother, as she wanted to sit in her lap during the interview.

Parental Interview (Jill's mother). Jill's mother stated that she felt very satisfied in her parenting role, but also frustrated because her children are so easy. Jill's mother stated, "sometimes I think that our relationship (with Jill) is too close. She needs to be more independent. Jill spends a great deal of time with me, and she does not want to share my attention with someone else." Jill's mother identified several skills she believed are critical to parenting such as "patience, listening ability, a proactive attitude when acting on problems, flexibility, and generosity with time."

References

Adams, C.D., Hillman, N., & Gaydos, G. R. (1994). Behavioral difficulties in toddlers: Impact of socio-cultural and biological risk factors. *Journal of Clinical Child Psychology, 23*, 373-381.

Brooks, R. B. (1994). Children at-risk. Fostering resilience and hope. *American Orthopsychiatric Association, 64*, 545-553.

Emery, R. E. (1982). Interpersonal conflict and the children of discord and divorce. *Psychological Bulletin, 92*, 310-330.

Entwisle, D. R., & Astone, N. M. (1994). Some practical guidelines for measuring youth's race/ethnicity and socioeconomic status. *Child Development.* 65, 1521-1540.

Fauber, R., Foreland, R., McCombs Thomas, A., & Wierson, M. (1990). A mediational model of the impact of marital conflict on adolescent adjustment in intact and divorced families: The role of disruptive parenting. *Child Development, 61*, 1112-1123.

Garmezy, N. (1993). Children in poverty: Resilience despite risk. *Psychiatry, 56*, 127-135.

Grizenko, N., & Pawliuk, M.A. 91994). Risk and protective factors for disruptive behavior disorders in children. *American Orthopsychiatric Association, 64*, 535-543.

Hauser, S.T., Vieyra, M.A., Jacobson. A.M., & Wertreib, D. 91985). Vulnerability and resilience in adolescence: Views from the family. *Journal of Early Adolescence, 5*, 81-100.

Honig, A. (1984). Research in review: Risk factors in infants and young children. *Young Children, 38*, 60-73.

Kaufman, A. S., & Kaufman, N. L. (1983a). *Administration and scoring manual for the Kaufman Assessment Battery for Children* . Minneapolis, MN: American Guidance Service.

Kaufman, A. S., & Kaufman, N. L. (1983b). *Interpretative manual for the Kaufman Assessment Battery for Children* . Minneapolis, MN: American Guidance Service.

Keogh, B.K. (1982). Children's temperament and teachers' decisions. In R. Porter & G. M. Collins (Eds.), *Ciba Foundation Symposium: Temperamental; differences in infants and young children, Vol. 89* (pp. 269-279). London: Pittman Books.

Kyrios, M., & Prior, M. (1990). Temperament, stress, and family factors in behavioral adjustment of 3-5 year-old children. *International Journal of Behavioral Development, 13*, 67-93.

Martin, R. P. (1988). *The Temperament Assessment Battery for Children.* Brandon, VT: Clinical Psychology Publishing.

McDevin, S.C., & Carey, W. B. (1978). The measurement of temperament in 3-to-7-year-old children. *Journal of Child Psychology and Psychiatry, 19*, 245-253.

Miller, C.L., Miceli, P.J., Whitman, T. L., & Borkowski, J. G. (1996). Cognitive readiness to parent and intellectual-emotional development in children of adolescent mothers. *Developmental Psychology, 32*, 533-541.

Neighbors, B., Forehand, R., & McVicar, D. (1993). Resilient adolescents and inter-parental conflict. *American Journal of Orthopsychiatry, 63*, 462-471.

Presley, R., & Martin, R. P. (1994). Towards a structure of preschool temperament: Factor structure of the Temperament Assessment Battery for Children. *Journal of Personality, 62*, 415-447.

Rak, C.F., & Patterson, L. E. (1996). Promoting resiliency in at-risk children. *Journal of Counseling and Development, 74*, 368-373.

Thomas, A., & Chess, A. (1992). Temperament and follow-up to adulthood. In R. Porter & G. M. Collins (Eds.), *Ciba Foundation Symposium: Temperamental differences in infants and young children , Vol. 89* (pp. 2268-273). London: Pittman Books.

Werner, E. (1989). Children of the Garden Island . *Scientific American, 49* , 106-111.

Wolfson, J., Fields, J., & Rose, S. (1987). Symptoms, temperament, resiliency, and control in anxiety-disordered preschool children. *Journal of American Academy of Child and Adolescent Psychiatry, 26*, 16-22.

Wyman, P. A., Cowan, E. L., Work, W. C. (1991). Developmental and family milieu correlates of resilience ion urban children who have experienced major life stresses. *American Journal of Community Psychology, 19*, 405-425.

Van Tassel-Baska, J. (1989). The role of family on the success of disadvantaged gifted learners. *Journal of the Education of the Gifted, 13*, 22-36.

Table 7.1.

Relationship Among Research Questions, Research Model,
Variables, and Research Design

Research Questions	Research Model	Variables	Research Design
1) What characteristics of early childhood temperament promote academic resilience in young children?	Descriptive	* Early childhood temperament * Academic resilience	Qualitative analysis
2) What qualities of the parent-child relationship promote academic resilience in young children?	Descriptive	* Quality of the parent-child relationship * Academic resilience	Qualitative analysis
3) Do early childhood temperament and the quality of the parent-child relationship interact to influence academic resilience in young children?	Descriptive	* Early childhood temperament * Quality of the parent-child relationship * Academic resilience	Qualitative analysis
4) Do early childhood temperament and the quality of the parent-child relationship interact to influence academic resilience in young children from advantaged as well as disadvantaged family backgrounds?	Descriptive	* Early childhood temperament * Quality of the parent-child relationship * Academic resilience * Family background	Qualitative analysis

Table 7.2.

Overall Categorization of Temperamental Domains

Temperamental Category	Description
Easy temperament	* Strongly approachable * Strongly adaptable * Strongly persistent * Positive emotionality * Low activity
Intermediate positive temperament	* Mostly to strongly approachable * Mostly to strongly adaptable * Mostly to strongly persistent * Low to slight activity * Slight negative emotionality
Slow to warm-up temperament	* Moderate (slow) approachability * Moderate (slow) adaptability * Slight negative emotionality
Intermediate negative temperament	* Slight to low approachability * Slight to low approachability * Slight to low persistence * Mostly to strongly active * Mostly to strongly negatively emotional
Difficult temperament	* Low approachability * Low adaptability * Low persistence * Strong negative emotionality * High activity

Table 7.3.
Temperamental Domains

Construct	Definition of Construct	Descriptive Adjectives
Approachability	Introversion or extroversion	* Low: quiet, reserved * High: talkative, outgoing
Negative emotionality	Affective reactions or mood	* Low: stable, calm * High: moody, irritable
Adaptability	Agreeableness, a djustment to new routines	* Low: unfriendly, cold * High: kind, warm
Activity level	Amount of daily vigor	* Low: shy, withdrawn High: outgoing, physical
Task orientation	Task persistence, attention span	* Low: Disorderly, irresponsible High: organized, efficient

Table 7.4.

Temperamental Domains and their Relationship to Projective
Technique Stories

Construct	Definition of Construct	Descriptive Adjectives	Stories
Approachability	Introversion or extroversion	Low: quiet, reserved High: talkative, outgoing	Child is approached by new child, What does child do?
Negative emotionality	Affective reactions, mood	* Low: stable, calm High: moody, irritable	Child is shopping with parent. Child sees a toy s/he wants, but parent says that s/he can not have not, What does child do?
Adaptability	Agreeableness, adjustment to new routines	* Low: unfriendly, cold High: kind, warm	Child is told by parent that there is going to be a new baby in the family, What does child do?
Activity level	Amount of daily vigor	* Low; shy, withdrawn High: outgoing, physical	Parent asks the child to choose what s/he wants to do during free time, What does child do?
Task persistence	Task persistence, attention span	* Low: disorderly, irresponsible High: organized, efficient	Child is working on a difficult task, What does child do?

Table 7.5.
Case Study 1: The Influence of Context, Informant, and Format on the Categorization of Temperament

Instruments	Context	Informant	Format	Approachability	Negative Emotionality	Adaptability	Activity	Task Persistence	Overall
TABC (parent) form	Informal	Parents	Closed	Mostly approachable	Slightly emotional	Moderately adaptable	Mostly active	Mostly persistent	Intermediate positive
TABC (teacher) form	Formal	Teacher	Closed	Moderately approachable	Moderately emotional	N/A	N/A	Mostly persistent	Slow to warm-up
	Informal	Researcher	Open	Mostly approachable	Moderately emotional	Mostly adaptable	Moderately active	Moderately persistent	Intermediate positive
	Formal	Researcher	Open	Moderately approachable	Moderately emotional	Moderately adaptable	Mostly active	Moderately persistent	Slow to warm-up
	Informal	Parents	Open	Moderately approachable	Strongly emotional	Moderately adaptable	Strongly active	Mostly persistent	Slow to warm-up

Table 7.6.

Case Study 2: The Influence of Context, Informant, and Format on the Categorization of Temperament

Instruments	Context	Informant	Format	Approachability	Negative Emotionality	Adaptability	Activity	Task Persistence	Overall
TABC (parent) form	Informal	Parents	Closed	Mostly approachable	Slightly emotional	Strongly adaptable	Mostly active	Mostly persistent	Easy
TABC (teacher) form	Formal	Teacher	Closed	Strongly approachable	Moderately emotional	N/A	N/A	Mostly persistent	Intermediate positive
	Informal	Researcher	Open	Strongly approachable	Moderately emotional	Strongly adaptable	Slightly active	Mostly persistent	Intermediate positive
	Formal	Researcher	Open	Strongly approachable	Not emotional	Strongly adaptable	Slightly active	Strongly persistent	Intermediate positive
	Informal	Parents	Open	Strongly approachable	Slightly emotional	Moderately adaptable	Moderately active	Mostly persistent	Intermediate positive

Table 7.7.

Case Study 3: The Influence of Context, Informant, and Format on the Categorization of Temperament

Instru-ments	Context	Informant	Format	Approacha-bility	Negative Emotion-ality	Adapta-bility	Activity	Task Persis-tence	Overall
TABC (parent) form	Informal	Parents	Closed	Mostly approachable	Slightly emotional	Strongly adaptable	Moder-ately ac-tive	Mostly persistent	Interme-diate positive
TABC (teacher) form	Formal	Teacher	Closed	Strongly approachable	Moderately emotional	N/A	N/A	Mostly persistent	Interme-diate positive
	Informal	Researcher	Open	Moderately approachable	Slightly emotional	Strongly adaptable	Slightly active	Mostly persistent	Interme-diate positive
	Formal	Researcher	Open	Moderately approachable	Slightly emotional	Strongly adaptable	Slightly active	Strongly persistent	Interme-diate positive
	Informal	Parents	Open	Moderately approachable	Slightly emotional	Strongly adaptable	Slightly active	Strongly persistent	Interme-diate positive

Table 7.8.

Case Study 4: The Influence of Context, Informant, and Format on the Categorization of Temperament

Instru-ments	Context	Informant	For-mat	Approacha-bility	Negative Emotiona-lity	Adapta-bility	Activity	Task Persistence	Overall
TABC (parent) form	Informal	Parents	Closed	Strongly approachable	Slightly emotional	Strongly adaptable	Mostly active	Mostly persistent	Interme-diate positive
TABC (teacher) form	Formal	Teacher	Closed	Strongly approachable	Slightly emotional	N/A	N/A	Mostly persistent	Interme-diate positive
	Informal	Researcher	Open	Strongly approachable	Slightly emotional	Mostly adaptable	Mostly active	Strongly persistent	Interme-diate positive
	Formal	Researcher	Open	Strongly approachable	Slightly emotional	Mostly adaptable	Strongly active	Strongly persistent	Interme-diate positive
	Informal	Parents	Open	Strongly approachable	Slightly emotional	Strongly adaptable	Mostly active	Strongly persistent	Interme-diate positive

8

CONCLUSIONS: PATTERNS AND
THEORETICAL AND EDUCATIONALLY
APPLIED IMPLICATIONS

ℬↄℭℛ

Virginia Gonzalez

After critically examining contemporary literature in Chapters 1 and 2, and presenting a collection of five data-based research studies conducted from an Ethnic Researcher perspective in Chapters 3 through 7, some concluding remarks in the form of patterns can be posed. The first pattern emerging across the contemporary literature critically discussed in Chapters 1 and 2, and the five data-based studies presented in this book, supports a theoretical and methodological framework that is ecological and multidimensional; which is closely connected with the major theme of the book: The study of the interaction of internal (i.e., biological, psychological—cognitive, social, emotional/affective) and external mediating factors (i.e., socio-cultural and socioeconomic status –SES- e.g., family structure and cultural factors, and school environments) affecting minority and mainstream children's developmental, learning processes, and academic achievement .

Secondly, this state-of-the-art philosophical and theoretical framework, has been coined by collaborators and I as the Ethnic Researcher paradigm (see Gonzalez, Brusca-Vega, & Yawkey, 1997; Gonzalez, Yawkey, & Minaya-Rowe, 2006 for further discussion of this perspective). The Ethnic Researcher perspective can serve as a context for opening new lines of research with the purpose of: (1) broadening our present understanding of mainstream children's internal (i.e., biological and psychological) and external (i.e., family and schooling) factors affecting their individual developmental patterns and variations in academic achievement, and (2) uncovering new developmental patterns, and unique culturally and linguistically diverse characteristics of the effect of SES and socio-cultural factors on minority children's development and academic achievement.

Third, the Ethnic Researcher perspective has opened a new line of research that can help study (at a deeper level) the particular ways in which socio-cultural factors (i.e., minority culture and language) act as external mediators for the effect of low SES on the developmental and academic achievement levels attained by minority young children. In addition, there is also need for attention towards deeper understanding of the cumulative interacting patterns among mediating factors, and how poverty can be scaffold by the presence of positive family factors or high-quality school environments, resulting in minority children being able to develop resilience for at-risk external conditions (and even at-risk internal –biological- conditions, such as premature and low weight at birth) associated with low SES. For instance, there is need to further study the interaction between low SES, minority parents' personality traits and their child's personality characteristics, its effect on the quality of the parent-child relationship, and ultimately on the minority children's resilience or vulnerability expressed in developmental and academic achievement levels attained.

Moreover, there is need to study the distinct aspects of poverty characteristics, such as initial disadvantage and depth of poverty. As noted in this book, income has been demonstrated to be just the tip of the iceberg of the complexity of the SES omnibus variable. The particular quality of the family and school environment encompasses multiple socio-cultural characteristics resulting in supportive or detrimental psychological and physical settings for biological, socio-emotional, and mental growth. Among the most important significant variables uncovered by contemporary traditional and Ethnic Research studies impacting low SES minority and mainstream children's development and academic achievement are: (1) degree of family cultural adaptation such as value and belief systems, attitudes, socialization goals, patterns of cultural adaptive strategies to the mainstream American social and school cultures, and home language use; (2) family structure characteristics such as number of sibling, continuous presence of a paternal figure, presence of extended family members—such as supporting grandparents; (3) parents' characteristics such as degree of literacy and education, occupation, degree of acculturation, and physical and mental health; and (4) quality of neighborhood and community resources such as availability of mentors (e.g., teachers; extended family, community or church members; peers and siblings, etc.), social services available such as federal or state programs for provision of health care ands nutritious food, etc.

Fourth, there is need to develop ecological and multidimensional research studies on recurrent or changing minority and mainstream low SES children's developmental characteristics affecting resilience to at-risk conditions for developmental or achievement problems. Researchers still need to uncover the different transitional or recurrent risks affecting minority children, and the characteristics and effects of protective internal and external mechanisms at different ages and points in development. We still need to uncover what are the protective internal (i.e., biological and psychological) and/or external (i.e., socio-cultural and SES factors present at home and school settings) mechanisms that function as scaffolds or mediators for at-risk low SES children to become resilient. The challenge is increased by scarcity of studies that control for confounding socio-cultural (i.e., cultural and linguistic) and low SES factors on these protective internal or external mechanisms. That is, there is need for conducting studies that broaden our understanding of the interacting effects of poverty with other internal and external mediating factors (i.e., biological, psychological, and family and community structure) on cognitive and socio-emotional *developmental processes* in minority and mainstream children. In contrast, much research has been conducted on performances or actual levels of skills and abilities developed: that is, research with a focus on products (instead of on developmental *processes*). For instance, conducting studies following an Ethnic Researcher perspective can hopefully be conducted at the *process* level on problem-solving, giftedness, creativity, bilingualism, biculturalism, cultural identity, self-esteem, self-concept, socio-cultural interpersonal and communication styles, cultural thinking styles, knowledge acquisition, and so forth. Examples of more permanent child's characteristics that can be studied at the *process* level and that need to be further studied are temperament and personality traits, unique individual needs, and self-regulation of attention, emotion, and behaviors. Examples of changing child's characteristics at the *process* level that need to be studied are developmental stages, interests, attitudes, perceptions, and values and belief systems. Examples of ecological factors that need to be studied at the *process* level that are open for research are the quality of parent-child relationships, parental cultural values about education and child rearing practices, the effect of home language, and the effect of mentors and other educational opportunities for success.

Fifth, we need to create opportunities for minority children to experience educational success, so that we increase the qualified pool of minority students who can have genuine access to higher education, and also increase their retention rates once admission is gained. Conducting more research on how to reduce the drop-out rate of minority students at the middle school and high school levels is instrumental for enabling them to gain a college degree and be able to enter middle class professional America, with all the SES and socio-cultural benefits that access to mainstream society entails. We need to generate more studies from an Ethnic Researcher perspective on how to integrate national high-academic standards for *all* students with high-quality education for meeting the cultural and linguistic needs of minority and mainstream low SES students.

Moreover, we need to discover ways of successfully integrating minority students' real-life experiences in their family and community environments with curriculums, educational methodologies and strategies, and educational materials across content areas in the U.S. public school system. By conducting further sound Ethnic Research we can generate high-quality educational programs delivered by caring mentors and advocates at school, who can act as external socio-cultural mediators and can provide minority students with genuine opportunities to actualize their potential for developing and achieving at high levels. By carrying out Ethnic Research we can uncover the bicultural identities of minority students and open up genuine communication channels with their minority families and communities in order to increase their adaptation and integration to the school system. In addition, we also need to generate more effective teacher training models for developing content knowledge about second-language (L2) learning and developmental *processes* in minority low SES children, as well as more sensitive and caring attitudes about their "holistic" development across cognitive, linguistic, social, and affective/emotional areas. That is, *for all* teachers (English as a second language—ESL, and mainstream) to help minority children by becoming caring mentors, committed advocates, and trusted adults who assume moral responsibility to help develop socio-cultural adaptation (i.e., integration of bicultural and bilingual cultural identities), reach their developmental potential, and become achievers within the mainstream American school culture and broader society.

The goal is not to acculturate minority students to assimilate into the status quo of mainstream school culture. Instead the goal is to initiate a process of reciprocal adaptation across school, family, and community environments in order to facilitate for minority students the engagement in an accommodation process of integration of their bicultural and bilingual identities. Both sides of the socio-cultural environments (i.e., home and school system) need to adapt and learn about minority and mainstream cultures and languages. That is, ESL and mainstream teachers need to become aware of the powerful effect of home minority culture and language on developmental and academic achievement   *processes*, and of the necessary integration with the curriculum content and instructional methodology across subject areas. ESL teachers need to function as mentors and increase their understanding of other cultures in order to develop rapport with minority children and their families. These understandings include: recognizing minority family concerns and feelings, discussions of issues of concern to minority families about school and community involvement activities, and family education originating from and based on the needs and interests of minority families.

Moreover, minority parents also need to become committed partners with teachers and the school system in order to support their children's ESL learning *process* and subsequent cultural integrative adaptation and progress that will lead to higher levels of academic achievement. Thus, the key to secure success for the educational experience of minority children is to integrate and increase the quality of external socio-cultural mediating schooling, family, and community factors.

Sixth, it seems important to conduct studies within the Ethnic Researcher paradigm for developing new research methodologies and procedures, such as research designs and assessment instruments. The creation of these new research tools can generate valid and reliable instruments for exploring socio-cultural factors (including linguistic diversity) acting as mediating external variables when studying the effect of poverty on the development and academic achievement of minority children. Then, these alternative measures need to represent accurately the social, cultural, and linguistic diverse characteristics of minority low SES children, while at the same time be sensitive to tap their individual differences and developmental changes.

For instance, the Ethnic Researcher perspective study presented in Chapter 3 contributes to the validation of a data-driven model explaining why and how bilingualism affects cognition, taking into account the interaction of multidimensional and interactive internal and external factors. In addition, this revised model also expands the findings into more specific developmental profiles in light of new data and more complex coding systems. Actually this revised model opens new windows to how potentially gifted Hispanic children form culturally-linguistically loaded and universal non-verbal concepts in their dominant and second languages.

Another example of the importance of using alternative assessments when evaluating young children, even mainstream Kindergartners is presented in Chapter 7. This study indicated that the mainstream young children's ability to perform adaptive behavior skills on a daily basis is highly related to their classroom performance. In fact, adaptive behavior, as measured by a standardized test (Vineland Adaptive Behavior Scale) and by teachers' ratings played an important role in the early screening of young children and in the prediction of future school performance. Moreover, while advanced problem-solving abilities and prior learning of factual knowledge (as measured by a standardized test, the Kauffman Assessment Battery for Children –K-ABC) predicted mainstream children's school performance, it appears that the ability to perform certain adaptive behavior skills on a regular basis (as evaluated with an alternative evaluation by the child's classroom teacher) is a better predictor of a child's readiness to learn and participate in a classroom setting.

However, presently we face in contemporary research literature that studies minority and mainstream low SES children, the presence of two contradictory paradigms: (1) the traditional methodological paradigm that uses primarily standardized discrete-point tests derived from research conducted with mainstream children; and (2) the Ethnic Researcher perspective, that endorses alternative qualitative measures and methodological procedures that tap the cultural and linguistic diversity of minority children. Thus, given the multidisciplinary backgrounds of researchers attempting to study minority children, the application of multiple theoretical paradigms and philosophies has resulted in a diverse set of measures and data analysis procedures and, in some instances, contradictory research findings.

This book has attempted to merge both theoretical perspectives (i.e., traditional and Ethnic Researcher paradigms) and to reach some conclusions about the confounding effect of poverty with socio-cultural external factors (i.e., diverse culture and language) and developmental internal factors (i.e., biological and psychological) that are present in both minority low SES and mainstream low SES children. The bottom line is that *all* poor children are at-risk or vulnerable for actualizing at some point in time, some developmental and achievement delays and difficulties. Research trends show that there is no "full proof" or "super" child, who *will not* be affected at all by poverty conditions. Instead, contemporary research has uncovered that internal and external mediational factors can interact positively or negatively with at-risk internal (i.e., biological and psychological) and external (i.e., mentors and healthy family environments, high-quality instruction) conditions to help poor children to become resilient and overcome developmental delays, premature births, lack or poor quality early stimulation, low-quality or inappropriate schooling, etc. Then, minority children are *not* at-risk of underachievement and developmental delays because of cultural/linguistic differences, but primarily because they are *poor*.

In a similar manner, *mainstream poor* children (e.g., Appalachian white children) suffer from high under-achievement and high school drop out rates as well. Thus, poverty has equal powerful negative effects across races, ethnicities, and monolingual or bilingual, mono-cultural mainstream or bicultural young children: Any poor child is at-risk of developmental delays and/or underachievement. In addition to poverty, minority children, have an additive effect of cultural/linguistic differences (i.e., ESL and lack of cultural adaptation to the mainstream school culture). However, in the same manner as minority children, mainstream poor children also lack proficiency in academic English (in comparison to middle and upper class peers), as well as are not prepared at home to develop socialization skills that respond to the expectations of the mainstream school culture. As a result, both groups of minority and mainstream poor children become vulnerable or at-risk for developmental delays and underachievement; and are in need of supporting external mediating factors at home and school to help them actualize their learning potential into skills and abilities at age level.

In sum, the critical literature review conducted in Chapters 1 and 2, and all the data-based research studies presented in Chapters 3 through 7 attest for some degree of progress achieved by contemporary Ethnic Researchers. We have been able to uncover the presence of some mediating factors when studying the effect of low SES on the development and academic achievement of minority children. However, still new lines of research need to be open in order to understand how these external mediating factors, stemming from socio-cultural and SES variables, interact with at-risk internal factors (i.e., biological and psychological) in minority-children. Finally, more research studies need to be conducted using new research methodologies, stemming from the Ethnic Researcher perspective, for measuring the effect of poverty and cultural and linguistic diversity on developmental processes and achievement levels attained by minority children. With the new millennium, a bright and broad future opens up for Ethnic Researchers who will pursue these challenging tasks. Table 8.1. presents a summary of all six patterns found across the theoretical framework and the five research studies presented in this book.

Theoretical and Practical Implications Found Across Data-Based Research Studies Presented in the Book

Most data-based studies presented in this book offer a contribution to the fields of ESL and bilingual education, special education, and school and developmental psychology in the form of theoretical and practical implications of using alternative assessments for accurately measuring minority low SES children's cognitive and language development. Alternative assessments used in the research studies presented in this book show construct and criterion-referenced validity, because they include: (1) different informants, (2) verbal and non-verbal tasks representing the children's minority culture, and (3) administrations in the dominant minority language of the children.

Some of these research studies presented in this book provide evidence for the significant relation between ecological variables and the cognitive and language development of Hispanic, young, low SES children. More specifically, family structure factors (i.e., home language of parents and siblings, the parents' Spanish and English language proficiency levels, the parents' educational levels and occupations, the number of siblings, and the child's birth order) were significantly related to the child's cognitive and language developmental level attained. Furthermore, the home language of parents and children, and the parents' number of years of US residence were related to the *degree of acculturation* present in the minority parents and their children. Having English as a home language also resulted in the child's higher English language proficiency levels (as rated by parents), language dominance that was reflected in the child's ability to form non-verbal concepts.

Furthermore, when alternative assessments methodologically control for conceptual differences introduced by cultural and linguistic factors, the significant relation of family structure factors can also be demonstrated in minority, low SES children's conceptual development. Thus, when alternative assessments are used, representing the cultural and linguistic factors affecting cognitive and language development in minority children, the advantages of bilingualism or of speaking a minority language can be shown.

In terms of practical educational implications, some of the studies present empirical evidence for the importance of involving parents in the referral process of potentially gifted, minority and mainstream children, who come from low SES backgrounds. Information provided by parents on family structure factors become of paramount importance for evaluators to understand how ecological variables are related to first-and-second-language learning processes, and to cognitive development in minority low SES children. For instance, the study presented in Chapter 6 found that parents do have certain perceptions about their child's cognitive abilities and what constitutes giftedness even *before* their children are identified as gifted. More importantly, parents also have certain beliefs about what internal and/or external factors influence the cognitive development (and possible giftedness) of their child. In fact, parental perceptions and beliefs about cognitive development and giftedness also form part of the home environment to which children are exposed to.

References

Gonzalez, V., Brusca-Vega, R., & Yawkey, T. (1997).   *Assessment and instruction of culturally and linguistically diverse students with or at-risk of learning problems: From research to practice.* Needham Heights, MA: Allyn & Bacon.

Gonzalez, V., Yawkey, T.D., & Minaya-Rowe, L. (2006).   *English-as-a-Second-Language (ESL) teaching and learning: Classroom applications for Pre-K-12th Grade students' academic achievement & development.* Needham Heights, MA: Allyn & Bacon.

Table 8.1.

Patterns Found Across Theoretical Framework and
Data-Based Research Studies

First pattern: Ecological and multidimensional theoretical and methodological framework, which encompasses an interaction of internal (i.e.,
biological, psychological -cognitive, social, emotional/affective) and
external mediating factors (i.e., SES and socio-cultural variables -e.g.,
family structure and cultural factors, and school environments) on developmental and learning processes, and subsequently on academic achievement in minority and mainstream young children.

Second pattern: The Ethnic Researcher perspective can serve as a philosophical and theoretical perspective for: (1) broadening our present understanding of mainstream children's internal (i.e., biological and psychological) and external (i.e., family and schooling) factors affecting
their individual developmental patterns and variations in academic
achievement; and (2) uncovering new developmental patterns, and
unique culturally and linguistically diverse characteristics of the effect of
SES and socio-cultural factors on minority children's development and
academic achievement.

Third pattern: The Ethnic Researcher perspective has opened a new line
of research that can help study (at a deeper level) the particular ways in
which socio-cultural factors (i.e., minority culture and language) act as
external mediators for the effect of low SES on the developmental and
academic achievement levels attained by minority young children.

Fourth pattern: Ecological and multidimensional Ethnic Researcher
studies on the interacting effects of *poverty* with other internal and external mediating factors (i.e., biological, psychological, and family and
community structure) on cognitive and socio-emotional   *developmental
processes* in minority and mainstream children. The bottom line is that
all poor children are at-risk or vulnerable for actualizing at some point in
time, some developmental and achievement delays and difficulties.
Then, minority children are *not* at-risk of underachievement and developmental delays because of cultural/linguistic differences, but primarily
because they are *poor*. As a result, both groups of minority and mainstream p *oor* children become vulnerable or at-risk for developmental

delays and underachievement; and are in need of supporting external mediating factors at home and school to help them actualize their learning potential into skills and abilities at age level.

Fifth pattern: Studies from an Ethnic Researcher perspective can help to understand how to integrate national high-academic standards for *all* students with high-quality education for meeting the cultural and linguistic needs of minority and mainstream low SES students. We need to conduct research on how to increase the effectiveness of teacher training programs for helping minority low SES students develop integrative cultural identities and social adaptation; for being able to adapt the instructional methodologies, strategies, and educational materials to their real-life socio-cultural experiences; and for develop partnerships with minority parents, families, and ethnic communities.

Sixth pattern: Studies from an Ethnic Researcher perspective can contribute to integrate national high-academic standards for *all* students with high-quality education, and valid and reliable assessments and research designs and procedures for meeting the cultural and linguistic needs of minority and mainstream low SES students.

INDEX

ABOUT THE AUTHOR

Virginia Gonzalez is a Professor of English as a second language (ESL) Education at the University of Cincinnati. She has an interdisciplinary professional and academic background, with a M.A. in Bilingual Special Education and a Ph. D. in Educational Psychology, both degrees from The University of Texas at Austin. She received a Bachelors degree in Clinical Psychology, with a minor in Educational Psychology from the Pontifical University of Lima, Peru. She was formerly a faculty member at Texas A&M University and at The University of Arizona. She is an expert in ESL/bilingual instruction and assessment.

One of Dr. Gonzalez's major areas of expertise is the generation of research models explaining cognitive and linguistic development in ESL Hispanic students, and its implications for assessment, learning processes, and instruction and teacher education programs. She has taught pre-and-in-service teacher education courses in child and human development, diversity in learners, assessment of mainstream and ESL students, second language development and learning, instructional methods in ESL/bilingual education, research methods in ESL, and development and achievement in ESL/bilingual students in the three universities where she has worked. Dr. Gonzalez has published multiple books and journal articles, which have been applied for the assessment and instruction of diverse students, and for the training of ESL/bilingual educators in higher education. She has served in national boards in major professional organizations and other research and advisory committees on ESL and bilingual education.

Dr. Gonzalez is multilingual with Spanish as her native language, and Italian and English as second languages. She was born and raised in Lima-Peru and came to the US in 1986 as a graduate international student, with Austin, Texas as her U.S. hometown. She is an immigrant, naturalized U.S. citizen, from a Hispanic background. She and her husband, Emmanuel, have a bilingual English/Spanish child, Christian who is first-generation Hispanic, born in Tucson, Arizona.